ISRAEL!
DO YOU KNOW?

D1627085

הֲלוֹא יָדַעְתָּ יִשְׂרָאֵל

ISRAEL! DO YOU KNOW?

By

LeGrand Richards

a member of

The Quorum of the Twelve Apostles

of

The Church of Jesus Christ of Latter-day Saints

> *And he shall set up an ensign for the nations, and shall assemble the outcasts of Israel, and gather together the dispersed of Judah from the four corners of the earth.*
>
> *The envy also of Ephraim shall depart, and the adversaries of Judah shall be cut off: Ephraim shall not envy Judah, and Judah shall not vex Ephraim.*
>
> *—Isaiah 11:12-13.*

Deseret Book Company
Salt Lake City, Utah

Paperback edition released 1990

ISBN 0-87579-314-2

Printed in the United States of America   18961-4653
10   9   8   7   6   5   4   3

PREFACE

A sincere love for the descendants of Judah; an unwavering faith in their destiny as a chosen people of noble birthright; an unbounded admiration for the manner in which they have maintained their racial identity through 2000 years of trial and abuse have combined to inspire in the author a deep-rooted desire to bring them hope and the feeling of good will and fellowship wherever they are throughout the world.

Hope for the descendants of Judah is predicated upon their willingness to recognize themselves in the picture which God has unerringly outlined in detail through His holy prophets almost since time began.

It is doubtful whether God has ever provided more detailed information, more divine signposts along the way of life, than He has provided for the descendants of Judah. No student of the scriptures will deny that the Jews, as a people, are dear to the heart of the Father of us all, else why would so much of prophecy be devoted to outlining their destiny and so many covenants be made to insure their eternal blessings?

Look up, O House of Judah! The divine promises which God made to your fathers Abraham, Isaac, and Jacob have spanned the centuries and their blessed fulfillment are upon you.

USE OF ITALICS

All italics used throughout the text have been employed by the author to emphasize certain words, phrases, and sentences as an aid to the reader in his study of this treatise.

BIBLICAL QUOTATIONS

All Biblical quotations have been taken from the Authorized (King James) Version.

ACKNOWLEDGMENTS

Several friends read manuscript copies of this book. To all of them, too numerous to mention, I express my gratitude for their time, their candid opinions and suggestions.

Since this book deals largely with the Jews, I invited some of my Jewish friends to read the manuscript and to express their reactions. All of them have been most cooperative and their suggestions have been invaluable. The manuscript was passed so freely from one to another among so many of them as to make it hazardous to mention names lest some are omitted. I am sure they will understand and will accept this expression of my appreciation for their friendly assistance.

The Embassy of Israel, Washington, D. C., gave me full cooperation in all requests made of them as detailed elsewhere.

Words cannot express my feelings of gratitude to my very dear friend and colleague, Lee A. Palmer, for his willingness to assist me with this book in so many ways. His tireless assistance, given without remuneration, in the editing of *A Marvelous Work and A Wonder*,* gave me courage to call upon him again. Since the time he so generously devoted to editing the manuscript, to proofreading, and to relieving me of the details of publication was taken from his family at home, I express to him and to them my profound appreciation.

Vella Wetzel, Frances Cardall, and Liliu Peery were so kind and helpful in typing the manuscript copy and reference material with such meticulous care.

LeGrand Richards

Salt Lake City, Utah
October 1, 1954

———

CONTENTS

CHAPTER 6

CHAPTER 7

CHAPTER 13

End Known from the Beginning—The Lord Works
Only Through His Prophets—Purposes of the Lord
Fail Not—A Summary of the Promises of the Lord to
Israel—The Last Shall be First and the First Shall be
Last—A Falling Away Foretold—A Marvelous Work and
a Wonder to Come Forth—The God of Heaven to Set up
His Kingdom—Gospel Sent First to the Gentiles
and Then to the Jews—Prophecies Concerning the Latter
Days and Their Fulfillment—The Dispensation of the
Fullness of Times—Israel No Longer to be Two Nations
—Knowledge From the Stick of Joseph—Jesus the Giver
of the Law of Moses—Christ's Message to the Descend-
ants of Judah—Remnants of Israel to be Grafted—Judah
to Believe in Christ—The Lord to Fight Judah's Battles—
A "Mystical Force" Seems to be Working with Judah—
A Modern Prophet Reassures the Descendants of Judah
—A Prophet of the Latter Days Speaks of Judah—Con-
clusion of the Summary

CHAPTER 1

ISRAEL! DO YOU KNOW?

Israel! Do you know why the Lord made so many great promises unto the House of Israel?

Do you know the Lord promised your forefathers, Abraham, Isaac and Jacob that through them and their seed "shall all the nations of the earth be blessed"?

Do you know the Lord changed Jacob's name to "Israel"? and that, therefore, all of his descendants are "Israelites"?

Israel! Do you know the House of Israel was divided into two great kingdoms—the Kingdom of Judah and the Kingdom of Israel?

Do you know that since Israel was divided, they have never been reunited to this day?

Do you know the Kingdom of Judah and the Kingdom of Israel, headed by Joseph and his seed, must be reunited before the Lord can fulfill all of his promises to the children of Israel?

Do you know that, during the long separation of the Kingdom of Judah and the Kingdom of Israel, Joseph was given a new land in "the utmost bound of the everlasting hills," or the land of America?

Israel! Do you know that, because of the division in the House of Israel, and because of their separation one from the other, the Lord commanded Ezekiel, a prophet in Judah, to keep a record of His hand-dealings with *each* of these two great kingdoms?

Do you know one record was referred to as the Stick of Judah (the Holy Bible), and that the other record was referred to as the Stick of Joseph? The Stick of Judah has been with us through the years, but *do you know* that only recently the Lord has brought forth the Stick of Joseph and joined it with the Stick of Judah? The Lord has made the two records as one in His hands for the purpose of establishing His Kingdom in the earth in these latter days, preparatory to reuniting the Kingdoms of Judah and of Israel into one great kingdom.

Do you know the Stick of Joseph contains many promises to the seed of Judah which will help them to accomplish all the Lord has decreed concerning them in the latter days?

Do you know the Stick of Joseph contains such valuable and definite information for the seed of Judah, concerning their promised Messiah, that they need no longer be confused or in doubt as to His identity?

Israel! Do you know the Lord promised, through Jeremiah, another prophet in Judah, that in the latter days He would "make a new covenant with the house of Israel, and with the house of Judah"?

Do you know the Stick of Joseph names the "choice seer . . . like unto Moses" whom the Lord promised to raise up "in the latter days"? and through whom He promised to establish His "new covenant"?

Israel! Do you know the Stick of Joseph makes it clear that "before the coming of the great and dreadful day of the Lord," as predicted by Malachi, a prophet of Judah, the Lord would establish His New Jerusalem in the land of Joseph (America)? that He would gather the seed of Judah back to the land of Palestine? that through the blessings and help of the Lord, Judah would rebuild the city of Jerusalem as of old?

Judah and Israel Must Come Together

It seems indisputable that the Kingdom of Judah and the Kingdom of Israel must come together with one heart and one mind that the promises of the Lord and the word of prophecy may be fulfilled and that truth may be established in the earth.

Are we not living "in the latter days" when so many of the prophecies of the prophets of Judah and other prophets are to be fulfilled?

Come—let us reason together and happily discover our common objectives—discover that neither Judah nor Israel can say, one to the other, "I have no need of thee."

CHAPTER 2

ISRAEL, GOD'S COVENANT PEOPLE

Israel to be a Special People

Great and mighty are the promises of the Lord unto the seed of Abraham, Isaac, and Jacob:

> For thou art an holy people unto the Lord thy God: the Lord thy God hath chosen thee to be a special people unto himself, above all people that are upon the face of the earth. (Deuteronomy 7:6.)

Since the Lord hath chosen the seed of Abraham "to be a special people unto himself, above all people that are upon the face of the earth," it is of the utmost importance that they fully understand why the Lord has chosen them, and to learn of their great mission in the earth.

The Lord has planned His work from the beginning, just as the architect plans a building before it is built. The Lord has made His plans known in advance through His prophets. His plans never fail. The Lord said to Isaiah:

> Remember the former things of old: for I am God, and there is none else! I am God, and there is none like me,
> *Declaring the end from the beginning,* and from ancient times the things that are not yet done, saying, My counsel shall stand, and I will do all my pleasure: (Isaiah 46:9-10.)

Isaiah fully understood that the Lord was working to a definite plan, "declaring the end from the beginning," and that His word would never fail:

> The grass withereth, the flower fadeth: but the word of our God shall stand forever. (Isaiah 40:8.)

The Prophet Amos declared:

> Surely the Lord God will do nothing, but he revealeth his secret unto his servants the prophets. (Amos 3:7.)

Since the Lord has declared "the end from the beginning," and since "the word of our God shall stand forever," it is important that the seed of Abraham, through the loins of Isaac and Jacob, familiarize themselves with the word of their God spoken through the mouths of His prophets. It is important that they understand the promises of the Lord unto them, what He expects of them, that He may fulfill His promises to their fathers that "in thy seed shall all the nations of the earth be blessed." (See Genesis 1:4; 18:18; 22:18.)

The Lord's Covenant with Abraham

Let us therefore consider the promises of the Lord unto Abraham and his seed, the children of Israel:

> And the Lord said, Shall I hide from Abraham that thing which I do;
> Seeing that Abraham shall surely become a great and mighty nation, and *all the nations of the earth shall be blessed in him?* (Genesis 18:17-18.)

Abraham's complete willingness to offer up his son Isaac as a burnt offering, as he had been commanded, brought forth a confirmation of the covenant and an enlargement thereof:

> And the angel of the Lord called unto Abraham out of heaven the second time,
> And said, By myself have I sworn, saith the Lord, for because thou hast done this thing, and hast not withheld thy son, thine only son:
> That in blessing I will bless thee, and in multiplying I will multiply thy seed as the stars of the heaven, and as the sand which is upon the sea shore; and thy seed shall possess the gate of his enemies;
> And *in thy seed shall all the nations of the earth be blessed;* because thou hast obeyed my voice. (Genesis 22:15-18.)

Covenant Renewed with Isaac

The covenant the Lord made with Abraham was renewed with Isaac, his son:

And there was a famine in the land, beside the first famine that was in the days of Abraham. And Isaac went unto Abimelech king of the Philistines unto Gerar.

And the Lord appeared unto him, and said, Go not down into Egypt; dwell in the land which I shall tell thee of:

Sojourn in this land, and I will be with thee, and will bless thee; for unto thee, and unto thy seed, I will give all these countries, and I will perform the oath which I sware unto Abraham thy father;

And I will make thy seed to multiply as the stars of heaven, and will give unto thy seed all these countries; and *in thy seed shall all the nations of the earth be blessed;*

Because that Abraham obeyed my voice, and kept my charge, my commandments, my statutes, and my laws. (Genesis 26:1-5.)

Covenant Renewed with Jacob

The Lord made the same covenant with Jacob, the son of Isaac:

And Jacob went out from Beersheba, and went toward Haran.

And he lighted upon a certain place, and tarried there all night, because the sun was set; and he took of the stones of that place, and put them for his pillows, and lay down in that place to sleep.

And he dreamed, and behold a ladder set up on the earth, and the top of it reached to heaven: and behold the angels of God ascending and descending on it.

And, behold, the Lord stood above it, and said, I am the Lord God of Abraham thy father, and the God of Isaac: the land whereon thou liest, to thee will I give it, and to thy seed;

And thy seed shall be as the dust of the earth, and thou shalt spread abroad to the west, and to the east, and to the north, and to the south: and *in thee and in thy seed shall all the families of the earth be blessed.* (Genesis 28:10-14.)

In summary, the promises made to Abraham, Isaac and Jacob were:

1. "Seeing that Abraham shall surely become a great and mighty nation."

2. "I will give unto thee all these countries."

3. "I will multiply thy seed as the stars of the heavens, and as the sand which is upon the seashore."

4. "And in thy seed shall all the nations of the earth be blessed."

Jacob's Name Changed to Israel

In keeping with the wonderful promises of the Lord to the posterity of Abraham and Isaac, through Jacob, He gave them a special name by which they would be known among all peoples, even the name "Israel" or "Israelites," which name or designation has continued with them to this day. Their God is referred to as the "God of Israel."

At the time Jacob wrestled with an angel at Peniel, the angel changed Jacob's name to Israel:

> And he said, Let me go, for the day breaketh. And he said, I will not let thee go, except thou bless me.
> And he said unto him, What is thy name? And he said, Jacob.
> And he said, *Thy name shall be called no more Jacob, but Israel* for as a prince hast thou power with God and with men, and hast prevailed. (Genesis 32:26-28.)

Jacob's new name, Israel, became the family name. The posterity of Abraham and Isaac, through Jacob came to be known variously as "Israel," "Children of Israel," "House of Israel," "Tribes of Israel." Their descendants are known as "Israelites" to this day.

The following scriptures suggest the varied usage of the name "Israel":

> And the sons of Jacob came out of the field when they heard it: and the men were grieved, and they were very wroth, because he had wrought folly in *Israel*. . . . (Genesis 34:7.)

> Now therefore hearken, *O Israel*, unto the statutes and unto the judgments, which I teach you, for to do them, that ye may live, and go in and possess the land which the Lord God of your fathers giveth you. (Deuteronomy 4:1.)

> The God of *Israel* said, the Rock of *Israel* spake to me, He that ruleth over men must be just, ruling in the fear of God. (II Samuel 23:3.)

> Ye daughters of *Israel*, weep over Saul, who clothed you in scarlet, with other delights, who put on ornaments of gold upon your apparel. (II Samuel 1:24.)

> Who is there among you of all his people? his God be with him, and let him go up to Jerusalem, which is in Judah, and build the house of the Lord God of *Israel*, (he is the God,) which is in Jerusalem. (Ezra 1:3.)

> And made him king over Gilead, and over the Ashurites, and over Jezreel, and over Ephraim, and over Benjamin, and over all *Israel*. (II Samuel 2:9.)

> And Pharaoh sent, and, behold, there was not one of the cattle of the *Israelites* dead. And the heart of Pharaoh was hardened, and he did not let the people go. (Exodus 9:7.)

> And these are the names of the children of *Israel*, which came into Egypt, Jacob and his sons: . . . (Genesis 46:8.)

A careful consideration of the 46th chapter of Genesis, naming the sons and daughters of Jacob and their families, will clearly establish the fact that all of the children of Jacob were called after his new name, "Israel," and were known as "Israelites." It should be emphasized that this designation applied to all the sons of Jacob, and not to the posterity of his son Judah only. Therefore, the fulfillment of the promises of the Lord unto Abraham, Isaac and Jacob, will not be realized through any one branch of the House of Israel, but through all of them.

Jacob's Sons Not to Share Equally in the Lord's Blessings

Through a careful study and consideration of the blessings of the Lord pronounced through Jacob, upon his twelve sons, it is evident that they were not to share equally in the promises of the Lord:

And Jacob called unto his sons, and said, Gather yourselves together, that I may tell you that which shall befall you in the last days.

Gather yourselves together and hear, ye sons of Jacob; and hearken unto Israel your father.

Reuben, thou art my firstborn, my might, and the beginning of my strength, the excellency of dignity, and the excellency of power:

Unstable as water, thou shalt not excel; because thou wentest up to thy father's bed; then defiledst thou it: he went up to my couch.

Simeon and *Levi* are brethren; instruments of cruelty are in their habitations.

O my soul, come not thou into their secret; unto their assembly, mine honour, be not thou united: for in their anger they slew a man, and in their selfwill they digged down a wall.

Cursed be their anger, for it was fierce; and their wrath, for it was cruel: I will divide them in Jacob, and scatter them in Israel.

Judah, thou art he whom thy brethren shall praise: thy hand shall be in the neck of thine enemies; thy father's children shall bow down before thee.

Judah is a lion's whelp: from the prey, my son, thou art gone up: he stooped down, he couched as a lion, and as an old lion; who shall rouse him up?

The sceptre shall not depart from Judah, nor a lawgiver from between his feet, until Shiloh come; and unto him shall the gathering of the people be.

Binding his foal unto the vine, and his ass's colt unto the choice vine; he washed his garments in wine, and his clothes in the blood of grapes:

His eyes shall be red with wine, and his teeth white with milk.

Zebulun shall dwell at the haven of the sea; and he shall be for an haven of ships; and his border shall be unto Zidon.

Issachar is a strong ass couching down between two burdens:

And he saw that rest was good, and the land that it was pleasant; and bowed his shoulder to bear, and became a servant unto tribute.

Dan shall judge his people, as one of the tribes of Israel.

Dan shall be a serpent by the way, an adder in the path, that biteth the horse heels, so that his rider shall fall backward.

I have waited for thy salvation, O Lord.

Gad, a troop shall overcome him: but he shall overcome at the last.

Out of *Asher* his bread shall be fat, and he shall yield royal dainties.

Naphtali is a hind let loose: he giveth goodly words.

Joseph is a fruitful bough, even a fruitful bough by a well; whose branches run over the wall:

The archers have sorely grieved him, and shot at him, and hated him:

But his bow abode in strength, and the arms of his hands were made strong by the hands of the mighty God of Jacob; (from thence is the shepherd, the stone of Israel:)

Even by the God of thy father, who shall help thee; and by the Almighty, who shall bless thee with blessings of heaven above, blessings of the deep that lieth under, blessings of the breasts, and of the womb:

The blessings of thy father have prevailed above the blessings of my progenitors unto the utmost bound of the everlasting hills: they shall be on the head of Joseph, and on the crown of the head of him that was separate from his brethren.

Benjamin shall ravin as a wolf: in the morning he shall devour the prey, and at night he shall divide the spoil.

All these are the twelve tribes of Israel: and this is it that their father spake unto them, and blessed them; every one according to his blessing he blessed them. (Genesis 49: 1-28. See Deuteronomy, Chapter 33, for a record of the blessings of Moses upon the twelve sons of Jacob.)

It is evident that the blessings given to Judah and Joseph were choice above the blessings pronounced upon their brothers.

Israel Divided into Two Kingdoms

Israel was divided into two kingdoms, the Kingdom of Judah, and the Kingdom of Israel — the "Kingdom of Israel" under the leadership of Joseph and his sons, Ephraim and Manasseh. This is in keeping with the promise of the Lord to the sons of Joseph, as they were blessed by Jacob, their grandfather:

> And Israel beheld Joseph's sons, and said, Who are these?
>
> And Joseph said unto his father, they are my sons, whom God hath given me in this place. And he said, Bring them, I pray thee, unto me, and I will bless them. . . .
>
> The Angel which redeemed me from all evil, bless the lads; and *let my name be named on them,* and the name of my fathers Abraham and Isaac; and let them grow into a multitude in the midst of the earth. (Genesis 48:8-9, 16.)

Note Jacob's words: "let my name be named on them, and the name of my fathers Abraham and Isaac." And what was Jacob's name? "Israel." Thus the descendants of Abraham and Isaac through Jacob were called Israelites. The descendants and followers of Joseph were variously called the Kingdom of Israel, the House of Israel, or the House of Joseph or Ephraim. All these designations will be found in the scriptures.

Another reason why the two sons of Joseph are to be counted among the twelve tribes of "Israel" is that the birthright was taken from Reuben, the firstborn of Jacob, because of his transgression, and was given to the sons of Joseph:

> Now the sons of Reuben the firstborn of Israel, (for he was the firstborn; but, forasmuch as he defiled his father's bed, his birthright was given unto the sons of Joseph the son of Israel: and the genealogy is not to be reckoned after the birthright.
>
> For Judah prevailed above his brethren, and of him came the chief ruler; but *the birthright was Joseph's:*)
> (I Chronicles 5:1-2.)

This foreshadows the division of Israel into two kingdoms: "For Judah prevailed above his brethren, and of him came the chief ruler, but the birthright was Joseph's."

The Lord, "the God of Israel," inspired the Prophet Ahijah to predict the division of Israel:

> And he said to Jeroboam, Take thee ten pieces: for thus saith the Lord, the God of Israel, Behold, I will rend the kingdom out of the hand of Solomon, and will give ten tribes to thee:
>
> (But he shall have one tribe for my servant David's sake, and for Jerusalem's sake, the city which I have chosen out of all the tribes of Israel:) (I Kings 11:31-32.)

Concerning the fulfillment of the words of the Lord that he would "rend the kingdom," we read the following:

> And the men of Judah came, and there *they anointed David king over the house of Judah.* . . .
>
> But Abner the son of Ner, captain of Saul's host, took Ishbosheth the son of Saul, and brought him over to Mahanaim;
>
> And made him king over Gilead, and over the Ashurites, and over Jazreel, and over Ephraim, and over Benjamin, and *over all Israel.*
>
> Ishbosheth Saul's son was forty years old when he began to *reign over Israel,* and reigned two years. *But the house of Judah followed David.*
>
> And the time that *David was king in Hebron over the house of Judah* was seven years and six months. (II Samuel 2:4, 8-11.)

From the above it is plain that Ishbosheth the son of Saul was made king "over all Israel . . . but the house of Judah followed David."

It later appears that half of the tribe of Benjamin and the House of Judah constituted the Kingdom of Judah, while the remainder of the tribes were called the Kingdom of Israel or Ephraim.

Then rose up the chief of the fathers of *Judah and Benjamin,* and the priests, and the Levites, with all them whose spirit God had raised, to go up to build the house of the Lord which is in Jerusalem. (Ezra 1:5.)

The following scriptures confirm the fact that the Twelve Tribes of Israel were divided into two kingdoms: Those of the Kingdom of Israel were often referred to as "the men of Ephraim," or "the Kingdom of Ephraim," since Ephraim was the son of Joseph, and since he and his brother Manasseh received the birthright of Reuben, the firstborn of the twelve sons of Jacob:

And the *men of Israel* answered the *men of Judah,* and said, We have ten parts in the king, and we have also more right in David than ye: why then did ye despise us, that our advice should not be first had in bringing back our king? And the words of the men of Judah were fiercer than the words of the men of Israel. (II Samuel 19:43.)

And the *men of Ephraim* said unto him, Why hast thou served us thus, that thou callest us not, when thou wentest to fight with the Midianites? And they did chide with him sharply. (Judges 8:1.)

And the *men of Ephraim* gathered themselves together, and went northward, and said unto Jephthah, Wherefore passedst thou over to fight against the children of Ammon, and didst not call us to go with thee? . . . (Judges 12:1.)

And Joab gave up the sum of the number of the people unto the king: and there were *in Israel* eight hundred thousand valiant men that drew the sword; and the *men of Judah* were five hundred thousand men. (II Samuel 24:9.)

So *Israel* rebelled against *the house of David* unto this day.

And it came to pass, when all Israel heard that Jeroboam was come again, that they sent and called him unto the congregation, and made him *king over all Israel:* there was none that followed *the house of David, but the tribe of Judah only.*

And when Rehoboam was come to Jerusalem, he assembled *all the house of Judah, with the tribe of Benjamin,*

an hundred and fourscore thousand chosen men, which were
warriors, to fight against the *house of Israel*, to bring the
kingdom again to Rehoboam the son of Solomon.

But the word of God came unto Shemaiah the man of
God saying,

Speak unto Rehoboam, the son of Solomon, *king of
Judah,* and unto *all the house of Judah and Benjamin,* and
to the remnant of the people, saying,

Thus saith the Lord, Ye shall not go up, nor fight against
your brethren *the children of Israel:* return every man to
his house; for this thing is from me. They hearkened therefore to the word of the Lord, and returned to depart, according to the word of the Lord. (I Kings 12:19-24.)

From the above quotations it will be noted that
the Lord commanded Judah: "Ye shall not go up, nor
fight against your brethren the children of Israel." And
that notwithstanding the wars, contentions and jeal-
ousies existing between the two kingdoms, the Lord
reminded them that they were "brethren," for they
were all descendants of Abraham, Isaac, and Jacob
and together constituted one great family, the House
of Israel.

It is important, therefore, in looking for the fulfillment of the promises of the Lord unto the Fathers,
that "in thy seed shall all nations of the earth be blessed,"
(Genesis 26:4) that we look not alone to the House
of Judah, but to the House of Israel through Joseph
and his sons Ephraim and Manasseh.

Notwithstanding the fact that the descendants of
Jacob, all of whom were called Israelites, were divided
into two kingdoms, nevertheless, the title "Israel" is
often used in the Bible referring to the whole House
of Israel, or all of the descendants of Jacob. By keeping this in mind, we will be less confused in our further
consideration of the words and predictions of the
prophets.

In our day, the term "Israel" often refers to the
descendants of Judah only, since they have maintained

their identity as a race, while the descendants of Joseph and the other sons of Jacob who constituted the Kingdom of Israel were sifted among the nations as the Prophet Amos declared they would be:

> . . . I will not utterly destroy the house of Jacob, saith the Lord.
>
> For, lo, I will command, and I will sift the house of Israel among all nations, like as corn is sifted in a sieve, yet shall not the least grain fall upon the earth. (Amos 9:8-9.)

CHAPTER 3

THE HOUSE OF JUDAH

Promises to Israel Should be Remembered

We have endeavored to show the promises of the Lord to the seed of Abraham, Isaac and Jacob, which included the promises that they would "surely become a great and mighty nation," that the Lord would multiply their seed "as the stars of the heaven, and as the sand which is upon the sea shore"; that in their seed "shall all the nations of the earth be blessed," and that the Lord promised to give unto them "all these countries."

We have called attention to the promises of the Lord made by Jacob to each of his twelve sons.

We have also shown how Israel was later divided into two great kingdoms; how they left the countries or lands the Lord gave unto them. However, we should remember that all the promises of the Lord are to be fulfilled which means that Israel shall eventually be reestablished in the lands given to their fathers; that the two kingdoms will ultimately be reunited and the Kingdom of God be established among them, that the Lord may fulfill His promises to their fathers that "in thy seed shall all the nations of the earth be blessed."

It is important that all the seed of the fathers, Abraham and Isaac through Jacob, keep these promises in mind and familiarize themselves with all the promises of the Lord through His prophets pertaining to them, that they fail not in doing their part in bringing about a complete fulfillment of the word of the Lord unto them.

The Lord Reassures Wayward and Scattered Israel

The Lord knew, and permitted the Prophet Moses to declare that, because of Israel's transgressions (1) they would not be permitted to remain in the promised land to which Moses led them, (2) they would be scattered among the nations, (3) they would serve false gods.

Then the Lord promised them, through Moses, that, if they would repent, they would "find Him":

> When thou shalt beget children, and children's children, and ye shall have remained long in the land, and shall corrupt yourselves, and make a graven image, or the likeness of any thing, and shall do evil in the sight of the Lord thy God, to provoke him to anger:
>
> I call heaven and earth to witness against you this day, that ye shall soon utterly perish from off the land whereunto ye go over Jordan to possess it; ye shall not prolong your days upon it, but shall utterly be destroyed.
>
> And the Lord shall scatter you among the nations, and ye shall be left few in number among the heathen, whither the Lord shall lead you.
>
> And there ye shall serve gods, the work of men's hands, wood and stone, which neither see, nor hear, nor eat, nor smell.
>
> But if from thence thou shalt seek the Lord thy God, thou shalt find him, if thou seek him with all thy heart and with all thy soul. (Deuteronomy 4:25-29.)

When Moses referred to the false gods to which Israel would turn, he indicated that they would neither be able to "see, nor hear, nor eat, nor smell," classifying them as "the works of men's hands, wood and stone."

In those days it was customary for men to make their own gods fashioned after things upon the earth. As evidence of this we refer to the children of Israel while in the wilderness following their freedom from Egyptian bondage. When Moses returned from the mountain where he communed with the God of Israel, he found the children of Israel had made a "molten calf" from the ear rings of their wives, their sons and their daughters, and were worshiping it. (See Exodus 32:2-8.) It was, no doubt, because of this tendency of the people that the Lord gave as the first and second commandments:

> Thou shalt have no other gods before me.
> Thou shalt not make unto thee any graven image, or any likeness of any thing that is in heaven above, or that is in the earth beneath, or that is in the water under the earth:
> Thou shalt not bow down thyself to them, nor serve them: for I the Lord thy God am a jealous God, visiting the iniquity of the fathers upon the children unto the third and fourth generation of them that hate me;
> And shewing mercy unto thousands of them that love me, and keep my commandments. (Exodus 20:3-6.)

Today, Israel does not worship gods of "wood and stone" who can "neither see, nor hear, nor eat, nor smell," but they have turned, as has the Christian world, to the worship of a spirit god or spirit essence which is said to be everywhere present in the universe, a god that can no more "see, nor hear, nor eat, nor smell," than could the gods of "wood and stone" to which Moses referred.

This is truly a departure from the worship of the true and living God, the God of Abraham, Isaac and Jacob, with whom Moses communed "face to face as a man speaketh unto his friend." (Exodus 33:9-11.)

The Lord permitted another one of His prophets

to foretell the removal of the children of Israel out of the promised land:

> And the Lord said, I will remove Judah also out of my sight, as I have removed Israel, and will cast off this city Jerusalem which I have chosen, and the house of which I said, My name shall be there. (II Kings 23:27.)

This prophecy, as history recounts, was literally fulfilled.

Israel was divided into two kingdoms, Judah and Israel, about 975 B.C. The Kingdom of Israel was overthrown and taken into captivity in the days of Shalmaneser, king of Assyria, and Hoshea, king of Israel about 721 B.C. It is supposed that early in their captivity they made their escape, the main body going northward into unknown lands. Since then they have been known as the "lost tribes."

About a century later, Nebuchadnezzar, king of Babylon, took Jerusalem and carried the tribe of Judah and part of the tribe of Benjamin to Babylon, where Judah served in captivity for seventy years:

> And I will smite the inhabitants of this city, both man and beast: they shall die of a great pestilence.
> And afterward, saith the Lord, I will deliver Zedekiah king of Judah, and his servants, and the people, and such as are left in this city from the pestilence, from the sword, and from the famine, into the hand of Nebuchadnezzar king of Babylon, and into the hand of their enemies, and into the hand of those that seek their life: and he shall smite them with the edge of the sword; he shall not spare them, neither have pity, nor have mercy. (Jeremiah 21:6-7.)
> And they burnt the house of God, and brake down the wall of Jerusalem, and burnt all the palaces thereof with fire, and destroyed all the goodly vessels thereof.
> And them that had escaped from the sword carried he away to Babylon; where they were servants to him and his sons until the reign of the kingdom of Persia:
> To fulfill the word of the Lord by the mouth of Jeremiah, until the land had enjoyed her sabbaths: for as long as she lay desolate she kept sabbath, to fulfil threescore and ten years. (II Chronicles 36:19-21.)

Judah Restored — The Temple Rebuilt

After this captivity the Kingdom of Judah was restored to its lands by Cyrus, king of Persia. They rebuilt the city and the temple:

> Now in the first year of Cyrus king of Persia, that the word of the Lord by the mouth of Jeremiah might be fulfilled, the Lord stirred up the spirit of Cyrus king of Persia, that he made a proclamation throughout all his kingdom, and put it also in writing, saying,
>
> Thus saith Cyrus king of Persia, The Lord God of heaven hath given me all the kingdoms of the earth; and he hath charged me to build him an house at Jerusalem, which is in Judah.
>
> Who is there among you of all his people? his God be with him, and let him go up to Jerusalem, which is in Judah, and build the house of the Lord God of Israel, (he is the God,) which is in Jerusalem. . . .
>
> Then rose up the chief of the fathers of Judah and Benjamin, and the priests, and the Levites, with all them whose spirit God hath raised, to go up to build the house of the Lord which is in Jerusalem. (Ezra 1:1-3, 5.)

This gathering of the House of Judah to their promised land, and the rebuilding of their city and temple under Cyrus, king of Persia, occurred about 538 B.C. They continued to occupy the land from this time on until 70 A.D. when Jerusalem was destroyed and the Jews taken captive under an order issued by Nero and executed by Titus, son of Vespasian. After an insurrection headed by Bar-Cochba, 132-135 A.D., Hadrian completely razed to the ground the remains of Jerusalem left by Titus, and erected in its place a Gentile city, with the title Aelia Capitolina. Jews were forbidden to enter this city on pain of death, and the name of Jerusalem was not revived until the time of Constantine.

This brief account of the House of Judah seems sufficient for our purpose to this point.

Judah's Population in the Nations of the Earth

Since the Jews, the House of Judah, have not intermarried, but have maintained their identity as a race, it is possible to follow them among the nations. The latest figures we have been able to obtain would indicate that there were about 16,000,000 Jews in the world in 1946 located in the various nations as follows:

United States	4,228,000
Russia	3,261,000
Poland	3,029,000
Rumania	984,000
Germany and Austria	690,000
Palestine	450,000
Hungary	445,000
Czechoslovakia	357,000
Great Britain	300,000
Argentina	260,000
France	240,000
Morocco	161,300
Netherlands	156,800
Canada	155,600
Lithuania	155,100
Algeria	110,000
Others	1,017,200
Total	16,000,000

It has been estimated that the Jewish population in Palestine increased in three years (1948 to 1951) from 651,000 to more than 1,350,000.

These figures will indicate approximately where the House of Judah (the Jews) may be found among the nations of today. Their treatment and persecutions are a sad commentary and reflection upon the supposed civilized nations of the earth. For an account of their persecutions during the recent world war, we refer the reader to the book *Behind the Silken Curtain,* by Bartley C. Crum, published by Simon and Schuster, Inc. in 1947, in which the author points out that in Germany alone six million Jews had been killed.

Judah and Israel to be Brought Together

The Jews (Judah) have maintained their identity as a people because they have not intermarried with other peoples, while those of the Kingdom of Israel have been sifted among the nations:

> For, lo, I will command, and I will sift the house of Israel among all nations, like as corn is sifted in a sieve, yet shall not the least grain fall upon the earth. (Amos 9:9.)

But the Lord, through His holy prophets, has made it clear that in the last days He would bring these two great kingdoms together again, and He would be their King:

> And say unto them, Thus saith the Lord God; Behold, I will take the children of Israel *from among the heathen,* whither they be gone, and will gather them on every side, and bring them into their own land:
>
> And I will make them one nation in the land *upon the mountains of Israel; and one king shall be king to them all: and they shall be no more two nations, neither shall they be divided into two kingdoms any more at all:*
>
> . . . so shall they be my people and I will be their God. (Ezekiel 37:21-23.)

How could the Lord make a more positive promise that He would bring these two kingdoms together "and they shall be no more two nations"? This promise should cause the descendants of Judah (the Kingdom of Judah) and the descendants of Joseph (the Kingdom of Israel) to realize that until the two kingdoms are brought together that neither can look for the complete fulfillment of the promises of the Lord unto their fathers, Abraham, Isaac and Jacob.

The Prophet Jeremiah speaks of reuniting the two kingdoms:

> In those days *the house of Judah shall walk with the house of Israel,* and they shall come together out of the land

of the north to the land that I have given for an inheritance unto your fathers. (Jeremiah 3:18.)

The Prophet Isaiah also speaks of the time when the Lord would establish His Kingdom among men. He indicates they would be brought back together so that a common understanding would exist between them as one nation and one people, even the whole House of Israel:

> And he shall set up an ensign for the nations, and shall assemble the outcasts of Israel, and gather together the dispersed of Judah from the four corners of the earth.
> The envy also of Ephraim shall depart, and the adversaries of Judah shall be cut off: *Ephraim shall not envy Judah,* and *Judah shall not vex Ephraim.* (Isaiah 11:12-13.)

Judah! "Turn to the Lord Thy God"

It is our purpose to help Israel find the true and living God, the God of Abraham, the God of Isaac, and the God of Jacob, as the Lord promised through Moses, with whom he spake face to face as one man speaketh with his friend:

> When thou art in tribulation, and all these things are come upon thee, even *in the latter days,* if thou turn to the Lord thy God, and shalt be obedient unto his voice;
> (For the Lord thy God is a merciful God;) he will not forsake thee, neither destroy thee, nor forget the covenant of thy fathers which he sware unto them. (Deuteronomy 4:30-31.)

Judah! Surely "thou art in tribulation." Surely we are living in "the latter days." It is, therefore, of the utmost importance that you "turn to the Lord thy God." By so doing, He has promised that "he will not forsake thee . . . nor forget the covenant of thy fathers which he sware unto them."

It is our purpose, therefore, Judah, to declare unto you the voice of the Lord, and what He is accomplishing in the earth looking to the complete fulfillment of all the promises of the Lord through His prophets. We remind you of the conditions imposed upon you by the Lord to entitle you to a complete fulfillment of His promises: "If thou turn to the Lord, thy God, and shalt be obedient unto his voice."

It is apparent therefore, that to apply the designation "Israel" and "Israelites" to the Jews alone is erroneous, since they constituted the small Kingdom of Judah when Israel was divided, while the followers of Ephraim and Manasseh, sons of Joseph, constituted the large Kingdom of Israel or Ephraim, and were as much the children of Israel as were the Jews. Therefore, if we are to find the fulfillment of the promises of the Lord unto the Fathers, Abraham, Isaac and Jacob, we must search the records and history of these two kingdoms, and the promises of the Lord through their prophets.

The Old Testament is generally conceded to contain the history of the Kingdom of Judah, and the words of her prophets to the time of Malachi about 420 B.C. However, the Old Testament contains only a part of the history of the Kingdom of Israel or Ephraim up to the time they were overthrown in the days of Shalmaneser, king of Assyria, about 721 B.C. We will, therefore, consider other records which give an account of the descendants of Joseph, through his sons Ephraim and Manasseh, the Kingdom of Israel.

CHAPTER 4

THE STICK OF JOSEPH

One Record of Judah — One Record of Joseph

The Bible contains no history of the House of Joseph after approximately 721 B.C. Since we have considered the wonderful promises of the Lord to Joseph and his seed, we cannot refrain from asking: "Where is the record of the fulfillment of these promises? Is it possible that the Lord would have given Joseph such outstanding promises, even above those given to any of his eleven brothers, and then have made no provision for a record of their fulfillment?" It should be kept in mind that the Lord promised Joseph a new land "unto the utmost bounds of the everlasting hills," and that this blessing would come upon the top of the head of him that was separated from his brethren." Let us see what the Lord has to say about a record of the House of Joseph.

Ezekiel was a prophet in Judah unto whom "the heavens were opened, and I saw visions of God." (Ezekiel 1:1.) He was living about 600 years B.C. Let us carefully consider a command Ezekiel received from the Lord, according to his own account:

> The word of the Lord came again unto me, saying,
> Moreover, thou son of man, take thee one stick, and write upon it, For Judah, and for the children of Israel his companions: then take another stick, and write upon it, For Joseph, the stick of Ephraim, and for all the house of Israel his companions:
> And join them one to another into one stick; and they shall become one in thine hand.
> And when the children of thy people shall speak unto thee, saying, Wilt thou not shew us what thou meanest by these?

> Say unto them, Thus saith the Lord God; Behold, I will take the stick of Joseph, which is in the hand of Ephraim, and the tribes of Israel his fellows, and will put them with him, even with the stick of Judah, and make them one stick, and they shall be one in mine hand.
>
> And the sticks whereon thou writest shall be in thine hand before their eyes. (Ezekiel 37:15-20.)

In ancient times, in addition to keeping records on metal plates, it was the custom to write upon parchment, which was then rolled upon sticks for preservation. Thus when Ezekiel was commanded by the Lord to "take thee one stick and write upon it, For Judah . . . then take another stick and write upon it, For Joseph, the stick of Ephraim," in our present day language it was the equivalent of commanding the prophet to write one record for Judah and a separate one for Joseph.

It is evident that when this commandment was given to Ezekiel, the Lord did not anticipate that all His promises made to Abraham, Isaac and Jacob, and to the twelve sons of Jacob, would be recorded in the record of Judah. Recall that at the time this command was given, the house of Joseph had already departed northward into unknown lands, where they had been for some one hundred twenty years. Nevertheless, the Lord wanted all Israel to know that there would be two records kept, one "For Judah, and for the children of Israel his companions," and the other "For Joseph, the stick of Ephraim, and for all the house of Israel his companions." The Lord made it plain that in His own due time He would "make them one stick, and they shall be one in mine hand."

Therefore, the earnest seeker after truth should realize that he cannot expect to have all the record of the Lord's hand-dealings with His children if he has but one of these records. Since we have had the record of Judah with us always, we must inquire, "Where is the record of Joseph?" Since the Lord promised that *He* would bring the two records together, other questions persist: "Has the Lord fulfilled this promise, or must we still look forward to its fulfillment? If the promise has been fulfilled, where is the record of Joseph?" Remember, the Lord considered them equal: *"And they shall be one in mine hand."*

Jerusalem to be Destroyed

As near as we can determine, the command of the Lord to Ezekiel that two records be kept was given about 600 B.C. Recall that when the kingdom of Israel was overthrown in the days of Shalmaneser, king of Assyria, the main body of the Kingdom of Israel, or the House of Joseph, escaped, going northward into unknown lands. A remnant of the House of Joseph remained with the House of Judah. Of this remnant, there was one named Lehi, a descendant of Joseph, who had dwelt in Jerusalem all his days.

In the beginning of the first year of the reign of Zedekiah, king of Judah, there came many prophets prophesying unto the people that they must repent or the great city Jerusalem would be destroyed. Lehi was greatly concerned about this matter and prayed unto the Lord with all his heart in behalf of his people:

> And it came to pass as he prayed unto the Lord, there came a pillar of fire and dwelt upon a rock before him; and he saw and heard much; and because of the things which he saw and heard he did quake and tremble exceedingly.
>
> And it came to pass that he returned to his own house at Jerusalem; and he cast himself upon his bed, being overcome with the Spirit and the things which he had seen.
>
> And being thus overcome with the Spirit, he was carried away in a vision, even that he saw the heavens open, and he thought he saw God sitting upon his throne, surrounded with numberless concourses of angels in the attitude of singing and praising their God.

And it came to pass that he saw one descending out of the midst of heaven, and he beheld that his luster was above that of the sun at noon-day.

And he also saw twelve others following him, and their brightness did exceed that of the stars in the firmament.

And they came down and went forth upon the face of the earth; and the first came and stood before my father, and gave unto him a book, and bade him that he should read.

And it came to pass that as he read, he was filled with the Spirit of the Lord.

And he read, saying: Wo, wo, unto Jerusalem, for I have seen thine abominations! Yea, and many things did my father read concerning Jerusalem — that it should be destroyed, and the inhabitants thereof; many should perish by the sword, and many should be carried away captive into Babylon. . . .

Therefore, I would that ye should know, that after the Lord had shown so many marvelous things unto my father, Lehi, yea, concerning the destruction of Jerusalem, behold he went forth among the people, and began to prophesy and to declare unto them concerning the things which he had both seen and heard. (I Nephi 1:6-13, 18.)

As Lehi went about among the people warning them of the judgments that would befall them and the city of Jerusalem, because of their wickedness, he incurred the displeasure of the people and they persecuted him and sought to take his life.

Lehi Commanded to Leave Jerusalem

In a dream, the Lord commanded Lehi that he take his family and depart into the wilderness. Lehi did as he had been commanded and, with his family, left his home, the land of his inheritance, his gold, his silver, his precious things, taking nothing with him save provisions, and tents. After three days travel in the wilderness, the Lord commanded Lehi that he send his sons back to Jerusalem to obtain from Laban the record of the Jews (the Stick of Judah), and also the genealogy of his forefathers, which was engraven upon plates of brass. Of the importance of taking these records with them into the wilderness, Nephi, son of Lehi, states:

> And behold, it is wisdom in God that we should obtain these records, that we may preserve unto our children the language of our fathers;
> And also that we may preserve unto them the words which have been spoken by the mouth of all the holy prophets, which have been delivered unto them by the Spirit and power of God, since the world began, even down unto this present time. (I Nephi 3:19-20.)

After Nephi and his brothers had succeeded in obtaining the records, Lehi examined them:

> And he beheld that they did contain the five books of Moses, which gave an account of the creation of the world, and also of Adam and Eve, who were our first parents;
> And also a record of the Jews from the beginning, even down to the commencement of the reign of Zedekiah, king of Judah;
> And also the prophecies of the holy prophets, from the beginning, even down to the commencement of the reign of Zedekiah; and also many prophecies which have been spoken by the mouth of Jeremiah.
> And it came to pass that my father, Lehi, also found upon the plates of brass a genealogy of his fathers; wherefore he knew that he was a descendant of Joseph; yea, even that Joseph who was the son of Jacob, who was sold into Egypt, and who was preserved by the hand of the Lord, that he might preserve his father, Jacob, and all his household from perishing with famine.
> And they were also led out of captivity and out of the land of Egypt, by that same God who had preserved them.
> And thus my father, Lehi, did discover the genealogy of his fathers. And Laban also was a descendant of Joseph, wherefore he and his fathers had kept the records. (I Nephi 5:11-16.)

From this account we learn that Lehi was a descendant of Joseph who was sold into Egypt and that the writings his sons obtained from Laban contained "a record of the Jews from the beginning even down

to the commencement of the reign of Zedekiah, king of
Judah." We also learn that Lehi left Jerusalem in the
beginning of the first year of the reign of Zedekiah,
which the Bible Commentary places at about 599 B.C.,
approximately the same time that the Lord commanded
Ezekiel that two records be kept.

We learn that, as the heavens were opened to Ezekiel, so were they opened to Lehi, who prophesied of
the destruction of Jerusalem and her inhabitants. To
escape this destruction, the Lord commanded Lehi to
leave Jerusalem with his family and flee into the wilderness. According to the Bible Chronological table, Jerusalem was destroyed and Judah carried captive about
588 B.C. as Lehi had prophesied, or from eleven to
twelve years following his prediction.

Since God knows "the end from the beginning,"
it seems reasonable and consistent that, in His planning,
Lehi and his family would be led to a new land; that
the Lord would make provision that a record be kept
of His hand-dealings with them; and that through them
would come the fulfillment of the promises made to
Joseph that he would be given a new land in "the utmost
bound of the everlasting hills." These important events
all seem to have taken place at approximately the same
time, showing it was the work of the Lord.

Beginning of the Stick of Joseph

Lehi and his righteous son Nephi were God-fear-
ing men. They were led out of Jerusalem by the hand
of the Lord to escape death at the hands of their per-
secutors, or to escape their destruction with the de-
destruction of Jerusalem. The Lord had shown Lehi
what would befall Jerusalem because of her wickedness. Under the same divine guidance, they were inspired with the importance of keeping a record of the

Lord's hand-dealings with them, and of their travels, etc. In other words, as the Lord commanded Ezekiel that two records be kept, one of Judah and one of Joseph, He inspired Lehi and Nephi to keep a record of what the Lord did for them and their families as part of the Stick of Joseph.

We quote from Nephi's own writings what he had to say about record keeping:

> I, Nephi, having been born of goodly parents, therefore I was taught somewhat in all the learning of my fathers; and having seen many afflictions in the course of my days, nevertheless, having been highly favored of the Lord in all my days; yea, having had a great knowledge of the goodness and the mysteries of God, therefore I make a record of my proceedings in my days.
>
> Yea, I make a record in the language of my father, which consists of the learning of the Jews and the language of the Egyptians.
>
> And I know that the record which I make is true; and I make it according to my knowledge. (I Nephi 1:1-3.)
>
> And now I, Nephi, do not give the genealogy of my fathers in this part of my record; neither at any time shall I give it after upon these plates which I am writing; for it is given in the record which has been kept by my father; wherefore, I do not write it in this work.
>
> For it sufficeth me to say that *we are a descendant of Joseph.*
>
> And it mattereth not to me that I am particular to give a full account of all the things of my father, for they cannot be written upon these plates, for I desire the room that I may write of the things of God.
>
> For the fulness of mine intent is that I may persuade men to come unto the God of Abraham, and the God of Isaac, and the God of Jacob, and be saved.
>
> Wherefore, the things which are pleasing unto the world I do not write, but the things which are pleasing unto God and unto those who are not of the world.
>
> Wherefore, I shall give commandment unto my seed, that they shall not occupy these plates with things which are not of worth unto the children of men. (I Nephi 6:1-6.)

From these quotations three important facts are established:

1. That Lehi and his people are descendants of Joseph. Therefore, their record is the "Stick of Joseph."

2. That Nephi testifies the record is true.

3. That the record was not written to be pleasing unto the world, i.e., to be of historical value only, "but the things which are pleasing unto God and unto those who are not of the world, for the fulness of mine intent is that I may persuade men to come unto the God of Abraham, and the God of Isaac, and the God of Jacob, and be saved."

Was not this the purpose the Lord had in mind when he commanded Ezekiel to keep two records, one of Judah and one of Joseph?

Thus, as the Stick of Judah, the Holy Bible, was to be an instrument in the hands of the Lord for the guidance of His children, so also was the Stick of Joseph when joined to the Stick of Judah. Let us not forget the Lord's command: "and make them one Stick, and they shall be one in mine hand." (See Ezekiel 37:18-19.)

Ishmael and His Family go into the Wilderness

The "Stick of Joseph" further reveals that after Lehi and his family had left Jerusalem, and after his sons had returned and obtained the brass plates from Laban, the Lord further commanded that he again send his sons back to Jerusalem, "saying that it was not meet for him, Lehi, that he should take his family into the wilderness alone; but that his sons should take daughters to wife, that they might raise up seed unto the Lord *in the land of promise*." They were therefore commanded that they "should again return unto the land of Jerusalem, and bring down Ishmael and his family into the wilderness:"

> And it came to pass that the Lord did soften the heart of Ishmael, and also his household, insomuch that they took their journey with us down into the wilderness to the tent of our father. (I Nephi 7:5.)

Journey to "the Promised Land"

After they had journeyed in the wilderness for the space of eight years, (See I Nephi 17:4) they pitched their tents by the seashore, and the Lord gave to Nephi a commandment that he build a ship. The Lord instructed him how it should be built, where he could find ore to make tools, etc. When the ship was completed according to the word of the Lord, Nephi's brothers, Laman and Lemuel, who had complained against him, "beheld that it was good, and that the workmanship thereof was exceeding fine; wherefore, they did humble themselves again before the Lord."

> And it came to pass that the voice of the Lord came unto my father, that we should arise and go down into the ship.
> And it came to pass that on the morrow, after we had prepared all things, much fruits and meat from the wilderness, and honey in abundance, and provisions according to that which the Lord had commanded us, we did go down into the ship, with all our loading and our seeds, and whatsoever thing we had brought with us, every one according to his age; wherefore we did all go down into the ship, with our wives and our children. (I Nephi 18:5-6.)

They spent many days upon the water, and after having been driven by the wind, they reached the shore of "the promised land."

> . . . and we went forth upon the land, and did pitch our tents; and did call it the promised land.
> And it came to pass that we did begin to till the earth, and we began to plant seeds; yea, we did put all our seeds

into the earth, which we had brought from the land of
Jerusalem. And it came to pass that they did grow exceedingly; wherefore, we were blessed in abundance.

And it came to pass that we did find upon the land of
promise, as we journeyed in the wilderness, that there
were beasts in the forests of every kind, both the cow and
the ox, and the ass and the horse, and the goat and the wild
goat, and all manner of wild animals, which were for the
use of man. And we did find all manner of ore, both of
gold, and of silver, and of copper. (I Nephi 18:23-25.)

In reading Nephi's description of how their seeds
did grow exceedingly, so that they were blessed in
abundance, and his further description of what they
found in the land upon their arrival in the Land of Promise, including animals of all kinds, and all manner of
ore, both of gold, and of silver, and of copper, we would
do well to refer again to the blessing pronounced by
Moses upon the head of Joseph, the son of Jacob:

And of Joseph he said, Blessed of the Lord be his land,
for the precious things of heaven, for the dew, and for the
deep that coucheth beneath,
And for the precious fruits brought forth by the sun,
and for the precious things brought forth by the moon,
And for the chief things of the ancient mountains, and
for the precious things of the lasting hills,
And for the precious things of the earth and fulness
thereof, and for the good will of him that dwelt in the bush:
let the blessing come upon the head of Joseph, and upon
the top of the head of him that was separated from his
brethren. (Deuteronomy 33:13-16.)

From this blessing, it is clear that Joseph was to
have a new land; that it was to be a choice land pro-
ducing "precious fruits," etc.; that it was to be "in the
ancient mountains"; and that it would produce "the
precious things of the lasting hills"; and that it would
abound with "the precious things of the earth and fulness
thereof." It is clear that this blessing was to come upon
the head of Joseph who "was separate from his brethren."

All these promises seem to have had a complete fulfillment when the Lord led Lehi and his company, descendants of Joseph, to the Land of Promise, the land of America. Their history seems to have been written largely in the western part of South, Central and North America, or in the Rocky Mountains—"the ancient mountains," and "the lasting hills."

As the people became better established in "the promised land," they were so prospered by the Lord, that they often called it "a land choice above all other lands." (See I Nephi 13:30; II Nephi 1:5.)

The Stick of Joseph covers a history of Lehi and his people from the time they left Jerusalem 600 years B.C. to 421 A.D., or a period of more than one thousand years.

The record of Joseph also gives an account of the people of Jared who were scattered at the time the Lord confounded the language of the people when they were building a tower to get to heaven: "So the Lord scattered them abroad from thence upon the face of all the earth: and they left off to build the city." (Genesis 11:8.) Some of these people were led by the Lord, under Jared and his brother, to the land of America, a part of "the face of all the earth."

Mulekites Discovered

This Stick of Joseph also gives an account of the people of Mulek, known as the Mulekites. Concerning the time when king Nebuchadnezzar took the inhabitants of Jerusalem captive to Babylon, we read the following:

> And they slew the sons of Zedekiah before his eyes, and put out the eyes of Zedekiah, and bound him with fetters of brass, and carried him to Babylon. (II Kings 25:7.)

Of this event, the Stick of Joseph states:

> And now will you dispute that Jerusalem was destroyed?
> Will ye say that the sons of Zedekiah were not slain, all
> except it were Mulek? Yea, and do ye not behold that the
> seed of Zedekiah are with us, and they were driven out
> of the land of Jerusalem? . . . (Helaman 8:21.)

It will thus be seen that one of the sons of Zedekiah
escaped and he and his people were led to the land of
America. This seems to have been about 588 B.C., or
twelve years after Lehi and his family left Jerusalem. It
seems that the people of Mulek did not keep records but
after a sojourn in the land of America for approximately
400 years, the Nephites discovered them, and the two
peoples were united under king Mosiah of the people
of Nephi:

> Behold, it came to pass that Mosiah discovered that
> the people of Zarahemla came out from Jerusalem at the
> time that Zedekiah, king of Judah, was carried away cap-
> tive into Babylon.
> And they journeyed in the wilderness, and were brought
> by the hand of the Lord across the great waters, into the
> land where Mosiah discovered them; and they had dwelt
> there from that time forth. . . .
> And it came to pass that the people of Zarahemla, (the
> Mulekites) and of Mosiah, did unite together; and Mosiah
> was appointed to be their king. (Omni 1:15-16, 19.)

American Indians are of Israel

Returning again to Lehi and his descendants who
were called Nephites after the prophet Nephi, righteous
son of Lehi, we learn that shortly after their arrival in
"the promised land," [the land of America], because
of the wickedness of the followers of two of the sons of
Lehi—Laman and Lemuel—the Lord placed the curse of
a dark skin upon them:

> And he had caused the cursing to come upon them,
> yea, even a sore cursing, because of their iniquity. For be-

hold, they had hardened their hearts against him, that they had become like unto a flint; wherefore, as they were white, and exceeding fair and delightsome, that they might not be enticing unto my people the Lord God did cause a skin of blackness to come upon them.

And thus saith the Lord God: I will cause that they shall be loathsome unto thy people, save they shall repent of their iniquities.

And cursed shall be the seed of him that mixeth with their seed; for they shall be cursed even with the same cursing. And the Lord spake it, and it was done. (II Nephi 5:21-23.)

Those who were thus cursed succeeded in destroying all the white people, save twenty-four souls, about 421 A.D., at which time, Moroni deposited in the Hill Cumorah, in the western part of the state of New York, the plates containing the history of this people, or the Stick of Joseph. The dark-skinned people who occupied this land of America from that time on were called "Lamanites," who are the people known generally as the American Indians, all of whom are of the house of Israel.

Stick of Joseph Speaks Low Out of the Dust

The Prophet Isaiah saw the coming forth of this record of Joseph as the voice of one that has a familiar spirit whispering out of the dust:

Woe, to Ariel, to Ariel, the city where David dwelt! add ye year to year, let them kill sacrifices.

Yet I will distress Ariel, and there shall be heaviness and sorrow: and it shall be unto me as Ariel.

And I will camp against thee round about, and will lay siege against thee with a mount, and I will raise forts against thee.

And thou shalt be brought down, and shalt speak out of the ground, and thy speech shall be low out of the dust, and thy voice shall be, as one that hath a familiar spirit, out of the ground, and thy speech shall whisper out of the dust. (Isaiah 29:1-4.)

Isaiah saw the downfall of Ariel, or Jerusalem, at a
time far in the future, "add ye year to year," or approximately 170 years before Jerusalem was destroyed as
prophesied by Lehi.   Then he seems to have been carried away in vision to witness a similar destruction of
the cities of Joseph, "and it shall be unto me as Ariel."
Then he describes how they would be besieged and
forts would be raised against them.   They would be
brought down and would speak "out of the ground."
Their speech would be low "out of the dust."   Now,
obviously, the only way a dead people could speak "out
of the ground" or "out of the dust" would be by the
written word which was accomplished through the
"Stick of Joseph."   Truly it has a familiar spirit, for it
contains the words of the Nephite and Lamanite prophets
of God.

The Prophet Nephi describes the coming forth of
this record, speaking from the dust in these words:

> After my seed and the seed of my brethren shall have
> dwindled in unbelief, and shall have been smitten by the
> Gentiles; yea, after the Lord God shall have camped against
> them round about, and shall have laid siege against them
> with a mount, and raised forts against them; and after they
> shall have been brought down low in the dust, even that
> they are not, yet the words of the righteous shall be written,
> and the prayers of the faithful shall be heard, and all those
> who have dwindled in unbelief shall not be forgotten.
>
> *For those who shall be destroyed shall speak unto them
> out of the ground, and their speech shall be low out of the
> dust, and their voice shall be as one that hath a familiar
> spirit; for the Lord God will give unto him power, that he
> may whisper concerning them, even as it were out of the
> ground; and their speech shall whisper out of the dust.*
>
> For thus saith the Lord God: They shall write the things
> which shall be done among them, and they shall be written
> and *sealed up in a book,* and those who have dwindled in
> unbelief shall not have them, for they seek to destroy the
> things of God. (II Nephi 26:15-17.)

Part of the Stick of Joseph is Sealed

It will be seen that Nephi was privileged to see in vision the final destruction of his people, and how they would be brought down and speak from the dust. He informs us that this would be done through their recording the things done among them, that they would "be written and sealed up in a book." This is in complete accord with the same vision given to Isaiah long before Nephi's time:

> And the vision of all is become unto you as the words of a book that is sealed, which men deliver to one that is learned, saying, Read this, I pray thee: and he saith, I cannot; for it is sealed: (Isaiah 29:11.)

A Marvelous Work and a Wonder

What Isaiah was privileged to see concerning the destruction of the Nephites and the coming forth of their record, as a sealed book, speaking from the ground, seems to have impressed him greatly:

> Wherefore the Lord said, Forasmuch as this people draw near me with their mouth, and with their lips do honour me, but have removed their heart far from me, and their fear toward me is taught by the precept of men:
> Therefore, behold, I will proceed to do a marvelous work among this people, even a marvellous work and a wonder: for the wisdom of their wise men shall perish, and the understanding of their prudent men shall be hid. (Isaiah 29:13-14.)

The bringing forth of the Stick of Joseph which the Lord has done, surely constitutes "a marvelous work and a wonder." It has truly caused "the wisdom of their wise men [to] perish, and the understanding of their prudent men [to] be hid." (Isaiah 29:14.) It is one of the great steps in the unfoldment of the Lord's eternal program looking to the uniting of the two great houses of Israel, Judah and Joseph, since now He has united their records.

The keeping of these two records, the Stick of Judah and the Stick of Joseph, was a very grave and important matter to the Lord. He commanded they be kept with the promise that He would join them together and make them one in His hand. We understand this to mean that when the "Stick of Joseph" would be joined to the "Stick of Judah," it would have the same significance to the Jews as their record, the Old Testament, the Stick of Judah, would have to the descendants of Joseph.

We of the House of Joseph cannot underestimate the value of the Stick of Judah. Of its importance, the Lord told Nephi, when they returned to Jerusalem to obtain the plates of Laban, that "it is better that one man should perish than that a nation should dwindle and perish in unbelief." (I Nephi 4:13.)

In the sight of the Lord, the Stick of Joseph was to be of equal importance and value to the House of Judah, at the time the Lord would see fit to bring it forth and join it to the Stick of Judah, and make them one in His hand.

We will, therefore, give consideration to some of the sayings of the prophets of Joseph, and their message to their brethren, the House of Judah, the Jews.

CHAPTER 5

JOSEPH'S MESSAGE TO JUDAH

Stick of Joseph Offered to Judah

Do the Jews have any information as to the whereabouts of the Stick of Joseph which the Lord commanded be kept, and which would be taken from the custody of Ephraim and joined to the Stick of Judah and become one in the hand of the Lord? This command of the Lord to his Prophet Ezekiel cannot be repudiated. The Jews must look for its fulfillment. The Stick of Joseph is here and we now offer it to the Jews. There should be great eagerness on their part to know what the Lord has said concerning them through the prophets of Joseph, their brethren.

The Lord understood that Satan would put it into the hearts of the children of men to refuse to accept this new volume of scripture, and so declared himself through the American prophet, Nephi:

> But behold, there shall be many—*at that day when I shall proceed to do a marvelous work among them,* that I may remember my covenants which I have made unto the children of men, that *I may set my hand again the second time to recover my people,* which are of the house of Israel;
> And also, that I may remember the promises which I have made unto thee, Nephi, and also unto thy father, that I would remember your seed; and that the words of your seed should proceed forth out of my mouth unto your seed; *and my words shall hiss forth unto the ends of the earth, for a standard unto my people, which are of the* house of Israel.
> And because my words shall hiss forth—many of the Gentiles shall say: A Bible! A Bible! We have got a Bible, and there cannot be any more Bible.
> But thus saith the Lord God: O fools, they shall have a Bible; and it shall proceed forth *from the Jews, mine an-*

cient covenant people. And what *thank they the Jews for the Bible, which they receive from them?* Yea, what do the Gentiles mean? *Do they remember the travels, and the labors, and the pains of the Jews, and their diligence unto me, in bringing forth salvation unto the Gentiles?*

O ye Gentiles, have ye remembered the Jews, mine ancient covenant people? *Nay; but ye have cursed them, and have hated them, and have not sought to recover them.* But behold, I will return all these things upon your own heads; *for I the Lord have not forgotten my people.*

Thou fool, that shall say: A Bible, we have got a Bible, and we need no more Bible. *Have ye obtained a Bible save it were by the Jews?*

Know ye not that there are more nations than one? Know ye not that I, the Lord your God, have created all men, and that I remember those who are upon the isles of the sea; and that I rule in the heavens above and in the earth beneath; and I bring forth my word unto the children of men, yea, even upon all the nations of the earth?

Wherefore murmur ye, because that ye shall receive more of my word? *Know ye not that the testimony of two nations is a witness unto you that I am God, that I remember one nation like unto another? Wherefore, I speak the same words unto one nation like unto another. And when the two nations shall run together the testimony of the two nations shall run together also.*

And I do this that I may prove unto many that I am the same yesterday, today, and forever; and that I speak forth my words according to mine own pleasure. And because that I have spoken one word ye need not suppose that I cannot speak another; for my work is not yet finished; neither shall it be until the end of man, neither from that time henceforth and forever.

Wherefore, because that ye have a Bible ye need not suppose that it contains all my words; neither need ye suppose that I have not caused more to be written.

For I command all men, both in the east and in the west, and in the north, and in the south, and in the islands of the sea, that they shall write the words which I speak unto them; for out of the books which shall be written I will judge the world, every man according to their works, according to that which is written.

For behold, I shall speak unto the Jews and they shall write it; and I shall also speak unto the Nephites and they shall write it; and I shall also speak unto the other tribes of the house of Israel, which I have led away, and they shall write it; and I shall also speak unto all nations of the earth and they shall write it.

And it shall come to pass that *the Jews shall have the words of the Nephites,* and *the Nephites shall have the words of the Jews;* and the Nephites and the Jews shall have the words of the lost tribes of Israel; and the lost tribes of Israel shall have the words of the Nephites and the Jews.

And it shall come to pass that my people, which are of the house of Israel, shall be gathered home unto the lands of their possessions; *and my word also shall be gathered in one.* And I will show unto them that fight against my word and against my people, who are of the house of Israel, that I am God, *and that I covenanted with Abraham that I would remember his seed forever.* (2 Nephi Chapter 29.)

It will thus be noted that as the Lord revealed to Isaiah that He would proceed to do "a marvelous work and a wonder" among the children of men, He also gave Nephi a similar revelation, in which He defined in more definite terms what this marvelous work and a wonder would consist of:

a. "That I may remember my covenant which I have made unto the children of men." (*Ibid.,* verse 1.)

b. "That I may set my hand again the second time to recover my people, which are of the house of Israel." (*Ibid.,* verse 1.)

c. "That I would remember your seed; and that the words of your seed should proceed forth out of my mouth unto your seed; and my words shall hiss forth unto the ends of the earth, for a standard unto my people, which are of the house of Israel." (*Ibid.,* verse 2.)

d. "And it shall come to pass *that the Jews shall have the words of the Nephites,* and the Nephites shall have the words of the Jews; and the Nephites and Jews shall have the words of the lost tribes of Israel; and the lost tribes of Israel shall have the words of the Nephites and the Jews." (*Ibid.,* verse 13.)

e. "And it shall come to pass that my people, which are of the house of Israel, shall be gathered home unto the lands of their possessions; *and my word also shall be gathered in one,* And I will show unto them that fight

against my word and against my people, who are of the
house of Israel, that I am God, and that *I covenanted
with Abraham that I would remember his seed forever.*"
(*Ibid.*, verse 14.)

The burden of this revelation, therefore, is that the
Lord would keep the covenant He had made with
Abraham that He would remember His seed forever.
We must not forget that this promise was made to Joseph
and his descendants, to the lost tribes of Israel, as well
as to the Jews. Therefore, we have the Lord's statement that He would set His hand again "the second
time" to recover His people, the House of Israel.

Prophets Provided to the Remnants of Israel

In order for the Lord to accomplish all He promised to Abraham and his seed, it was necessary that
He raise up prophets to the various branches of the
House of Israel; that they keep their records; that these
records be "gathered in one"; that the Jews have the
words of the Nephites; and that the Nephites have the
words of the Jews. As has been pointed out, the words
of the Jews have been among us through the Holy Bible.
Now, if the Jews are willing to do their part in fulfilling
the promises of the Lord unto Abraham that through
him and his seed "should all the nations of the earth be
blessed," it becomes necessary that they accept the
words of the Nephites, or the Stick of Joseph.

Judah and Joseph to Walk Together

From the Stick of Judah, the Holy Bible, it is evident that the marvelous work and a wonder the Lord
promised to bring forth, connotes a reuniting of the
House of Judah and the House of Israel, or Joseph. This

reunion presupposes a new movement under the God of Israel looking to this great achievement:

> Behold, the days come, saith the Lord, that *I will make a new covenant with the house of Israel, and with the House of Judah*: (Jeremiah 31:31.)

> Say unto them, Thus saith the Lord God; Behold, I will take the stick of Joseph, which is in the hand of Ephraim, and the tribes of Israel his fellows, and will put them with him, even with the stick of Judah, and make them one stick, and they shall be one in mine hand.
> And the sticks whereon thou writest shall be in thine hand before their eyes.
> And say unto them, Thus saith the Lord God; Behold, I will take the children of Israel from among the heathen, whither they be gone, and will gather them on every side, and bring them into their own land:
> And I will make them one nation in the land upon the mountains of Israel; and one king shall be king to them all: and *they shall be no more two nations, neither shall they be divided into two kingdoms* any more at all: (Ezekiel 37:19-22.)

> In those days *the house of Judah shall walk with the house of Israel,* and they shall come together out of the land of the north to the land that I have given for an inheritance unto your fathers. (Jeremiah 3:18.)

> And he shall set up an ensign for the nations, and shall assemble the outcasts of Israel, and *gather together the dispersed of Judah* from the four corners of the earth.
> The envy also of Ephraim shall depart, and the adversaries of Judah shall be cut off. *Ephraim shall not envy Judah, and Judah shall not vex Ephraim.* (Isaiah 11:12-13.)

> *And I will strengthen the house of Judah, and I will save the house of Joseph, and I will bring them again to place them;* for I have mercy upon them: and they shall be as though I had not cast them off: for I am the Lord their God, and will hear them.
> And they of Ephraim shall be like a mighty man, and their heart shall rejoice as through wine: yea, their children shall see it, and be glad; their heart shall rejoice in the Lord.
> *I will hiss for them, and gather them;* for I have redeemed them; and they shall increase as they have increased.

> And I will sow them among the people: and they shall remember me in far countries; and they shall live with their children, and turn again. . . .
>
> And I will strengthen them in the Lord; *and they shall walk up and down in his name,* saith the Lord. (Zechariah 10:6-9, 12.)

From these scriptures, it is evident the Lord had definitely in mind that no matter how Israel would be scattered, He would eventually bring them together again. How could His promises to Abraham be fulfilled without accomplishing this objective.

Zechariah called attention to the fact that "Ephraim shall be like a mighty man . . . and I will sow them among the people . . . and they shall remember me in far countries." This prophecy seems to attach importance to the House of Joseph, and to what their prophets might have to say, as recorded in the Stick of Joseph, since Jeremiah definitely states that "In those days the house of Judah shall walk with the house of Israel." (Jeremiah 3:18.) This implies that Israel will point the way to Judah, and that in this accomplishment, the Stick of Joseph would perform a great mission in making plain unto Judah many important matters which they hitherto have not understood. Since we have had the Stick of Judah with us these many years, and since the Stick of Joseph has only recently been given to us, it seems proper that we consider the important truths Joseph has to offer his brother Judah through the record which the Lord commanded Ezekiel to keep.

Is Jesus of Nazareth the Promised Messiah?

No greater question has ever presented itself to the House of Judah, than the question: "Is Jesus Christ of Nazareth the promised Messiah?" If He is, how important that the House of Judah should know it, since

His mission would be of far greater importance to them than the mission of any of the prophets. While most of the Jews today do not accept Jesus Christ as their promised Messiah, yet there are many among them who do. If this question could be resolved in definite form, what a bone of contention would be removed not only from between the Jews and the Gentiles (the House of Joseph) but from among the Jews themselves. This great and important question must sooner or later find a definite answer. This question must be resolved before "the house of Judah shall walk with the house of Israel." (Jeremiah 3:18.)

It seems reasonable to assume that the clarification of this often disputed question might logically come at the time spoken of by Jeremiah when he said: "Behold, the days come, saith the Lord, that I will make a new covenant with the house of Israel, and with the house of Judah:" (Jeremiah 31:31.) In this promise, Jeremiah puts Israel or Joseph first; hence it seems logical that Judah listen to Joseph.

If, therefore, Judah will but listen to Joseph at this time, he will discover that what Joseph has to offer his brother Judah, and the other tribes of the House of Israel, is of far greater value to them than was the grain given them and their father Jacob, by their brother Joseph from the granaries of Pharaoh. (Genesis Chapter 42.) It will also give Judah a greater understanding of Joseph's dreams when he saw all his brothers' sheaves do obeisance to his sheaf, and when he saw the sun and the moon and the eleven stars do obeisance to him. (See Genesis 37:5-11.) Recall, it was the Lord who gave Joseph his dreams.

Since all things were known to God from the beginning, (Isaiah 46:9-10.) He understood just what part Joseph and his seed would play in establishing "A new covenant with the house of Israel, and with the house of Judah," in the latter days. God knew what the Stick of Joseph would be able to contribute to the House of Judah, and all the children of Israel, when the Lord would bring it forth as declared by Ezekiel:

> . . . Behold, I will take the stick of Joseph, which is in the hand of Ephraim, and the tribes of Israel his fellows, and will put them with him, even with the stick of Judah, and make them one stick, and they shall be one in mine hand. (Ezekiel 37:19.)

Since they are to become one in the hand of the Lord, Judah would do well to give attention to what the Stick of Joseph has to say.

Messiah to be Raised Up from Among the Descendants of Judah

Nephi, in the Stick of Joseph, gives us an account of the words of his father Lehi, a great prophet of the Lord, concerning the promised Messiah. Admittedly, the quotations are long but the reward for patience in carefully reading them will be rich indeed:

> And now I, Nephi, proceed to give an account upon these plates of my proceedings, and my reign and ministry; wherefore, to proceed with mine account, I must speak somewhat of the things of my father, and also of my brethren.
>
> For behold, it came to pass after my father had made an end of speaking the words of his dream, and also of exhorting them to all diligence, *he spake unto them concerning the Jews—*
>
> That after they should be destroyed, even that great city of Jerusalem, and many be carried away captive into Babylon, according to the own due time of the Lord, they should return again, yea, even be brought back out of captivity; and after they should be brought back out of captivity they should possess again the land of their inheritance.
>
> *Yea, even six hundred years from the time that my father left Jerusalem, a prophet would the Lord God raise up*

among the Jews—even a Messiah, or, in other words, a Savior of the world.

And he also spake concerning the prophets, how great a number had testified of these things, concerning this Messiah, of whom he had spoken, or this Redeemer of the world.

Wherefore, all mankind were in a lost and in a fallen state, and ever would be save they should rely on this Redeemer.

And he spake also concerning a prophet who should come before the Messiah, to prepare the way of the Lord—

Yea, even he should go forth and cry in the wilderness: Prepare ye the way of the Lord, and make his paths straight; for there standeth one among you whom ye know not; and he is mightier than I, whose shoe's latchet I am not worthy to unloose. And much spake my father concerning this thing.

And my father said he should baptize in Bethabara, beyond Jordan; and he also said he should baptize with water; even that he should baptize the Messiah with water.

And after he had baptized the Messiah with water, he should behold and bear record that he had baptized the Lamb of God, who should take away the sins of the world.

And it came to pass after my father had spoken these words *he spake unto my brethren concerning the gospel which should be preached among the Jews,* and also concerning the dwindling of the Jews in unbelief. And after they had slain the Messiah, who should come, and after he had been slain he should rise from the dead, and should make himself manifest, by the Holy Ghost, unto the Gentiles.

Yea, even my father spake much concerning the Gentiles, and also concerning the house of Israel, that they should be compared like unto an olive-tree, whose branches should be broken off and should be scattered upon all the face of the earth.

Wherefore, he said it must needs be that we should be led with one accord into the land of promise, unto the fulfilling of the word of the Lord, that we should be scattered upon all the face of the earth.

And after the house of Israel should be scattered they should be gathered together again; or, in fine, *after the Gentiles had received the fulness of the Gospel,* the natural branches of the olive-tree or the remnants of the house of Israel, should be grafted in, or *come to the knowledge of the true Messiah, their Lord and their Redeemer.* (1 Nephi 10:1-14.)

Nephi Desired Knowledge of the Messiah

Nephi was so impressed with the things his father had seen in his dream, that he was desirous also that he be privileged to see, and hear, and know of these things:

> And it came to pass after I, Nephi, having heard all the words of my father, concerning the things which he saw in the vision, and also the things which he spake by the power of the Holy Ghost, which power he received by faith on the Son of God—and the Son of God was the Messiah who should come—I, Nephi, was desirous also that I might see, and hear, and know of these things, by the power of the Holy Ghost, which is the gift of God unto all those who diligently seek him, as well in times of old as in the time that he should manifest himself unto the children of men. (1 Nephi 10:17.)

Vision of Nephi Concerning the Messiah

Let Nephi now describe the things he saw and heard because of his great faith and his desire:

> For it came to pass after I had desired to know the things that my father had seen, and believing that the Lord was able to make them known unto me, as I sat pondering in mine heart I was caught away in the Spirit of the Lord, yea, into an exceeding high mountain, which I never had before seen, and upon which I never had before set my foot.
> And the Spirit said unto me: Behold, what desirest thou?
> And I said: I desire to behold the things which my father saw.
> And the Spirit said unto me. Believest thou that thy father saw the tree of which he hath spoken?
> And I said: Yea, thou knowest that I believe all the words of my father.
> And when I had spoken these words, the Spirit cried with a loud voice, saying: Hosanna to the Lord, the most high God; for he is God over all the earth, yea, even above all. And blessed art thou, Nephi, because thou believest in the Son of the most high God; wherefore, thou shalt behold the things which thou hast desired.
> And behold this thing shall be given unto thee for a sign, that after thou hast beheld the tree which bore the fruit which thy father tasted, thou shalt also behold a man

descending out of heaven, and him shall ye witness; and after ye have witnessed him ye shall bear record that it is the Son of God.

And it came to pass that the Spirit said unto me: Look! and I looked and beheld a tree; and it was like unto the tree which my father had seen; and the beauty thereof was far beyond, yea, exceeding of all beauty; and the whiteness thereof did exceed the whiteness of the driven snow.

And it came to pass after I had seen the tree, I said unto the Spirit: I behold thou hast shown unto me the tree which is precious above all.

And he said unto me: What desirest thou?

And I said unto him: To know the interpretation thereof—for I spake unto him as a man speaketh; for I beheld that he was in the form of a man; yet nevertheless, I knew that it was the Spirit of the Lord; and he spake unto me as a man speaketh with another.

And it came to pass that he said unto me: Look! And I looked as if to look upon him, and I saw him not; for he had gone from before my presence.

And it came to pass that I looked and beheld the great city of Jerusalem, and also other cities. *And I beheld the city of Nazareth; and in the city of Nazareth I beheld a virgin, and she was exceeding fair and white.*

And it came to pass that I saw the heavens open; and an angel came down and stood before me; and he said unto me: Nephi, what beholdest thou?

And I said unto him: A virgin, most beautiful and fair above all other virgins.

And he said unto me: Knowest thou the condescension of God?

And I said unto him: I know that he loveth his children; nevertheless, I do not know the meaning of all things.

And he said unto me: *Behold, the virgin whom thou seest is the mother of the Son of God,* after the manner of the flesh.

And it came to pass that I beheld that she was carried away in the Spirit; and after she had been carried away in the Spirit for the space of a time the angel spake unto me, saying: Look!

And I looked and beheld the virgin again, bearing a child in her arms.

And the angel said unto me: *Behold the Lamb of God, yea, even the Son of the Eternal Father!* Knowest thou the meaning of the tree which thy father saw?

And I answered him, saying: Yea, it is the love of God, which sheddeth itself abroad in the hearts of the children of men; wherefore, it is the most desirable above all things.

And he spake unto me, saying: Yea, and the most joyous to the soul.

And after he had said these words, he said unto me: Look! And I looked, and *I beheld the Son of God going forth among the children of men;* and I saw many fall down at his feet and worship him.

And it came to pass that I beheld that the rod of iron, which my father had seen, was the word of God, which led to the fountain of living waters, or to the tree of life; which waters are a representation of the love of God; and I also beheld that the tree of life was a representation of the love of God.

And the angel said unto me again: Look and behold the condescension of God!

And I looked and beheld the Redeemer of the world, of whom my father had spoken; and I also beheld the prophet who should prepare the way before him. *And the Lamb of God went forth and was baptized of him; and after he was baptized, I beheld the heavens open, and the Holy Ghost come down out of heaven and abide upon him in the form of a dove.*

And I beheld that he went forth ministering unto the people, in power and great glory; and the multitudes were gathered together to hear him; and I beheld that they cast him out from among them.

And I also beheld twelve others following him. And it came to pass that they were carried away in the Spirit from before my face, and I saw them not.

And it came to pass that the angel spake unto me again, saying: Look! And I looked, and I beheld the heavens open again, and I saw angels descending upon the children of men; and they did minister unto them.

And he spake unto me again, saying: Look! And I looked, and beheld the Lamb of God going forth among the children of men. And I beheld multitudes of people who were sick, and who were afflicted with all manner of diseases, and with devils and unclean spirits; and the angel spake and showed all these things unto me. And they were healed by the power of the Lamb of God; and the devils and the unclean spirits were cast out.

And it came to pass that the angel spake unto me again, saying, *Look! And I looked and beheld the Lamb of God, that he was taken by the people; yea, the Son of the ever-*

lasting God was judged of the world; and I saw and bear record.

And I, Nephi, saw that he was lifted up upon the cross and slain for the sins of the world. And after he was slain I saw the multitudes of the earth, that they were gathered together to fight against the apostles of the Lamb; for thus were the twelve called by the angel of the Lord.

And the multitude of the earth was gathered together; and I beheld that they were in a large and spacious building, like unto the building which my father saw. And the angel of the Lord spake unto me again, saying: Behold the world and the wisdom thereof; yea, behold the house of Israel hath gathered together to fight against the twelve apostles of the Lamb.

And it came to pass that I saw and bear record, that the great and spacious building was the pride of the world; and it fell, and the fall thereof was exceeding great. And the angel of the Lord spake unto me again, saying: Thus shall be the destruction of all nations, kindreds, tongues, and people, that shall fight against the twelve apostles of the Lamb. (1 Nephi, Chapter 11.)

In this glorious vision Nephi was also shown many things concerning his seed and the seed of his brethren, and many important things that would come to pass concerning the land of promise (America) which the Lord gave to Lehi and his seed forever—the land of Joseph.

Nephi's Vision Extended

The Lord further showed Nephi the future coming of the Messiah to the people of Nephi, and the destruction that would take place in this promised land preceding his appearance.

He also showed Nephi how the people would finally depart from the plain and simple truths taught by the Son of God, the Redeemer of the world, and His twelve apostles, and how their leaders would "[take] away from the gospel of the Lamb many parts which are plain and most precious; and also many covenants of the Lord have they taken away." (I Nephi 13:26.)

Then Nephi adds:

> And it came to pass that I beheld the remnant of the seed of my brethren, and also the book of the Lamb of God, *which had proceeded forth from the mouth of the Jew,* that it came forth from the Gentiles unto the remnant of the seed of my brethren.
>
> And after it had come forth unto them *I beheld other books,* which came forth by the power of the Lamb, from the Gentiles unto them, unto the convincing of the Gentiles and the remnant of the seed of my brethren, and *also the Jews* who were scattered upon all the face of the earth, that the records of the prophets and of the twelve apostles of the Lamb are true.
>
> And the angel spake unto me, saying: *These last records, which thou hast seen among the Gentiles, shall establish the truth of the first, which are of the twelve apostles of the Lamb, and shall make known the plain and precious things which have been taken away from them; and shall make known to all kindreds, tongues, and people, that the Lamb of God is the Son of the Eternal Father, and the Savior of the world; and that all men must come unto him, or they cannot be saved.*
>
> And they must come according to the words which shall be established by the mouth of the Lamb; and *the words of the Lamb shall be made known in the records of thy seed, as well as in the records of the twelve apostles of of the Lamb; wherefore they both shall be established in one;* for there is one God and one Shepherd over all the earth. (1 Nephi 13:38-41.)

From these quotations, it is evident (1) that Jesus Christ was the promised Messiah; (2) that He was born of the Virgin Mary; (3) "that he was lifted up upon the cross and slain for the sins of the world"; (4) that the record given of Him in the New Testament is true, as far as it has been unaltered and unchanged; (5) that we are indebted to the Jews for this record; (6) that other books were to come forth from the Gentiles (the House of Joseph) "unto the convincing of the Gentiles and the remnant of the seed of my brethren and also the Jews who were scattered upon all the face of the earth; (7)

that the records of the prophets and of the twelve apostles of the Lamb are true."

We emphasize:

> And they must come according to the words which shall be established by the mouth of the Lamb; and the words of the Lamb shall be made known in the records of thy seed, as well as in the records of the twelve apostles of the Lamb; wherefore they both shall be established in one; for there is one God and one Shepherd over all the earth. (*Ibid.*, verse 41.)

How wonderful it is that God, knowing the end from the beginning, made provision for these two records, each bearing witness to the truth of the other, that His children may come to a full knowledge of the truth and the divine mission of the Redeemer of the world.

The Last Shall be First, and the First Shall be Last

In further consideration of what the Stick of Joseph has to say regarding the Messiah, we remind the Jews, our brothers, that Nephi was shown that Jesus would come first to the Jews, but that since they were not ready to receive Him, He would later manifest himself first to the Gentiles and then to the Jews:

> And the time cometh that he shall manifest himself unto all nations, both unto the Jews and also unto the Gentiles; and after he has manifested himself unto the Jews and also unto the Gentiles, then he shall manifest himself unto the Gentiles and also unto the Jews, and the last shall be first, and the first shall be last. (1 Nephi 13:42.)

It is important that the Jews understand the true meaning of this statement, "the last shall be first, and the first shall be last." If they do, they will realize that the time was to come when they would have to look to the House of Joseph, gathered from the Gentile nations, and the Stick of Joseph, to bring to them a true knowledge of their Messiah, and the work He would accomplish in the latter days in preparation for His final coming to reign over all nations as King of kings and Lord of lords. (Revelation 19:16.)

This is the message Joseph has for Judah at this time.

Jesus Christ, the True Messiah

We will now consider what the Stick of Joseph has to say regarding the Messiah. The Prophet Nephi prophesied concerning the Jews, the destruction of Jerusalem, and the coming and work of the Messiah in these words:

> Wherefore, *the Jews shall be scattered among all nations;* yea, and also Babylon shall be destroyed; wherefore, the Jews shall be scattered by other nations.
>
> And after they have been scattered, and the Lord God hath scourged them by other nations for the space of many generations, yea, even down from generation to generation *until they shall be persuaded to believe in Christ, the Son of God, and the atonement, which is infinite for all mankind —and when that day shall come that they shall believe in Christ, and worship the Father in his name, with pure hearts and clean hands, and look not forward any more for another Messiah,* then, at that time, the day will come that it must needs be expedient that they should believe these things.
>
> And the Lord will set his hand again the second time to restore his people from their lost and fallen state. Wherefore, he will proceed to do a marvelous work and a wonder among the children of men.
>
> Wherefore, he shall bring forth his words unto them, which words shall judge them at the last day, for *they shall be given them for the purpose of convincing them of the true Messiah, who was rejected by them; and unto the convincing of them that they need not look forward any more for a Messiah to come, for there should not any come, save it should be a false Messiah which should deceive the people; for there is save one Messiah spoken of by the prophets, and that Messiah is he who should be rejected of the Jews.*
>
> For according to the words of the prophets, the Messiah cometh in six hundred years from the time that my

father left Jerusalem; and according to the words of the prophets, and also the word of the angel of God, *his name shall be Jesus Christ, the Son of God.*

And now, my brethren, I have spoken plainly that ye cannot err. And as the Lord God liveth that brought Israel up out of the land of Egypt, and gave unto Moses power that he should heal the nations after they had been bitten by the poisonous serpents, if they would cast their eyes unto the serpent which he did raise up before them, and also gave him power that he should smite the rock and the water should come forth; yea, behold I say unto you, that as these things are true, and *as the Lord God liveth, there is none other name given under heaven save it be this Jesus Christ, of which I have spoken, whereby man can be saved.* (2 Nephi 25:15-20.)

This prophecy clearly sets forth how the Jews would be scattered among all nations where they would be scourged for many generations until they are persuaded to believe in Christ, the Son of God as their Messiah, at which time the Lord shall set His hand the second time to restore them from their lost and fallen state, even by the doing of a marvelous work and a wonder among the children of men, even through the bringing forth of His word for the purpose of convincing them of the true Messiah, who was rejected by them. And this is the purpose of this presentation to offer unto the Jews the marvelous work and a wonder the Lord has accomplished in bringing forth His word, even the Stick of Joseph.

While this prophecy was given nearly 600 years before the birth of the Messiah, it was given in great plainness, even indicating that the name of the Messiah would be Jesus Christ, the Son of God.

Law of Moses to be Fulfilled in Christ

Every member of the House of Judah will do well to give particular attention to the words of Nephi concerning the law of Moses and its fulfillment in Christ.

Like the Jews, the Nephites were loyal to the law of Moses. However, the Nephites recognized, through the word of prophecy, that the law of Moses would be fulfilled and done away with when Christ was born and His law given as prophesied:

And, notwithstanding we believe in Christ, we keep the law of Moses, and look forward with steadfastness unto Christ, *until the law shall be fulfilled.*

For, for this end was the law given; wherefore *the law hath become dead unto us,* and *we are made alive in Christ* because of our faith; yet we keep the law because of the commandments.

And we talk of Christ, we rejoice in Christ, we preach of Christ, we prophesy of Christ, and we write according to our prophecies, that our children may know to what source they may look for a remission of their sins.

Wherefore, we speak concerning the law that our children may know the deadness of the law; and they, by knowing the deadness of the law, may look forward unto that life which is in Christ, and know for what end the law was given. And after the law is fulfilled in Christ, that they need not harden their hearts against him when the law ought to be done away.

And now behold, my people, ye are a stiffnecked people; wherefore, I have spoken plainly unto you, that ye cannot misunderstand. And the words which I have spoken shall stand as a testimony against you; for they are sufficient to teach any man the right way; for *the right way is to believe in Christ and deny him not; for by denying him ye also deny the prophets and the law.*

And now behold, I say unto you that the right way is to believe in Christ, and deny him not; and Christ is the Holy One of Israel; wherefore ye must bow down before him, and worship him with all your might, mind, and strength, and your whole soul; and if ye do this ye shall in no wise be cast out.

And, inasmuch as it shall be expedient, ye must keep the performances and ordinances of God until the law shall be fulfilled which was given unto Moses. (2 Nephi 25:24-30.)

Christ to Appear to the House of Joseph

Nephi further declared that after Christ shall have risen from the dead, He would show himself unto the Nephites and that signs would be given them of the birth, death, and resurrection of the Christ:

And after Christ shall have risen from the dead he shall show himself unto you, my children, and my beloved brethren; and the words which he shall speak unto you shall be the law which ye shall do.

For behold, I say unto you that I have beheld that many generations shall pass away, and there shall be great wars and contentions among my people.

And after the Messiah shall come there shall be signs given unto my people of his birth, and also of his death and resurrection; and great and terrible shall that day be unto the wicked, for they shall perish; and they perish because they cast out the prophets, and the saints, and stone them, and slay them; wherefore the cry of the blood of the saints shall ascend up to God from the ground against them. (2 Nephi 26:1-3.)

Destruction to be Visited upon the Unrighteous

Nephi then described the destruction which would come upon his people because they kill the prophets and saints:

And they that kill the prophets, and the saints, the depths of the earth shall swallow them up, saith the Lord of Hosts; and mountains shall cover them, and whirlwinds shall carry them away, and buildings shall fall upon them and crush them to pieces and grind them to powder.

And they shall be visited with thunderings, and lightnings, and earthquakes, and all manner of destructions, for the fire of the anger of the Lord shall be kindled against them, and they shall be as stubble, and the day that cometh shall consume them, saith the Lord of Hosts. (2 Nephi 26: 5-6.)

All these prophecies of Nephi did come to pass.

Signs of Christ's Birth and Death Predicted

One Lamanite prophet, Samuel, foretold the signs that would be given in this land of America at the time of Christ's birth and at the time of His death:

And now it came to pass that Samuel, the Lamanite, did prophesy a great many more things which cannot be written.

And behold, he said unto them: *Behold, I give unto you a sign; for five years more cometh, and behold, then cometh the Son of God to redeem all those who shall believe on his name.*

And behold, this will I give unto you for a sign at the time of his coming; for behold, there shall be great lights in heaven, insomuch that in the night before he cometh there shall be no darkness, insomuch that it shall appear unto man as if it was day.

Therefore, there shall be one day and a night and a day, as if it were one day and there were no night; and this shall be unto you for a sign; for ye shall know of the rising of the sun and also of its setting; therefore they shall know of a surety that there shall be two days and a night; nevertheless the night shall not be darkened; and it shall be the night before he is born.

And behold, there shall be a new star arise, such an one as ye never have beheld; and this also shall be a sign unto you.

And behold this is not all, there shall be many signs and wonders in heaven.

And it shall come to pass that ye shall all be amazed, and wonder, insomuch that ye shall fall to the earth.

And it shall come to pass that whosoever shall believe on the Son of God, the same shall have everlasting life.

And behold, thus hath the Lord commanded me, by his angel, that I should come and tell this thing unto you; yea, he hath commanded that I should prophesy these things unto you; yea, he hath said unto me: Cry unto this people, repent and prepare the way of the Lord.

And now, because I am a Lamanite, and have spoken unto you the words which the Lord hath commanded me, and because it was hard against you, ye are angry with me and do seek to destroy me, and have cast me out from among you.

And ye shall hear my words, for, for this intent have I come up upon the walls of this city, that ye might hear and know of the judgments of God which do await you because of your iniquities, and also that ye might know the conditions of repentance;

And also that ye might know of the coming of Jesus Christ, the Son of God, the Father of heaven and of earth, the Creator of all things from the beginning; and that ye might know of the signs of his coming, to the intent that ye might believe on his name.

And if ye believe on his name ye will repent of all your sins, that thereby ye may have a remission of them through his merits.

And behold, again, another sign I give unto you, yea, a sign of his death.

For behold, he surely must die that salvation may come; yea, it behooveth him and becometh expedient that he dieth, to bring to pass the resurrection of the dead, that thereby men may be brought into the presence of the Lord.

Yea, behold, this death bringeth to pass the resurrection, and redeemeth all mankind from the first death—that thereby men may be brought into the presence of the Lord.

Yea, behold, this death bringeth to pass the resurrection, and redeemeth all mankind from the first death—that spiritual death; for all mankind, by the fall of Adam being cut off from the presence of the Lord, are considered as dead, both as to things temporal and to things spiritual.

But behold, the resurrection of Christ redeemeth mankind, yea, even all mankind, and bringeth them back into the presence of the Lord.

Yea, and it bringeth to pass the condition of repentance, that whosoever repenteth the same is not hewn down and cast into the fire; but whosoever repenteth not is hewn down and cast into the fire; and there cometh upon them again a spiritual death, yea, a second death, for they are cut off again as to things pertaining to righteousness.

Therefore repent ye, repent ye, lest by knowing these things and not doing them ye shall suffer yourselves to come under condemnation, and ye are brought down unto this second death.

But behold, as I said unto you concerning another sign, *a sign of his death,* behold, in that day that he shall suffer death the sun shall be darkened and refuse to give his light unto you; and also the moon and the stars; and there shall be no light upon the face of this land, even from the time that he shall suffer death, for the space of three days, to the time that he shall rise again from the dead.

Yea, at the time that he shall yield up the ghost there

shall be thunderings and lightnings for the space of many
hours, and the earth shall shake and tremble; and the rocks
which are upon the face of this earth which are above the
earth and beneath, which ye know at this time are solid,
or the more part of it is one solid mass, shall be broken up;

Yea, they shall be rent in twain, and shall ever after
be found in seams and in cracks, and in broken fragments
upon the face of the whole earth, yea, both above the earth
and beneath.

And behold, there shall be great tempests, and there
shall be many mountains laid low, like unto a valley, and
there shall be many places which are now called valleys
which shall become mountains, whose height is great.

And many highways shall be broken up, and many
cities shall become desolate.

And many graves shall be opened, and shall yield up
many of their dead; and many saints shall appear unto
many.

And behold, thus hath the angel spoken unto me; for
he said unto me that there should be thunderings and lightnings for the space of many hours.

And he said unto me that while the thunder and the
lightning lasted, and the tempest, that these things should
be, and that darkness should cover the face of the whole
earth for the space of three days.

And the angel said unto me that many shall see greater
things than these, to the intent that they might believe
that these signs and these wonders should come to pass upon
all the face of this land, to the intent that there should be
no cause for unbelief among the children of men. (Helaman
14:1-28.)

Predicted Signs of Christ's Birth Fulfilled

The signs predicted by Samuel, the Lamanite
prophet, did surely come to pass as recorded by the
Nephite prophet:

Now it came to pass that the ninety and first year had
passed away and it was six hundred years from the time
that Lehi left Jerusalem; and it was in the year that La-
choneus was the chief judge and the governor over the land.
. . .

And it came to pass that in the commencement of the
ninety and second year, behold, the prophecies of the

prophets began to be fulfilled more fully; for there began
to be greater signs and greater miracles wrought among
the people.

But there were some who began to say that the time
was past for the words to be fulfilled, which were spoken
by Samuel, the Lamanite.

And they began to rejoice over their brethren, saying:
Behold the time is past, and the words of Samuel are not
fulfilled; therefore, your joy and your faith concerning this
great thing hath been vain.

And it came to pass that they did make a great uproar
throughout the land; and the people who believed began to
be very sorrowful, lest by any means those things which
had been spoken might not come to pass.

But behold, they did watch steadfastly for that day
and that night and that day which should be as one day
as if there were no night, that they might know that their
faith had not been vain.

Now it came to pass that there was a day set apart by
the unbelievers, that all those who believed in these traditions should be put to death except the sign should come
to pass, which had been given by Samuel the prophet.

Now it came to pass that when Nephi, the son of Nephi,
saw this wickedness of his people, his heart was exceedingly sorrowful.

Now it came to pass that he went out and bowed himself down upon the earth, and cried mightily to his God in
behalf of his people, yea, those who were about to be destroyed because of their faith in the tradition of their
fathers.

And it came to pass that he cried mightily unto the
Lord, all the day; and behold, the voice of the Lord came
unto him, saying:

*Lift up your head and be of good cheer; for behold,
the time is at hand, and on this night shall the sign be
given, and on the morrow come I into the world,* to show
unto the world that I will fulfill all that which I have caused
to be spoken by the mouth of my holy prophets.

Behold, *I come unto my own,* to fulfil all things which
I have made known unto the children of men from the foundation of the world, and to do the will, both of the Father
and the Son—of the Father because of me, and of the
Son because of my flesh. And behold, the time is at hand
and this night shall the sign be given.

And it came to pass that the words which came unto
Nephi were fulfilled, according as they had been spoken;

for behold, at the going down of the sun there was no darkness; and the people began to be astonished because there
was no darkness when the night came.

And there were many, who had not believed the words
of the prophets, who fell to the earth and became as if they
were dead, for they knew that the great plan of destruction
which they had laid for those who believed in the words
of the prophets had been frustrated; for the signal which
had been given was already at hand.

And they began to know that the Son of God must
shortly appear; yea, in fine, all the people upon the face of
the whole earth from the west to the east, both in the land
north and in the land south, were so exceedingly astonished
that they fell to the earth.

For they knew that the prophets had testified of those
things for many years, and that the sign which had been
given was already at hand; and they began to fear because
of their iniquity and their unbelief.

And it came to pass that there was no darkness in all
that night, but it was as light as though it was mid-day.
And it came to pass that the sun did rise in the morning
again, according to its proper order; and they knew that it
was the day that the Lord should be born, because of the
sign which had been given.

And it had come to pass, yea, all things, every whit, according to the words of the prophets.

And it came to pass also that a new star did appear,
according to the word. (III Nephi 1:1, 4-21.)

Because of the signs that were given, the more part
of the people did believe and were converted unto the
Lord. The people began again to have peace in the
land.

Predicted Signs of Christ's Death Fulfilled

After thirty-three years had passed since the signs
were given of the birth of Jesus Christ, the signs foretold by Samuel which would occur at the time of Christ's
death, were given:

And now it came to pass that according to our record,
and we know our record to be true, for behold, it was a
just man who did keep the record—for he truly did many

miracles in the name of Jesus; and there was not any man who could do a miracle in the name of Jesus save he were cleansed every whit from his iniquity—

And now it came to pass, if there was no mistake made by this man in the beginning of our time, *the thirty and third year had passed away;*

And the people began to look with great earnestness for the sign which had been given by the prophet Samuel, the Lamanite, yea, for the time that there should be darkness for the space of three days over the face of the land.

And there began to be great doubtings and disputations among the people, notwithstanding so many signs had been given.

And it came to pass in the thirty and fourth year, in the first month, on the fourth day of the month, there arose a great storm, such an one as never had been known in all the land.

And there was also a great and terrible tempest; and there was terrible thunder, insomuch that it did shake the whole earth as if it was about to divide asunder.

And there were exceeding sharp lightnings, such as never had been known in all the land.

And the city of Zarahemla did take fire.

And the city of Moroni did sink into the depths of the sea, and the inhabitants thereof were drowned.

And the earth was carried up upon the city of Moronihah that in the place of the city there became a great mountain.

And there was a great and terrible destruction in the land southward.

But behold, there was a more great and terrible destruction in the land northward; for behold, the whole face of the land was changed, because of the tempest and the whirlwinds and the thunderings and lightnings, and the exceeding great quaking of the whole earth;

And the highways were broken up, and the level roads were spoiled, and many smooth places became rough.

And many great and notable cities were sunk, and many were burned, and many were shaken till the buildings thereof had fallen to the earth, and the inhabitants thereof were slain, and the places were left desolate.

And there were some cities which remained; but the damage thereof was exceeding great, and there were many of them who were slain.

And there were some who were carried away in the

whirlwind; and whither they went no man knoweth, save they know that they were carried away.

And thus the face of the whole earth became deformed, because of the tempests, and thunderings, and the lightnings, and the quaking of the earth.

And behold, the rocks were rent in twain; they were broken up upon the face of the whole earth, insomuch that they were found in broken fragments, and in seams and in cracks, upon all the face of the land.

And it came to pass that when the thunderings, and the lightnings, and the storm, and the tempest, and the quakings of the earth did cease—for behold, they did last for about the space of three hours; and it was said by some that the time was greater; nevertheless, all these great and terrible things were done in about the space of three hours — and then behold, there was darkness upon the face of the land.

And it came to pass that there was thick darkness upon all the face of the land, insomuch that the inhabitants thereof who had not fallen could feel the vapor of darkness;

And there could be no light, because of the darkness, neither candles, neither torches; neither could there be fire kindled with their fine and exceedingly dry wood, so that there could not be any light at all;

And there was not any light seen, neither fire, nor glimmer, neither the sun, nor the moon, nor the stars, for so great were the mists of darkness which were upon the face of the land.

And it came to pass that it did last for the space of three days that there was no light seen; and there was great mourning and howling and weeping among all the people continually; yea, great were the groanings of the people, because of the darkness and the great destruction which had come upon them.

And in one place they were heard to cry, saying: O that we had repented before this great and terrible day, and then would our brethren have been spared, and they would not have been burned in that great city Zarahemla.

And in another place they were heard to cry and mourn, saying: O that we had repented before this great and terrible day, and had not killed and stoned the prophets, and cast them out; then would our mothers and our fair daughters, and our children have been spared, and not have been buried up in that great city Moronihah. And thus were the howlings of the people great and terrible. (3 Nephi, Chapter 8.)

Jesus Appears to the House of Joseph

Following the death of Jesus Christ, and His resurrection, He appeared to the people of Nephi in the land of Joseph (America) as the multitude were gathered together in the land Bountiful, and did minister unto them. On this wise did He show himself unto them, and teach them:

And now it came to pass that there were a great multitude gathered together, of the people of Nephi, round about the temple which was in the land Bountiful; and they were marveling and wondering one with another, and were showing one to another the great and marvelous change which had taken place.

And they were also conversing about this Jesus Christ, of whom the sign had been given concerning his death.

And it came to pass that while they were thus conversing one with another, *they heard a voice as if it came out of heaven;* and they cast their eyes round about, for they understood not the voice which they heard; and it was not a harsh voice, neither was it a loud voice, nevertheless, and notwithstanding it being a small voice it did pierce them that they did hear to the center, insomuch that there was no part of their frame that it did not cause to quake; yea, it did pierce them to the very soul, and did cause their hearts to burn.

And it came to pass that *again they heard the voice,* and they understood it not.

And *again the third time they did hear the voice,* and did open their ears to hear it; and their eyes were towards heaven, from whence the sound came.

And behold, the third time they did understand the voice which they heard; and it said unto them:

Behold my Beloved Son, in whom I am well pleased, in whom I have glorified my name—hear ye him.

And it came to pass, as they understood they cast their eyes up again towards heaven; and behold, they saw a Man descending out of heaven; and he was clothed in a white robe; and he came down and stood in the midst of them; and the eyes of the whole multitude were turned upon him, and they durst not open their mouths, even one to another,

and wist not what it meant, for they thought it was an
angel that had appeared unto them.

And it came to pass that he stretched forth his hand
and spake unto the people, saying:

*Behold, I am Jesus Christ, whom the prophets testified
shall come into the world.*

And behold, I am the light and the life of the world;
and I have drunk out of that bitter cup which the Father
hath given me, and have glorified the Father in taking
upon me the sins of the world, in the which I have suffered
the will of the Father in all things from the beginning.

And it came to pass that when Jesus had spoken these
words the whole multitude fell to the earth; for they remembered that it had been prophesied among them that
Christ should show himself unto them after his ascension
into heaven.

And it came to pass that the Lord spake unto them
saying:

*Arise and come forth unto me, that ye may thrust your
hands into my side, and also that ye may feel the prints of
the nails in my hands and in my feet, that ye may know that
I am the God of Israel, and the God of the whole earth,
and have been slain for the sins of the world.*

And it came to pass that the multitude went forth, and
thrust their hands into his side, and did feel the prints of
the nails in his hands and in his feet; and this they did do,
going forth one by one until they had all gone forth, and
did see with their eyes and did feel with their hands, and
did know of a surety and did bear record, that it was he,
of whom it was written by the prophets, that should come.

And when they had all gone forth and had witnessed
for themselves, they did cry out with one accord, saying:

Hosanna! Blessed be the name of the Most High God!
And they did fall down at the feet of Jesus, and did worship
him.

And it came to pass that he spake unto Nephi (for
Nephi was among the multitude) and he commanded him
that he should come forth.

And Nephi arose and went forth, and bowed himself
before the Lord and did kiss his feet.

And the Lord commanded him that he should arise.
And he arose and stood before him.

And the Lord said unto him: I give unto you power
that ye shall baptize this people when I am again ascended
into heaven.

And again the Lord called others, and said unto them likewise; and he gave unto them power to baptize. And he said unto them: On this wise shall ye baptize; and there shall be no disputations among you.

Verily I say unto you, that whoso repenteth of his sins through your words and desireth to be baptized in my name, on this wise shall ye baptize them — Behold, ye shall go down and stand in the water, and in my name shall ye baptize them.

And now behold, these are the words which ye shall say, calling them by name, saying:

Having authority given me of Jesus Christ, I baptize you in the name of the Father, and of the Son, and of the Holy Ghost. Amen.

And then shall ye immerse them in the water, and come forth again out of the water.

And after this manner shall ye baptize in my name; for behold, verily I say unto you, that the Father, and the Son, and the Holy Ghost are one; and I am in the Father, and the Father in me, and the Father and I are one.

And according as I have commanded you thus shall ye baptize. And there shall be no disputations among you, as there have hitherto been; neither shall there be disputations among you concerning the points of my doctrine, as there have hitherto been.

For verily, verily I say unto you, he that hath the spirit of contention is not of me, but is of the devil, who is the father of contention, and he stirreth up the hearts of men to contend with anger, one with another.

Behold, this is not my doctrine, to stir up the hearts of men with anger, one against another; but this is my doctrine, that such things should be done away.

Behold, verily, verily, I say unto you, I will declare unto you my doctrine.

And this is my doctrine, and it is the doctrine which the Father hath given unto me; and I bear record of the Father, and the Father beareth record of me, and the Holy Ghost beareth record of the Father and me; and I bear record that the Father commandeth all men, everywhere, to repent and believe in me.

And whoso believeth in me, and is baptized, the same shall be saved; and they are they who shall inherit the kingdom of God.

And whoso believeth not in me, and is not baptized, shall be damned.

Verily, verily, I say unto you, that this is my doctrine, and I bear record of it from the Father; and whoso believeth in me believeth in the Father also; and unto him will the Father bear record of me, for he will visit him with fire and with the Holy Ghost.

And thus will the Father bear record of me, and the Holy Ghost will bear record unto him of the Father and me; for the Father, and I, and the Holy Ghost are one.

And again I say unto you, ye must repent, and become as a little child, and be baptized in my name, or ye can in nowise receive these things.

And again I say unto you, ye must repent, and be baptized in my name, and become as a little child, or ye can in nowise inherit the kingdom of God.

Verily, verily, I say unto you, that this is my doctrine, and whoso buildeth upon this buildeth upon my rock, and the gates of hell shall not prevail against them.

And whoso shall declare more or less than this, and establish it for my doctrine, the same cometh of evil, and is not built upon my rock; but he buildeth upon a sandy foundation, and the gates of hell stand open to receive such when the floods come and the winds beat upon them.

Therefore, go forth unto this people, and declare the words which I have spoken, unto the ends of the earth. (3 Nephi, Chapter 11.)

And it came to pass that when Jesus had spoken these words unto Nephi, and to those who had been called, (now the number of them who had been called, and received power and authority to baptize, was twelve) and behold, he stretched forth his hand unto the multitude, and cried unto them, saying: Blessed are ye if ye shall give heed unto the words of these twelve whom I have chosen from among you to minister unto you, and to be your servants; and unto them I have given power that they may baptize you with water; and after that ye are baptized with water, behold, I will baptize you with fire and with the Holy Ghost; therefore blessed are ye if ye shall believe in me and be baptized, after that ye have seen me and know that I am.

And again, more blessed are they who shall believe in your words because that ye shall testify that ye have seen me, and that ye know that I am. Yea, blessed are they who shall believe in your words, and come down into the depths of humility and be baptized, for they shall be visited with fire and with the Holy Ghost, and shall receive a remission of their sins. (3 Nephi 12:1-2.)

Law of Moses Fulfilled in Christ

Then Jesus continued to teach them many things, many of which He had already taught His children the Jews while He ministered among them in Jerusalem. It seems wise to quote His sayings regarding the law of Moses:

And now it came to pass that when Jesus had ended these sayings he cast his eyes round about on the multitude, and said unto them: Behold, ye have heard the things which I taught before I ascended to my Father; therefore, whoso remembereth these sayings of mine and doeth them, him will I raise up at the last day.

And it came to pass that when Jesus had said these words he perceived that there were some among them who marveled, and wondered what he would concerning the law of Moses; for they understood not the saying that old things had passed away, and that all things had become new.

And he said unto them: *Marvel not that I said unto you that old things had passed away, and that all things had become new.*

Behold, I say unto you that the law is fulfilled that was given unto Moses.

Behold, I am he that gave the law, and I am he who covenanted with my people Israel; therefore, the law in me is fulfilled, for I have come to fulfil the law; therefore it hath an end.

Behold, I do not destroy the prophets, for as many as have not been fulfilled in me, verily I say unto you, shall all be fulfilled.

And because I said unto you that old things have passed away, I do not destroy that which hath been spoken concerning things which are to come.

For behold, the covenant which I have made with my people is not all fulfilled; but *the law which was given unto Moses hath an end in me.*

Behold, I am the law, and the light. Look unto me, and endure to the end, and ye shall live; for unto him that endureth to the end will I give eternal life.

Behold, I have given unto you the commandments; therefore keep my commandments. And this is the law and the prophets, for they truly testified of me. (3 Nephi 15:1-10.)

Stick of Joseph Given with a Promise

Sufficient of the sacred scriptures in the Stick of Joseph have been presented in this chapter to indicate the great message of truth which the House of Joseph now offers to the House of Judah. Since the Stick of Joseph is the companion volume of scripture to the Stick of Judah, the Holy Bible, Judah would do well to accept the Stick of Joseph, offered in humility. The Stick of Joseph is a volume of scripture of over 500 pages as translated from the original gold plates prepared and preserved by the Nephite prophets. This record has now been printed in 22 languages and translated in eight other languages awaiting publication. Millions of copies have been distributed.

When the records of the Stick of Joseph were sealed up by the hand of Moroni, and deposited in a stone box in the earth, as commanded by the Lord, pending the time when he would bring them forth among the Gentiles or the descendants of Joseph, Moroni recorded this wonderful promise to those who would read it as suggested:

> And when ye shall receive these things, I would exhort you that ye would ask God, the Eternal Father, in the name of Christ, if these things are not true; and if ye shall ask with a sincere heart, with real intent, having faith in Christ, he will manifest the truth of it unto you, by the power of the Holy Ghost. (Moroni 10:4.)

Thousands have put this promise to the test and testify that the Lord has manifested unto them the truth of this record, by the power of the Holy Ghost.

CHAPTER 6

THE FIRST COMING OF
JESUS CHRIST

One of the principal reasons why the Jews rejected Jesus Christ, as their promised Messiah, was because they failed to differentiate between the prophecies concerning His first coming, and those relating to His second coming. They seem always to have expected a complete fulfillment of all of the promises of the prophets concerning the Messiah when He came the first time. When this did not happen, they were disappointed and refused to accept Him as their Redeemer.

The Messiah Described

The Prophet Nephi describes who the Messiah would be:

> And behold he cometh, according to the words of the angel, in six hundred years from the time my father left Jerusalem.
>
> And the world, because of their iniquity, shall judge him to be a thing of naught; wherefore they scourge him, and he suffereth it; and they smite him, and he suffereth it. Yea, they spit upon him, and he suffereth it, because of his loving kindness and his long-suffering towards the children of men.
>
> And the God of our fathers, who were led out of Egypt, out of bondage, and also were preserved in the wilderness by him, yea, the God of Abraham, and of Isaac, and the God of Jacob, yieldeth himself, according to the words of the angel, as a man, into the hands of wicked men, to be lifted up, according to the words of Zenock, and to be crucified, according to the words of Neum, and to be buried in a sepulchre, according to the words of Zenos, which he spake concerning the three days of darkness, which should be a sign given of his death unto those who

should inhabit the isles of the sea, more especially given
unto those who are of the house of Israel. (I Nephi 19:8-
10.)

This Messiah, therefore, was to be "the God of our
fathers . . . yea, the God of Abraham, and of Isaac, and
the God of Jacob," for it was by Him that the Father
created this world, and through whom He has directed
all His prophets, and through whom the law was given
to Moses.

Confirming this statement, we find in the writings
of Abraham, that he received instructions from Jehovah
who was the promised Messiah. (The writings of Abraham are contained in The Pearl of Great Price the origin
of which will be explained later.)

> And his voice was unto me: Abraham, Abraham, be-
> hold, my name is Jehovah, and I have heard thee, and have
> come down to deliver thee, and to take thee away from
> thy father's house, and from all thy kins-folk, into a strange
> land which thou knowest not of; (Pearl of Great Price,
> Abraham 1:16.)

Again, from the writings of Abraham:

> My name is Jehovah and I know the end from the be-
> ginning; therefore my hand shall be over thee.
> And I will make of thee a great nation, and I will bless
> thee above measure, and make thy name great among all
> nations, and thou shalt be a blessing unto thy seed after
> thee, that in their hands they shall bear this ministry and
> Priesthood unto all nations; (Pearl of Great Price, Abra-
> ham 2:8-9.)

Prophecies Concerning the First Advent
of the Messiah

We should keep in mind the truth made plain in
the Stick of Joseph that Jesus Christ is not only the
promised Messiah but that He is literally the Son of

God, the Jehovah of the Old Testament, manifest in the flesh:

> For behold, the time cometh, and is not far distant, that with power, *the Lord Omnipotent who reigneth, who was, and is from all eternity to all eternity, shall come down from heaven among the children of men, and shall dwell in a tabernacle of clay,* and shall go forth amongst men, working mighty miracles, such as healing the sick, raising the dead, causing the lame to walk, the blind to receive their sight, and the deaf to hear, and curing all manner of diseases.
>
> And he shall cast out devils, or the evil spirits which dwell in the hearts of the children of men.
>
> And lo, he shall suffer temptations, and pain of body, hunger, thirst, and fatigue, even more than men can suffer, except it be unto death; for behold, blood cometh from every pore, so great shall be his anguish for the wickedness and abominations of his people.
>
> *And he shall be called Jesus Christ, the Son of God, the Father of heaven and earth, the Creator of all things from the beginning* and *his mother shall be called Mary.* (Mosiah 3:5-8.)

The above were the words of King Benjamin, recorded by his son Mosiah, from which we learn that Jesus Christ was "the Lord Omnipotent who reigneth, who was, and is from all eternity, . . . the Son of God, the Father of heaven and earth, the Creator of all things from the beginning,"—indeed the Jehovah of the Jews.

The Prophet Nephi spoke with great plainness concerning the coming of "the God of Israel," and His rejection by His own, as a result of which they would "perish, and become a hiss and a by-word, and be hated among all nations." Nephi further declared that when "they no more turn aside their hearts against the Holy One of Israel, then will He remember the covenants which He made to their fathers:"

> And as for those who are at Jerusalem, saith the prophet, they shall be scourged by all people, because they crucify the God of Israel, and turn their hearts aside, rejecting signs and wonders, and the power and glory of the God of Israel.

And because they turn their hearts aside, saith the prophet, and have despised the Holy One of Israel, they shall wander in the flesh, and perish, and become a hiss and a by-word, and be hated among all nations.

Nevertheless, when that day cometh, saith the prophet, that they no more turn aside their hearts against the Holy One of Israel, then will he remember the covenants which he made to their fathers.

Yea, then will he remember the isles of the sea; yea, and all the people who are of the house of Israel, will I gather in, saith the Lord, according to the words of the prophet Zenos, from the four quarters of the earth.

Yea, and all the earth shall see the salvation of the Lord, saith the prophet; every nation, kindred, tongue and people shall be blessed. (1 Nephi 19:13-17.)

Jesus Christ Fulfilled the Law of Moses

When Jesus Christ appeared to the Nephites in the land of America, following His resurrection and ascension, He explained to them that He had come to fulfill the law of Moses, and that it was He who gave the law, thus indicating that He was the Jehovah of the Jews:

Behold, I say unto you that the law is fulfilled that was given unto Moses.

Behold, I am he that gave the law, and I am he who covenanted with my people Israel; therefore, the law in me is fulfilled, for I have come to fulfill the law; therefore it hath an end. (3 Nephi 15:4-5.)

Because the Jews have not understood that Jehovah of the Old Testament and Jesus Christ of the New Testament are one and the same person, they have felt there was no need for the coming of the Savior, the Redeemer. In this conclusion they have felt sustained by the following scriptures:

But now thus saith the Lord that created thee, O Jacob, and he that formed thee, O Israel, Fear not: for I have redeemed thee, I have called thee by thy name; thou art mine.

For I am the Lord thy God, the Holy One of Israel, thy Saviour: I gave Egypt for thy ransom, Ethiopia and Seba for thee.

WHY Jews DiDN't Accept Jesus

I, even I, am the Lord; and beside me there is no saviour.

I am the Lord, your Holy One, the creator of Israel, your King. (Isaiah 43:1, 3, 11, 15.)

Verily thou art a God that hidest thyself, O God of Israel, the Saviour. (Isaiah 45:15.)

Tell ye, and bring them near; yea, let them take counsel together: who hath declared this from ancient time? who hath told it from that time? have not I the Lord? and there is no God else beside me; a just God and a Saviour; there is none beside me.

Look unto me, and be ye saved, all the ends of the earth: for I am God, and there is none else.

I have sworn by myself, the word is gone out of my mouth in righteousness, and shall not return, That unto me every knee shall bow, every tongue shall swear. (Isaiah 45:21-23.)

I, even I, am he that blotteth out thy transgressions for mine own sake, and will not remember thy sins. (Isaiah 43:25.)

Thus saith the Lord, thy redeemer, and he that formed thee from the womb, I am the Lord that maketh all things; that stretcheth forth the heavens alone; that spreadeth abroad the earth by myself. (Isaiah 44:24.)

Because of this misunderstanding, the Jews felt no need of their Savior and Redeemer coming in the flesh, notwithstanding the fact that their prophets had clearly indicated that He would come and give His life for their redemption.

God the Father and the Son

There seems to be a feeling among the Jews that, according to the teachings of the prophets of the Old Testament, reference is made to but one God, while the New Testament clearly refers to God the Father, and to God the Son or Jesus Christ the Son of God.

We call attention to the following scripture:

And God said, Let us make man in *our* image, after *our* likeness: and let them have dominion over the fish of the sea, and over the fowl of the air, and over the cattle, and over all the earth, and over every creeping thing that creepeth upon the earth. (Genesis I:26.)

Clearly God was speaking to one or more associated with Him in the creation. This statement can be better understood by referring to the following:

In the beginning was the Word, and the Word was with God, and the Word was God.

The same was in the beginning with God.

All things were made by him; and without him was not anything made that was made. . . .

And the Word was made flesh, and dwelt among us, (and we beheld his glory, the glory as of the *only begotten of the Father,*) full of grace and truth. (St. John 1:1-3, 14.)

And I, the Lord God, said unto *mine Only Begotten:* Behold, the man is become as one of us to know good and evil; and now lest he put forth his hand and partake also of the tree of life, and eat and live forever,

Therefore I, the Lord God, will send him forth from the Garden of Eden, to till the ground from whence he was taken. (Pearl of Great Price, Moses 4:28:29.)

Thus, in the Old Testament is recorded the fact that the Lord said: "Let us make man in *our* image." He surely was not talking to Himself. The person to whom He was talking was in the image of God, for He said: "Let *us* make man in *our* image." Therefore, He must have been talking to his Son, as is made very plain in the New Testament reference above quoted, and also the statement of the Lord found in the Book of Moses: "And I, the Lord God, said unto *mine Only Begotten.*"

We quote further from the words of Moses:

And behold, the glory of the Lord was upon Moses, so that Moses stood in the presence of God, and talked with him face to face. And the Lord God said unto Moses: For mine own purpose have I made these things. Here is wisdom and it remaineth in me.

And by *the word of my power,* have I created them, *which is mine Only Begotten Son,* who is full of grace and truth.

> And worlds without number have I created; and I also created them for mine own purpose; and *by the Son I created them, which is mine Only Begotten.* (Pearl of Great Price, Moses 1:31-33.)

The oneness that existed between God the Father and his Only Begotten Son was clearly a oneness of purpose, for they were united in all things. Therefore the Son carried out the purposes and plans of his Father, and through Him, the Father created "worlds without number."

As the Son was the instrument in the hands of the Father in creating worlds, including the one upon which we live, so He was the Father's instrument in giving commandments to the children of men in various dispensations. Note His own declaration to the Nephites when He appeared to them following His crucifixion and resurrection:

> Behold, I am he that gave the law, and I am he who covenanted with my people Israel; therefore, the law in me is fulfilled, for I have come to fulfil the law; therefore it hath an end. (3 Nephi 15:5.)

> Behold, I am Jesus Christ the Son of God. I created the heavens and the earth, and all things that in them are. I was with the Father from the beginning. I am in the Father, and the Father in me; and in me hath the Father glorified his name. (3 Nephi 9:15.)

In speaking of the work of the Messiah, the Prophet Isaiah fully understood that God would direct the work of his Son:

> Surely he hath borne our griefs, and carried our sorrows: yet we did esteem him stricken, smitten of God, and afflicted. (Isaiah 53:4.)

The statement that He would bear Israel's griefs, carry their sorrows, and that he would be "smitten of God," indicates that there were two Gods and not one. How could this Redeemer be smitten by Himself?

Consider also Isaiah's further statement:

> All we like sheep have gone astray; we have turned every one to his own way; and the Lord hath laid on him the iniquity of us all. (Isaiah 53:6.)

Of course the Lord did not lay upon Himself "the iniquity of us all," but upon his Only Begotten Son whom He sent into the world to redeem the world.

Again, Isaiah states: "Yet it pleased the Lord to bruise him." (Isaiah 53:10.) Surely it did not please the Lord "to bruise" Himself.

The Prophet Isaiah further states the word of the Lord: "Therefore will I divide him a portion with the great." (Isaiah 53:12.) Who, except God, his Father, could "divide him a portion with the great?"

Consider further this statement of Isaiah:

> Therefore the Lord himself shall give you a sign; Behold, a virgin shall conceive, and bear a son, and shall call his name Immanuel. (Isaiah 7:14.)

The "Lord himself" promised to give a sign, that a virgin would conceive, "and bear a son." Surely this is plain enough that there were two—the Lord who made the promise, and the Son who was to be born.

The Prophet Isaiah speaks of the ministry of the Messiah in these words:

> I the Lord have called thee in righteousness, and will hold thine hand, and will keep thee, and give thee for a covenant of the people, for a light of the Gentiles. (Isaiah 42:6.)

Here the Lord speaks of what He would do through Him whom He promised to send. There were, therefore, two persons.

Again, the Prophet Isaiah states:

> The Spirit of the Lord God is upon me; because the Lord hath anointed me to preach good tidings unto the meek;

he hath sent me to bind up the broken hearted, to proclaim liberty to the captives, and the opening of the prison to them that are bound. (Isaiah 61:1.)

Surely the Lord did not anoint Himself "to preach good tidings unto the meek." He did not send himself "to bind up the brokenhearted."

The ancient prophets of Judah understood without a question that the promised Messiah would be sent by God. Thus there were two Gods—one to send, and one to be sent.

Birth and Mission of the Messiah Foretold in Stick of Judah

As we consider the words of the prophets of the Old Testament concerning the coming of Jesus Christ as the Redeemer of the world, we should keep in mind that prophecy is but history in reverse. Since all things are known to God from the beginning, as declared by the prophet Isaiah, He directed His prophets to speak from time to time declaring events which would come to pass in the unfoldment of the Lord's plan pertaining to the inhabitants of this earth, and the destiny of the earth itself.

Consider the following prophecy of Isaiah. It would seem that these words might have been written following the birth and life of Jesus Christ the Savior of the world instead of some 750 years before His birth:

Who hath believed our report? and to whom is the arm of the Lord revealed?

For he shall grow up before him as a tender plant, and as a root out of a dry ground: he hath no form nor comeliness; and when we shall see him, there is no beauty that we should desire him.

He is despised and rejected of men; a man of sorrows, and acquainted with grief: and we hid as it were our faces from him; he was despised, and we esteemed him not.

Surely he hath borne our griefs, and carried our sorrows: yet we did esteem him stricken, smitten of God, and afflicted.

But he was wounded for our transgressions, he was bruised for our iniquities: the chastisement of our peace was upon him; and with his stripes we are healed.

All we like sheep have gone astray; we have turned every one to his own way; and the Lord hath laid on him the iniquity of us all.

He was oppressed, and he was afflicted, yet he opened not his mouth: he is brought as a lamb to the slaughter, and as a sheep before her shearers is dumb, so he openeth not his mouth.

He was taken from prison and from judgment: and who shall declare his generation? for he was cut off out of the land of the living: for the transgression of my people was he stricken.

And he made his grave with the wicked, and with the rich in his death; because he had done no violence, neither was any deceit in his mouth.

Yet it pleased the Lord to bruise him; he hath put him to grief: when thou shalt make his soul an offering for sin, he shall see his seed, he shall prolong his days, and the pleasure of the Lord shall prosper in his hand.

He shall see of the travail of his soul, and shall be satisfied: by his knowledge shall my righteous servant justify many; for he shall bear their iniquities.

Therefore will I divide him a portion with the great, and he shall divide the spoil with the strong; because he hath poured out his soul unto death: and he was numbered with the transgressors; and he bare the sins of many, and made intercession for the transgressors. (Isaiah, Chapter 53.)

In the life and mission of Jesus Christ He met every requirement necessary to fulfill all the prophet Isaiah predicted He would do, as herein set forth. Can anyone deny that Jesus Christ was "despised and rejected of men . . . wounded for our transgressions, bruised for our iniquities . . . oppressed, . . . afflicted, yet He opened not his mouth . . . brought as a lamb to the slaughter . . . cut off out of the land of the living . . . numbered with the transgressors; and He bare the sins of many, and made intercession for the transgressors?" Isaiah further declared how universal His rejection would be in these words: "All we like sheep have gone astray; we have turned every one to his own way; and the Lord hath laid on him the iniquity of us all."

Isaiah understood that a son would be born of woman, and that His name would be called Immanuel:

> Therefore the Lord himself shall give you a sign; Behold, a virgin shall conceive, and bear a son, and shall call his name Immanuel. (Isaiah 7:14.)

According to this statement, God himself promised to give a sign. Surely the birth of Jesus by the Virgin Mary was a complete fulfillment of this prediction. When Isaiah stated that His name would be called "Immanuel," he understood the meaning of that name, "God with us." (St. Matthew 1:23.) Therefore, he knew that the son to be born of the virgin would be the God of Heaven:

> For unto us a child is born, unto us a son is given: and the government shall be upon his shoulders: and his name shall be called Wonderful, Counsellor, The mighty God, the everlasting Father, The Prince of Peace. (Isaiah 9:6.)

The child to be born of the virgin was to be "The Mighty God," or the God of Israel, the Jehovah, as declared by the Nephite prophets in the Stick of Joseph.

In this prophecy, Isaiah stated: "And the government shall be upon his shoulder." This statement was not understood by the Jews; they assumed that He would immediately take over their civil government and free them from the yoke of their oppressors. The government, however, to which Isaiah referred, was the organization of His Church, which was decreed to ultimately fill the whole earth, as we shall explain more in detail in the next chapter.

Prophet to be Raised Up Like unto Moses

The Lord promised that He would raise up a prophet like unto Moses:

> I will raise them up a Prophet from among their brethren, like unto thee, and will put my words in his mouth; and he shall speak unto them all that I shall command him.
>
> And it shall come to pass, that whosoever will not hearken unto my words which he shall speak in my name, I will require it of him. (Deuteronomy 18:18-19.)

Who among all the ancient prophets could be likened unto Moses except Jesus Christ? There was a great similarity in their ministries. On this parallel, the following quotation is illuminating:

MOSES — MESSIAH: A PARALLEL

1. Both Knew God Face to Face

Moses: And there arose not a prophet since in Israel like unto Moses, whom the Lord knew face to face. (Deuteronomy 34:10.)

Messiah: "As the Father knoweth me, even so know I the Father" (St. John 10:15). "Not that any man hath seen the Father (God), save he which is of God, he hath seen the Father." (St. John 6:46).

2. The Life of Each Was Sought in Infancy

Moses: Pharaoh sought the destruction of all the male children born of the Israelites, "and Pharaoh charged all his people saying, every son that is born ye shall cast into the river, and every daughter ye shall save alive." But Moses by faith of his mother had his life preserved, and became the adopted son of Pharaoh's daughter. (Exodus 1:22.)

Messiah: Herod ordered the slaughter of all the children of Bethlehem and in all the coasts thereof; but Jesus was preserved by the intervention of the Lord, for in a dream of the night, Joseph was commanded "to take the young child and his mother and flee into Egypt." Thus was his life preserved. (St. Matthew Chapter 2.)

3. Both Had Command Over the Sea

Moses: And Moses stretched out his hand over the sea; and the Lord caused the sea to go back by a strong east wind all that night, and made the sea dry land, and the waters were divided. (Exodus 14:21.)

Messiah: Crossing the Sea of Galilee there arose a great storm while the Christ slept in the boat until he was awakened by his frightened disciples. "Then he arose and rebuked the winds and the sea; and there was a great calm. But the men marvelled, saying, What manner of man is this, *that even the winds and the sea obey him!*" (St. Matthew, Chapter 8.)

4. Both Were Subject to Transfiguration

Moses: When Moses came down from the mountain with the tables of stone, whereon the ten commandments were written, "Moses wist not that the skin of his face shone," while he talked with him (i.e. with God), and the elders of Israel fled from him, and he (Moses) put a veil on his face. (Exodus 34:29-33.)

Messiah: The Christ went up into the mountain with Peter, James and John, "and was transfigured before them: and his face did shine as the sun, and his raiment was white as the light." (St. Matthew 17:2.)

5. Families of Each Sometimes Opposed Them

Moses: And Miriam and Aaron, sister and brother to Moses, spake against Moses because of the Ethiopian woman he had married; and they said: "Hath the Lord indeed spoken only by Moses? Hath he not spoken also by us?" But the Lord vindicated Moses. (Numbers 12:1-2.)

Messiah: His brethren mockingly challenged Jesus to go into the world and show himself — "for neither did his brethren believe in him." (St. John 7:5.)

6. Both Moses and Christ Were Meek

Moses: "Now the man Moses was very meek, above all the men which were upon the face of the earth." (Numbers 12:3.)

Messiah: "Take my yoke upon you, and learn of me; for I am meek and lowly in heart: and ye shall find rest unto your souls" (St. Matthew 11:29).

7. ...

8. Both Rejected the Glory of the World

Moses: "By faith Moses, when he was come to years refused to be called the son of Pharaoh's daughter; choosing rather to suffer affliction with the people of God, than to enjoy the pleasures of sin for a season; esteeming the reproach of Christ greater riches than the treasures of Egypt." (Hebrews 11:24, 26.)

Messiah: "The devil taketh him up into an exceedingly high mountain, and sheweth him all the kingdoms of the world, and the glory of them; and saith unto him: All these things will I give unto thee, if thou wilt fall down and worship me. Then saith Jesus unto him: Get thee hence, satan; for it is written thou shalt worship the Lord thy God, and him only shalt thou serve. Then the devil leaveth him." (St. Matthew 4:8-11.) (B. H. Roberts, *Rasha The Jew*, pp. 45-47.)

Surely Jesus Christ, the Son of God, met all the requirements necessary to justify our accepting Him as the promised prophet like unto Moses. When He came He was rejected by His own, and in this respect He was also like unto Moses, for when Moses went up into the mountain to commune with the Lord, the children of Israel turned away from Moses and made a molten calf from their jewels, and said:

These be thy Gods, O Israel, which have brought thee up out of the land of Egypt. (Exodus 32:8.)

The prophet Nephi, as recorded in the Stick of Joseph, tells us who this prophet was, who was like unto Moses, whom the Lord promised to send:

And the Lord will surely prepare a way for his people, unto the fulfilling of the words of Moses, which he spake saying: A prophet shall the Lord your God raise up unto you, like unto me; him shall ye hear in all things whatsoever he shall say unto you. And it shall come to pass that all those who will not hear that prophet shall be cut off from among the people.

And now I, Nephi, declare unto you, that this prophet of whom Moses spake was the Holy One of Israel; wherefore, he shall execute judgment in righteousness. (I Nephi 22:20-21.)

Location of the Messiah's Birth Foretold

Concerning the coming of the promised Messiah, the prophets gave many details, that in their fulfillment He would be recognized. They even foretold the city in which He would be born:

> But thou, Bethlehem Ephratah, though thou be little among the thousands of Judah, yet out of thee shall he come forth unto me that is to be ruler in Israel; *whose goings forth have been from of old, from everlasting.* (Micah 5:2.)

It must be more than a coincidence that Jesus Christ, the Son of God, who answers all the requirements of the prophecies, should have been born in "Bethlehem Ephratah." How much better could Micah have described Him who was to be "ruler in Israel?"

The Messiah's Death Foretold

Details pertaining to His death were given by the Psalmist in these words:

> . . . they pierced my hands and my feet. . . .
> They part my garments among them, and cast lots upon my vesture. (Psalms 22:16, 18.)

That they pierced the hands and feet of the Christ is a well recorded fact of history. The prophets in declaring the second coming of the Messiah indicated that He would present the wounds that He received in the house of His friends as evidence that He was the promised Messiah whom they had rejected:

> And I will pour upon the house of David, and upon the inhabitants of Jerusalem, the spirit of grace and of supplications: *and they shall look upon me whom they have pierced,* and they shall mourn for him, as one mourneth for his only son, and shall be in bitterness for him, as one that is in bitterness for his firstborn. (Zachariah 12:10.)
>
> And one shall say unto him, *What are these wounds in thine hands?* Then he shall answer, *Those with which I was wounded in the house of my friends.* (Zachariah 13:6.)

Consider the account of how they parted His garments and cast lots for His vesture:

And they crucified him, and parted his garments, casting lots: that it might be fulfilled which was spoken by the prophet, They parted my garments among them, and upon my vesture did they cast lots. (St. Matthew 27:35.)

The Prophet Zechariah even foretold the price that would be put upon His head:

So they weighed for my price thirty pieces of silver. (Zechariah 11:12.)

Matthew gives this account of the fulfillment of Zechariah's prophecy:

Then Judas, which had betrayed him, when he saw that he was condemned, repented himself, and brought again the *thirty pieces of silver* to the chief priests and elders,

Saying, I have sinned in that I have betrayed the innocent blood. And they said, What is that to us? see thou to that.

And he cast down the pieces of silver in the temple, and departed and went and hanged himself. (St. Matthew 27:3-5.)

The Messiah to be Called Out of Egypt

The Prophet Hosea foretold that the Lord would call His Son out of Egypt:

When Israel was a child, then I loved him, and called my son out of Egypt. (Hosea 11:1.)

Concerning the fulfillment of this prophecy, we read:

And when they were departed, behold, the angel of the Lord appeareth to Joseph in a dream, saying, Arise, and take the young child and his mother, and flee into Egypt, and be thou there until I bring thee word: for Herod will seek the young child to destroy him.

When he arose, he took the young child and his mother by night, and departed into Egypt:

And was there until the death of Herod: that it might

be fulfilled which was spoken of the Lord by the prophet, saying, Out of Egypt have I called my son. (St. Matthew 2: 13-15.)

Herod Slays the Children of Bethlehem

The Prophet Jeremiah foretold the sorrow among the people because of the children who would be put to death by Herod:

Thus saith the Lord; A voice was heard in Ramah, lamentation, and bitter weeping; Rachel weeping for her children refused to be comforted for her children, because they were not. (Jeremiah 31:15.)

The fulfillment of Jeremiah's prophecy is recorded as follows:

Then Herod, when he saw that he was mocked of the wise men, was exceeding wroth, and sent forth, and slew all the children that were in Bethlehem, and in all the coasts thereof, from two years old and under, according to the time which he had diligently enquired of the wise men.

Then was fulfilled that which was spoken by Jeremy [Jeremiah] the prophet, saying,

In Rama was there a voice heard, lamentation, and weeping, and great mourning, Rachel weeping for her children, and would not be comforted because they are not. St. Matthew 2:16-18.)

The Ministry of the Messiah

The Prophet Isaiah spoke of the ministry of the Messiah:

I the Lord have called thee in righteousness, and will hold thine hand, and will keep thee, and give thee for a covenant of the people for a light of the Gentiles;

To open the blind eyes, to bring out the prisoners from the prison, and them that sit in darkness out of the prison house.

I am the Lord: that is my name: and my glory will I not give to another, neither my praise to graven images. (Isaiah 42:6-8.)

Luke gives us an account of Zacharias, the father of John the Baptist, and how John would be sent to prepare the way for the coming of the Messiah:

> And his father Zacharias was filled with the Holy Ghost and prophesied, saying,
> Blessed be the Lord God of Israel; for he hath visited and redeemed his people,
> And hath raised up an horn of salvation for us in the house of his servant David;
> As he spake by the mouth of his holy prophets, which have been since the world began:
> That we should be saved from our enemies, and from the hand of all that hate us;
> To perform the mercy promised to our fathers, and to remember his holy covenant;
> The oath which he sware to our father Abraham.
> That he would grant unto us, that we being delivered out of the hand of our enemies might serve him without fear,
> In holiness and righteousness before him, all the days of our life.
> And thou, child, shalt be called the prophet of the Highest; for thou shalt go before the face of the Lord to prepare his ways;
> To give knowledge of salvation unto his people, by the remission of their sins,
> Through the tender mercy of our God; whereby the dayspring from on high hath visited us,
> To give light to them that sit in darkness and in the shadow of death, to guide our feet into the way of peace.
> And the child grew and waxed strong in spirit, and was in the deserts till the day of his shewing unto Israel. (St. Luke 1:67-80.)

Under the promptings of the spirit, Isaiah further spoke of the ministry of the Messiah:

> The Spirit of the Lord God is upon me; because the Lord hath anointed me to preach good tidings unto the meek; he hath sent me to bind up the broken-hearted, to proclaim liberty to the captives, and the opening of the prison to them that are bound;
> To proclaim the acceptable year of the Lord, and the day of vengeance of our God; to comfort all that mourn;

To appoint unto them that mourn in Zion, to give unto them beauty for ashes, the oil of joy for mourning, the garment of praise for the spirit of heaviness; that they might be called trees of righteousness, the planting of the Lord, that he might be glorified. (Isaiah 61:1-3.)

Luke gives the following account of the commencement of the ministry of Jesus Christ, the Messiah, after He had fasted forty days, and after He had been tempted by the devil:

And Jesus being full of the Holy Ghost returned from Jordan, and was led by the Spirit into the wilderness, . . .

And he came to Nazareth, where he had been brought up: and, as his custom was, he went into the synagogue on the sabbath day, and stood up for to read.

And there was delivered unto him the book of the prophet Esaias. And when he had opened the book, he found the place where it was written,

The Spirit of the Lord is upon me, because he hath anointed me to preach the gospel to the poor; he hath sent me to heal the broken-hearted, to preach deliverance to the captives, and recovering of sight to the blind, to set at liberty them that are bruised,

To preach the acceptable year of the Lord.

And he closed the book, and he gave it again to the minister, and sat down. And the eyes of all them that were in the synagogue were fastened on him.

And he began to say unto them, This day is this scripture fulfilled in your ears. (Luke 4:1, 16-21.)

Jacob's Promise to Judah Concerning the Messiah

Concerning the coming of the promised Messiah, let us consider the promise of Jacob to his son Judah:

Judah, thou art he whom thy brethren shall praise: thy hand shall be in the neck of thine enemies; thy father's children shall bow down before thee.

Judah is a lion's whelp: from the prey, my son, thou art gone up; he stooped down, he couched as a lion, and as an old lion; who shall rouse him up?

The sceptre shall not depart from Judah, nor a lawgiver from between his feet, until Shiloh come; and unto him shall the gathering of the people be. (Genesis 49:8-10.)

"Judah, thou art he whom thy brethren shall praise
. . . thy father's children shall bow down before thee."
This promise clearly looks to the coming of the Messiah
through the loins of Judah.

Time of the Messiah's Coming Foretold

Let us now consider the statement of Jacob as to
the time of the Messiah's coming.

> The sceptre shall not depart from Judah, nor a law-
> giver from between his feet, until Shiloh come. (*Ibid.*)

For an explanation and discussion of this promise,
the following scholarly excerpt is presented:

> This passage by the Jews, in ancient times, who be-
> lieved in the coming of the Messiah at all, was allowed to
> have reference to the coming of their Messiah, and as in
> some way fixing the time and circumstances of his coming.
>
> It is evident that by "Judah" is meant, not the person,
> but the tribe, and by "Sceptre" and "lawgiver" are obviously
> intended the legislative and ruling power. In the course of
> time this commenced in David, and for centuries afterwards
> was continued in his descendants. Whatever variety the
> form of government assumed the law and polity were the
> same.
>
> "The versions," it is said, "generally read 'Shiloh' in-
> stead of 'Shilow,' and the words 'until Shiloh come' should
> be, 'till he come whose it is' i.e., whose the Sceptre is."
>
> "Rabbi Johannan referring to Genesis 49:10 asked what
> was the name of the Messiah; they of the school of Rabbi
> Schilo, 1490 A.D., answered: 'his name shall be Shilo, ac-
> cording to that which is written — 'until Shilo come.'"
>
> Again: Lesser's Bible — Hebrew translator — not a
> Christian convert, 1900 A.D. — says: "The Scepter will re-
> turn, when the Shilo, the King Messiah shall come, and to
> him shall be both the obedience and assemblance of the
> people or nations."
>
> The Jewish Targums paraphrase the passage thus: "The
> Sceptre shall not depart from Judah until the King Messiah
> comes, to whom it belongeth." This is supported by the
> rabbis noted above.

This prediction of Genesis 49:10, all the older Jewish commentators, referred to as Messiah. Ben Uzzel, whose Commentaries are among the most ancient Targums, renders the passage: "Until the time when the King Messiah shall come." The Targum of Onkelos speaks of it to the same effect, and the Targum of Jerusalem paraphrases it thus: "Kings shall not cease, from the House of Judah, nor doctors that teach the law from his children until that the King, Messiah, do come, whose the kingdom is: and all nations of the earth shall be subject unto him."

For modern Jewish commentators, these admissions represent tremendous consequences. If the integrity of the prophecy be regarded, then, since the Sceptre — symbol of the legislative and ruling power — has departed from Judah, the Messiah must have come, and long since come, for Judah has not held legislative authority, nor the Sceptre of power for two thousand years! The last trace of legislative power in the Sanhedrin, and all administrative authority departed from Judah with the coming of Jesus, the Christ, and with the destruction of the temple and Jerusalem under the Romans, 70 A.D. (B. H. Roberts, *Rasha The Jew*, pp. 40-41.)

"Thy Dead Men Shall Live — Together With My Dead Body Shall They Arise"

There is another very important statement by the Prophet Isaiah when he takes the sorrows and afflictions of Israel to Jehovah which we should consider:

Lord, in trouble have they visited thee, they poured out a prayer when thy chastening was upon them.

Like as a woman with child, that draweth near the time of her delivery, is in pain, and crieth out in her pangs; so have we been in thy sight, O Lord. (Isaiah 26:16-17.)

To comfort Israel, the Lord replied:

Thy dead men shall live, together with my dead body shall they arise. Awake and sing, ye that dwell in dust: for thy dew is as the dew of herbs, and the earth shall cast out the dead. (Isaiah 26:19.)

We are informed:

This is Jehovah speaking. "Thy dead men," O Israel, "shall live"—the resurrection of the dead proclaimed!

Together with Jehovah's dead body shall they arise! Jehovah, then, is to have a "body"! He is to become "*dead*", and to "arise". Jehovah is to dwell with men in the flesh, to be "Immanuel", to live with men, to die, to arise from the dead, and the dead men of Israel to rise with him! Can language more clearly outline the incarnation of Jehovah in the flesh, his death and his resurrection! Blasphemy this? Then it is Isaiah, the great Hebrew prophet who blasphemes; or rather, Jehovah, for it is he who is speaking. And who but the Christ of the New Testament fulfills, or can fulfill the inspired prophecy of Isaiah, on the incarnation of Jehovah, his death in that mortal state, his resurrection to immortality in that incarnation, and the resurrection of men to an immortality with him—"together with my dead body shall they arise"! (B. H. Roberts, *Rasha the Jew*, p. 16.)

Through Judah Came the "Chief Ruler"

It was through the coming of the promised Messiah through the loins of Abraham that the Lord promised His prophet that all the nations of the earth would be blessed:

Seeing that Abraham shall surely become a great and mighty nation, and all the nations of the earth shall be blessed in him? (Genesis 18:18.)

And I will make of thee a great nation, and I will bless thee, and make thy name great; and thou shalt be a blessing:

And I will bless them that bless thee, and curse him that curseth thee: and in thee shall all families of the earth be blessed. (Genesis 12:2-3.)

And in thy seed shall all the nations of the earth be blessed; because thou hast obeyed my voice. (Genesis 22:18.)

The Lord further promised that the "Chief Ruler" would come through Judah:

For Judah prevailed above his brethren, and of him came the chief ruler; but the birthright was Joseph's: (I Chronicles 5:2.)

Kingdom to be Established Through the Seed of David

David was promised by the Lord that through his seed He would set up His Kingdom which would stand forever:

And when thy days be fulfilled, and thou shalt sleep with thy fathers, I will set up thy seed after thee, which shall proceed out of thy bowels, and I will establish his kingdom.

He shall build an house for my name, and I will establish the throne of his kingdom for ever.

I will be his father, and he shall be my son. If he commit iniquity, I will chasten him with the rod of men, and with the stripes of the children of men:

But my mercy shall not depart away from him, as I took it from Saul, whom I put away before thee.

And thine house and thy kingdom shall be established for ever before thee: thy throne shall be established for ever.

According to all these words, and according to all this vision, so did Nathan speak unto David. (II Samuel 7:12-17. This same promise is also recorded in I Chronicles 17:11-15.)

Prophecies Fulfilled

The prophecies we have considered foretelling the coming of the Messiah, the Jehovah of the Old Testament, have all been fulfilled in the coming of Jesus Christ, the Son of God, the Redeemer of the World, the King of Israel. He did establish His Kingdom in the meridian of time as was foretold.

Kingdom Removed — To be Restored

But His Kingdom (His Church) was not destined to remain upon the earth uninterrupted until the fulfillment of all the promises of the Lord through all His holy prophets. Because of the wickedness of the House of Israel, the Lord took His Kingdom from the earth until

it would be restored "in the latter days" that it may prepare the way for the second coming of the Messiah, who
will possess the Kingdom to rule and reign forever and
ever as "King of kings and Lord of lords." (Revelation
19:16; See also Zech. 14:9.)

Much would have to be done, according to the
words of the prophets, to prepare Christ's Kingdom for
His second coming. However, the Lord has made ample
provision for the fulfillment of all His promises through
His prophets.

In our next chapter we will consider the work necessary to prepare for the second coming of the Messiah,
as foretold by the prophets.

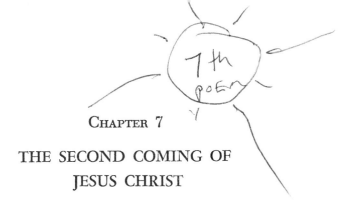

CHAPTER 7

THE SECOND COMING OF
JESUS CHRIST

Christ's Second Coming Distinguished from His First Coming

Having considered the prophecies relating to His first coming, including those contained in the Stick of Joseph, we will now consider those pertaining to His second coming. Let us begin this consideration with the words of the Christ in answer to the question of the high priest when He was brought before Caiaphas:

> But Jesus held his peace. And the high priest answered and said unto him, I adjure thee by the living God, that thou tell us whether thou be the Christ, the Son of God.
>
> Jesus saith unto him, Thou hast said: nevertheless I say unto you, Hereafter shall ye see the Son of man sitting on the right hand of power, and coming *in the clouds of heaven.* (St. Matthew 26:63-64.)

The Prophet Daniel saw this coming "in the clouds of heaven" to which Jesus referred:

> I saw in the night visions, and, behold, one like the Son of man came with the *clouds of heaven,* and came to the Ancient of days, and they brought him near before him.
>
> And there was given him dominion, and glory, and a kingdom, that all people, nations, and languages, should serve him: his dominion is an everlasting dominion, which shall not pass away, and his kingdom that which shall not be destroyed. (Daniel 7:13-14.)

Jesus' coming in the "clouds of heaven" to receive the kingdom prepared for Him, as described by Daniel,

is quite different from His first coming as described by
the Prophet Isaiah:

> . . . unto us a child is born, unto us a son is given: and
> the government shall be upon his shoulder: and his name
> shall be called Wonderful, Counsellor, The mighty God,
> The everlasting Father, The Prince of Peace. (Isaiah 9:6.)

Christ's coming in the "clouds of heaven" to which
Daniel referred was to be at a much later date than
"when a child is born" to which Isaiah referred. There
was no kingdom prepared for Him when He was born of
the virgin Mary. But when He shall come in the
"clouds of heaven," the kingdom will already have
been prepared for Him. Unless a kingdom is prepared
how can it be given to Him?

Christ Will Come to His Temple

Speaking of the second coming of the Lord, and the
preparation to be made therefor, the Prophet Malachi
states:

> Behold, I will send my messenger, and he shall pre-
> pare the way before me: and the Lord, whom ye seek, *shall
> suddenly come to his temple,* even the messenger of the
> covenant, whom ye delight in: behold, he shall come, saith
> the Lord of hosts.
> But who may abide the day of his coming? and who
> shall stand when he appeareth? for he is like a refiner's
> fire, and like fullers' soap:
> And he shall sit as a refiner and purifier of silver: and
> he shall purify the sons of Levi, and purge them as gold and
> silver, that they may offer unto the Lord an offering in
> righteousness.
> Then shall the offering of Judah and Jerusalem be
> pleasant unto the Lord, as in the days of old, and as in
> former years.
> And I will come near to you to judgment; and I will be
> a swift witness against the sorcerers, and against the adulter-
> ers and against false swearers, and against those that oppress
> the hireling in his wages, the widow, and the fatherless,
> and that turn aside the stranger from his right, and fear not
> me, saith the Lord of hosts.

For I am the Lord, I change not; therefore ye sons of Jacob are not consumed. (Malachi 3:1-6.)

Jesus testified that the messenger herein promised who would be sent to prepare the way before Him was John the Baptist:

For this is he, of whom it is written, Behold, I send my messenger before thy face, which shall prepare thy way before thee. (St. Matthew 11:10.)

From the reading of Malachi's prophecy, it is apparent that he saw far beyond the time of Christ's first coming, for he states that he shall "suddenly come to his temple." This He did not do at His first coming.

Then Malachi adds: "But who may abide the day of his coming?" All were able to abide the day of His first coming.

The Wicked Shall Cry

When He shall come the second time, *"in the clouds of heaven,"* the wicked shall cry out for the mountains and rocks to fall upon them, to hide them from His face:

And the kings of the earth, and the great men, and the rich men, and the chief captains, and the mighty men, and every bondman, and every free man, hid themselves in the dens and in the rocks of the mountains;

And said to the mountains and rocks, Fall on us, and hide us from the face of him that sitteth on the throne, and from the wrath of the Lamb:

For the great day of his wrath is come; and who shall be able to stand? (Revelations 6:15-17.)

The Lord to Judge His People

Again Malachi saw the coming of the Lord when He should come in power to judge His people:

For, behold, the day cometh that shall burn as an oven; and all the proud, yea, and all that do wickedly, shall be stubble: and the day that cometh shall burn them up, saith the Lord of hosts, that it shall leave them neither root nor branch. (Malachi 4:1.)

The prophecy of Isaiah is added in support of the words of Malachi:

7th Poem

> The earth shall reel to and fro like a drunkard, and shall be removed like a cottage; and the transgression thereof shall be heavy upon it; and it shall fall, and not rise again.
>
> And it shall come to pass in that day, that the Lord shall punish the host of the high ones that are on high, and the kings of the earth upon the earth.
>
> And they shall be gathered together, as prisoners are gathered in the pit, and shall be shut up in the prison, and after many days shall they be visited.
>
> Then the moon shall be confounded, and the sun ashamed, when the Lord of hosts shall reign in mount Zion, and in Jerusalem, and before his ancients gloriously. (Isaiah 24:20-23.)

In describing what would happen to the earth and the moon and the inhabitants of the earth "when the Lord of hosts shall reign in mount Zion," it is very apparent that Isaiah was referring to His second coming and not to His first coming.

The Lord to Reward His People

Isaiah further describes the coming of the Lord to reward His people:

7th Poem

> Behold, the Lord God will come with strong hand, and his arm shall rule for him: behold, *his reward is with him,* and his work before him. (Isaiah 40:10.)

> Behold, the Lord hath proclaimed unto the end of the the world, Say ye to the daughter of Zion, Behold, thy salvation cometh; behold, *his reward is with him,* and his work before him. (Isaiah 62:11.)

> Who is this that cometh from Edom, with dyed garments from Bozrah? this that is glorious in his apparel, travelling in the greatness of his strength? *I that speak in righteousness, mighty to save.*
>
> Wherefore art thou red in thine apparel, and thy garments like him that treadeth in the winefat?
>
> I have trodden the winepress alone; and of the people there was none with me: for I will tread them in mine anger,

and trample them in my fury; and their blood shall be sprinkled upon my garments, and I will stain all my raiment.

For the day of vengeance is in mine heart, and the year of my redeemed is come. (Isaiah 63:1-4.)

Time of the Second Coming Foretold

The Prophet Isaiah foresees the coming of the "Redeemer" to the seed of Jacob:

7th poem *And the Redeemer shall come to Zion,* and unto them that turn from transgression in Jacob, saith the Lord. (Isaiah 59:20.)

Isaiah gives us further light pertaining to the time of the coming of the Redeemer, and gives us some idea of the period in the world's history when this glorious event would occur:

Arise, shine; for thy light is come, and the glory of the Lord is risen upon thee.

For, behold, the darkness shall cover the earth, and gross darkness the people: but the Lord shall arise upon thee, and his glory shall be seen upon thee.

And the Gentiles shall come to thy light, and kings to the brightness of thy rising. (Isaiah 60:1-3.)

Note particularly these words of Isaiah:

Who are these that fly as a cloud, and as the doves to their windows? (Isaiah 60:8.)

Clearly, Isaiah was referring to individuals and not to birds. Surely there has never been a time in the history of this world when men flew "as a cloud" or "as the doves to their windows," until our present time since the advent of the airplane.

Again, in referring to the time of the second coming of the Messiah, Isaiah said:

And there shall come forth, a rod out of the stem of Jesse, and a Branch shall grow out of his roots:

And the spirit of the Lord shall rest upon him, the

spirit of wisdom and understanding, the spirit of counsel
and might, the spirit of knowledge and of the fear of the
Lord;

And shall make him of quick understanding in the fear
of the Lord: and he shall not judge after the sight of his
eyes, neither reprove after the hearing of his ears:

But with righteousness shall he judge the poor, and reprove with equity for the meek of the earth: and he shall
smite the earth with the rod of his mouth, and with the
breath of his lips shall he slay the wicked.

And righteousness shall be the girdle of his loins, and
faithfulness the girdle of his reins.

The wolf also shall dwell with the lamb, and the
leopard shall lie down with the kid; and the calf and the
young lion and the fatling together; and the little child shall
lead them.

And the cow and the bear shall feed; their young ones
shall lie down together: and the lion shall eat straw like the
ox.

And the sucking child shall play on the hole of the
asp, and the weaned child shall put his hand on the cocka-
trice' den.

They shall not hurt nor destroy in all my holy mountain: for the earth shall be full of the knowledge of the
Lord, as the waters cover the sea.

And in that day there shall be a root of Jesse, which
shall stand for an ensign of the people; to it shall the Gentiles seek: and his rest shall be glorious.

And it shall come to pass in that day, that the Lord
shall set his hand again *the second time* to recover the
remnant of his people, which shall be left, from Assyria,
and from Egypt, and from Pathros, and from Cush, and
from Elam, and from Shinar, and from Hamath, and from
the islands of the sea.

And he shall set up an ensign for the nations, and shall
assemble the outcasts of Israel, and gather together the
dispersed of Judah from the four corners of the earth.

The envy also of Ephraim shall depart, and the adversaries of Judah shall be cut off: Ephraim shall not envy
Judah, and Judah shall not vex Ephraim. (Isaiah 11:1-13.)

The promises declared by Isaiah did not have their
fulfillment in the first coming of Christ as the promised
Messiah. They relate to the time of the establishment
of His latter-day kingdom which Daniel saw would be

set up in the earth by the God of Heaven to prepare the way for Christ's second coming when he would come "in the clouds of heaven."

Of the second coming of the Messiah, the Prophet Jeremiah foretells the day when the Lord would raise up unto David a righteous branch, and a King whose name is, "The Lord Our Righteousness," who would reign and prosper, and execute judgment and justice in the earth:

> Behold, the days come, saith the Lord, that I will raise unto David a righteous Branch, and a King shall reign and prosper, and shall execute judgment and justice in the earth.
> In his days Judah shall be saved, and Israel shall dwell safely: and this is his name whereby he shall be called, THE LORD OUR RIGHTEOUSNESS.
> Therefore, behold, the days come, saith the Lord, that they shall no more say, The Lord liveth, which brought up the children of Israel out of the land of Egypt.
> But, the Lord liveth, which brought up and which lead the seed of the house of Israel out of the north country, and from all countries whither I had driven them; and they shall dwell in their own land. (Jeremiah 23:5-8.)

We include verses 7 and 8 in the above quotation to fix the time when the Lord would "raise unto David a righteous Branch" and a King who would "execute judgment and justice in the earth."

The Psalmist saw the coming of the Lord to judge His people, which vision clearly relates to His second coming—not to His first coming:

> The mighty God, even the Lord, hath spoken, and called the earth from the rising of the Sun unto the going down thereof.
> Out of Zion, the perfection of beauty, God hath shined.
> *Our God shall come*, and shall not keep silence: a fire shall devour before him, and it shall be very tempestuous around about him.
> He shall call to the heavens from above, and to the earth, that he may judge his people.

Gather my saints together unto me; those that have made a covenant with me by sacrifice.

And the heavens shall declare his righteousness: *for God is judge himself.* Selah. (Psalms 50:1-6.)

Second Coming to be "at the Latter Day"

In Job's great physical distress, he bore testimony that he knew his Redeemer would stand upon the earth at the *latter day*:

For I know that my redeemer liveth, and that *he shall stand at the latter day upon the earth:*

And though after my skin worms destroy this body, yet in my flesh shall I see God:

Whom I shall see for myself, and mine eyes shall behold, and not another; though my reins be consumed within me. (Job 19:25-27.)

What Job was given to know was that his Redeemer would stand upon the earth at the latter day and that in his flesh, though it had been destroyed by the worms, he would see God, his Redeemer. This, of course, has reference to Christ's second coming.

"And They Shall Look upon Me Whom They Have Pierced"

Zechariah clearly foretold the second coming of our Lord:

In that day will I make the governors of Judah like an hearth of fire among the wood, and like a torch of fire in a sheaf; and they shall devour all the people round about, on the right hand and on the left: and Jerusalem shall be inhabited again in her own place, even in Jerusalem.

The Lord also shall save the tents of Judah first, that the glory of the house of David and the glory of the inhabitants of Jerusalem do not magnify themselves against Judah.

In that day shall the Lord defend the inhabitants of Jerusalem; and he that is feeble among them at that day shall be as David; and the house of David shall be as God, as the angel of the Lord, before them.

And it shall come to pass in that day, that I will seek to destroy all the nations that come against Jerusalem.

And I will pour upon the house of David, and upon the inhabitants of Jerusalem, the spirit of grace and of supplication: *and they shall look upon me whom they have pierced*, and they shall mourn for him, as one mourneth for his only son, and shall be in bitterness for him, as one that is in bitterness for his firstborn. (Zechariah 12:6-10.)

Obviously, the words of Zechariah could only have reference to Christ's second coming since at His first coming, He was born a little child, as the prophets had foretold. Zechariah further described what he meant when he said: "and they shall look upon me whom they have pierced":

And one shall say unto him, What are these wounds in thine hands? Then he shall answer, *Those with which I was wounded in the house of my friends.* (Zechariah 13:6.)

"Forgive Them, for They Know Not What They Do"

Surely there will never be another who will have met all the requirements foretold by the prophets as did Jesus the Christ, even to the wounds which He received in the house of His friends. Even though they pierced and crucified Him, yet He loved them for they were His chosen people. That He loved them dearly is evidenced by His statement as He hung upon the cross:

Then said Jesus, Father, forgive them; for they know not what they do. And they parted his raiment, and cast lots. (St. Luke 23:34.)

"Blessed are They that Have Not Seen and Yet Have Believed"

It will be wonderful for those of the House of Judah who accept their Messiah without having to wait to see the wounds in His hands. Consider the words of Jesus to His Apostle Thomas, who doubted Christ's resurrection when told thereof by the disciples:

> Jesus saith unto him, Thomas, because thou hast seen me, thou hast believed: blessed are they that have not seen, and yet have believed. (St. John 20:29.)

Jerusalem Shall Be Safely Inhabited

The Prophet Zechariah made other important predictions concerning the coming of the Lord in the latter days, His second coming, and the winding up scenes and the preparation therefor:

> Behold, the day of the Lord cometh, . . .
> For I will gather all nations against Jerusalem to battle; . . .
> Then shall the Lord go forth, and fight against those nations, as when he fought in the day of battle. . . .
> . . . and the Lord my God shall come, and all the Saints with thee. . . .
> And the Lord shall be king over all the earth: in that day shall there be one Lord, and his name one. . . .
> And men shall dwell in it, and there shall be no more utter destruction; but Jerusalem shall be safely inhabited. . . .
> And Judah also shall fight at Jerusalem; and the wealth of all the heathen round about shall be gathered together, gold, and silver, and apparel, in great abundance. (Zechariah 14:1-3, 5, 9, 11, 14.)

Thus Zechariah saw, as did Daniel, that "the Lord my God shall come, and all the Saints with thee, and the Lord shall be king over all the earth." This had no reference to His first coming, but referred only to His second coming.

Stick of Joseph Predicts Second Coming of the Messiah

Of this final triumphant coming of the Lord to deliver and save His people, the Prophet Jacob, the brother of Nephi, as recorded in the Stick of Joseph, declared what the Lord had shown him:

And now I, Jacob, would speak somewhat concerning these words. For behold, the Lord has shown me that those who were at Jerusalem, from whence we came, have been slain and carried away captive.

Nevertheless, the Lord has shown unto me that they should return again. And he also has shown unto me that the Lord God, the Holy One of Israel, should manifest himself unto them in the flesh; and after he should manifest himself they should scourge him and crucify him, according to the words of the angel who spake it unto me.

And after they have hardened their hearts and stiffened their necks against the Holy One of Israel, behold, the judgments of the Holy One of Israel shall come upon them. And the day cometh that they shall be smitten and afflicted.

Wherefore, after they are driven to and fro, for thus saith the angel, many shall be afflicted in the flesh, and shall not be suffered to perish, because of the prayers of the faithful; they shall be scattered, and smitten, and hated; nevertheless, the Lord will be merciful unto them, that when they shall come to the knowledge of their Redeemer, they shall be gathered together again to the lands of their inheritance. . . .

And behold, according to the words of the prophet, *the Messiah* will set himself again *the second time* to recover them; wherefore, *he will manifest himself unto them in power and great glory,* unto the destruction of their enemies, when that day cometh *when they shall believe in him;* and none will he destroy that believe in him.

And they that believe not in him shall be destroyed, both by fire, and by tempest, and by earthquakes, and by bloodsheds, and by pestilence, and by famine. *And they shall know that the Lord is God, the Holy One of Israel.* (2 Nephi 6:8-11, 14-15.)

Thus the angel of the Lord showed Jacob the coming of the Holy One of Israel and His crucifixion, and the scattering and scourging of His people, and their gathering to Jerusalem prior to His second coming. He showed Jacob how those who would not be willing to accept Him would be destroyed until they who remained would "know that the Lord is God, the Holy One of Israel." It is of great importance, therefore, that *The House of Judah* come to this knowledge.

Jesus Ascends — He Will Come Again

Even the Apostles of Jesus seemed to be looking for the literal coming of His kingdom while He was with them. After His crucifixion and resurrection, and the forty days while He ministered among them following His resurrection, His apostles inquired again regarding the restoration of His kingdom:

> When they therefore were come together, they asked of him, saying, Lord, wilt thou at this time restore again the kingdom to Israel?
>
> And he said unto them, it is not for you to know the times or the seasons, which the Father hath put in his own power.
>
> But ye shall receive power, after that the Holy Ghost is come upon you: and ye shall be witnesses unto me both in Jerusalem, and in all Judaea, and in Samaria, and unto the uttermost part of the earth.
>
> And when he had spoken these things, while they beheld, he was taken up; and a cloud received him out of their sight.
>
> And while they looked stedfastly toward heaven as he went up, behold, two men stood by them in white apparel;
>
> Which also said, Ye men of Galilee, why stand ye gazing up into heaven? this same Jesus which is taken up from you into heaven, shall so come in like manner as ye have see him go into heaven. (Acts 1:6-11.)

Parley P. Pratt, an apostle of the Lord Jesus Christ, in this dispensation, summarized, in verse, a moving account of both the first and the second coming of our Lord:

> Jesus, once of humble birth,
> Now in glory comes to earth;
> Once he suffered grief and pain,
> Now he comes on earth to reign.

Once a meek and lowly Lamb,
Now the Lord, the great I AM:
Once upon the cross He bowed,
Now His chariot is the cloud.

Once he groaned in blood and tears,
Now in glory he appears;
Once rejected by His own,
Now their King He shall be known.

Once forsaken, left alone,
Now exalted to a throne;
Once all things He meekly bore,
But he now will bear no more.

CHAPTER 8

EVENTS TO TRANSPIRE BEFORE CHRIST'S SECOND COMING

A Choice Seer to be Raised Up "in the latter days"

We have pointed out that John the Baptist was the messenger sent to prepare the way for the first coming of our Lord. (St. Matthew 11:10.) It seems consistent that the Messiah would also send His messenger to prepare the way for His second coming. We have the promise of the Lord to this effect as recorded in the Stick of Joseph in the words of the Prophet Lehi to his son Joseph:

And now, Joseph, my last-born, whom I have brought out of the wilderness of mine afflictions, may the Lord bless thee forever, for thy seed shall not utterly be destroyed.

For behold, thou art the fruit of my loins; and I am a descendant of Joseph who was carried captive into Egypt. *And great were the covenants of the Lord which he made unto Joseph.*

Wherefore, Joseph truly saw our day. And he obtained a promise of the Lord, that out of the fruit of his loins the Lord God would raise up a righteous branch unto the house of Israel; not the Messiah, but a branch which was to be broken off, nevertheless, to be remembered in the covenants of the Lord *that the Messiah should be made manifest unto them in the latter days,* in the spirit of power, unto the bringing of them out of darkness unto light—yea, out of hidden darkness and out of captivity unto freedom.

For Joseph truly testified, saying: *A seer shall the Lord my God raise up, who shall be a choice seer unto the fruit of my loins.*

Yea, Joseph truly said: Thus saith the Lord unto me: *A choice seer* will I raise up out of the fruit of thy loins; and he shall be esteemed highly among the fruit of thy loins. And unto him will I give commandment that he shall do a work for the fruit of thy loins, his brethren, which shall be of great worth unto them, even to the bringing of them to the knowledge of the covenants which I have made with thy fathers.

And I will give unto him a commandment that he shall do none other work, save the work which I shall command him. *And I will make him great in mine eyes; for he shall do my work.*

And he shall be great like unto Moses, whom I have said I would raise up unto you, to deliver my people, O house of Israel.

And Moses will I raise up, to deliver thy people out of the land of Egypt.

But a seer will I raise up out of the fruit of thy loins; *and unto him will I give power to bring forth my word unto the seed of thy loins*—and not to the bringing forth my word only, saith the Lord, *but to the convincing them of my word, which shall have already gone forth among them.*

Wherefore, the fruit of thy loins shall write; and the fruit of the loins of Judah shall write; and that which shall be written by the fruit of thy loins, and also that which shall be written by the fruit of the loins of Judah, shall grow together, unto the confounding of false doctrines and laying down of contentions, and establishing peace among the fruit of thy loins, and bringing them to the knowledge of their fathers *in the latter days,* and also to the knowledge of my covenants, saith the Lord.

And out of weakness he shall be made strong, *in that day when my work shall commence among all my people, unto the restoring thee, O house of Israel, saith the Lord.*

And thus prophesied Joseph, saying: Behold, that seer will the Lord bless; and they that seek to destroy him shall be confounded; for this promise, which I have obtained of the Lord, of the fruit of my loins, shall be fulfilled. *Behold, I am sure of the fulfilling of this promise;*

And his name shall be called after me; and it shall be after the name of his father. And he shall be like unto me; for the thing, which the Lord shall bring forth by his hand, by the power of the Lord shall bring my people unto salvation.

Yea, thus prophesied Joseph: I am sure of this thing, even as I am sure of the promise of Moses; for the Lord hath said unto me, I will preserve thy seed forever. (2 Nephi 3:3-16.)

The mighty work to be done to prepare the way for
the second coming of the Messiah could not be accomplished without such a prophet and seer being raised
up by the Lord for this very purpose. Remember the
words of Amos:

> Surely the Lord God will do nothing, but he revealeth
> his secret unto his servants the prophets. (Amos 3:7.)

Judah Divided into Many Groups

Obviously, there would be no need of the Lord
sending a prophet "in the latter-days" if His children
of the House of Judah and Israel were already under the
leadership of a prophet.

Consider the condition of the House of Judah. If
the Lord had a seer and prophet among them "like unto
Moses," or like any of the ancient Hebrew prophets, the
Lord could speak to that prophet who, in turn, could
speak to the entire House of Judah. But such is impossible today, for Judah is divided into many groups, each
with its own interpretations of the written word of the
Lord, and with its own leaders, none of whom profess to
speak in the name of the Lord, as did the prophets of old.
All this, notwithstanding the statement of Amos: "Surely
the Lord God will do nothing, but he revealeth his secret
unto his servants the prophets." (Amos 3:7.)   Under
such divided leadership, how could the Lord establish
His kingdom preparatory to the second coming of the
Messiah?

"A Famine in the Land"

The Lord declared unto Joseph that from his seed
he would raise up a "choice seer . . . like unto Moses"
in the latter days. He also inspired others of His prophets to declare how the leaders of His people would go

astray and how spiritual darkness would spread over the earth as witness the words of Amos:

> Behold, the days come, saith the Lord God, that I will send a famine in the land, not a famine of bread, nor a thirst for water, but of hearing the words of the Lord:
>
> And they shall wander from sea to sea, and from the north even to the east, they shall run to and fro to seek the word of the Lord, and shall not find it. (Amos 8:11-12.)

If there were any place in the world where the word of the Lord could be heard, surely the Prophet Amos would not have made such a statement.

"No Answer of God"

The Prophet Micah also foresaw the day when there would be "no answer of God." He described the apostate condition of Israel as follows:

> Thus saith the Lord concerning the prophets that make my people err, that bite with their teeth, and cry, Peace; and he that putteth not into their mouths, they even prepare war against him.
>
> Therefore night shall be unto you, that ye shall not have a vision; and it shall be dark unto you, that ye shall not divine; and the sun shall go down over the prophets, and the day shall be dark over them.
>
> Then shall the seers be ashamed, and the diviners confounded: yea, they shall all cover their lips; *for there is no answer of God.* . . .
>
> *The heads thereof judge for reward, and the priests thereof teach for hire, and the prophets thereof divine for money: yet will they lean upon the Lord, and say, Is not the Lord among us?* none evil can come upon us. (Micah 3:5-7, 11.)

Can anyone question the fact that such a condition exists in Judah today? Yet their leaders "lean upon the Lord, and say, Is not the Lord among us?"

The Prophet Isaiah was also privileged to see this apostate condition of Israel and described it in these words:

> Behold, the Lord maketh the earth empty, and maketh it waste, and turneth it upside down, and scattereth abroad the inhabitants thereof.
>
> And it shall be, as with the people, so with the priest; as with the servant, so with his master; as with the maid, so with her mistress; as with the buyer, so with the seller; as with the lender, so with the borrower; as with the taker of usury, so with the giver of usury to him.
>
> The land shall be utterly emptied, and utterly spoiled: for the Lord hath spoken this word.
>
> The earth mourneth and fadeth away, the world languisheth and fadeth away, the haughty people of the earth do languish.
>
> *The earth also is defiled under the inhabitants thereof; because they have transgressed the laws, changed the ordinance, broken the everlasting covenant.*
>
> Therefore hath the curse devoured the earth, and they that dwell therein are desolate: therefore the inhabitants of the earth are burned, and few men left. (Isaiah 24:1-6.)

The need of a new prophet "like unto Moses" to be sent by the Lord "in the latter days" can well be understood when one considers the condition of Israel as described by the Prophet Isaiah. What an indictment!: "They have transgressed the laws, changed the ordinances, broken the everlasting covenant." And as Micah stated: "There is no answer of God."

Apostate Condition of the Christian World

The Apostles of the Christ had foretold this condition also, as had the prophets of Judah, with respect to the condition of the descendants of Judah. Paul declared:

> This know also, that *in the last days* perilous times shall come.
>
> For men shall be lovers of their own selves, covetous, boasters, proud, blasphemers, disobedient to parents, unthankful, unholy,

Without natural affection, trucebreakers, false accusers, incontinent, fierce, despisers of those that are good,

Traitors, heady, highminded, lovers of pleasure more than lovers of God;

Having a form of godliness, but denying the power thereof: from such turn away. (II Timothy 3:1-5.)

From this statement we are given to understand that it takes more than "a form of godliness," to constitute worship acceptable to God. Paul declared this would be the condition that would exist "in the last days." We repeat the admonition of Paul: "From such turn away."

A Falling Away Foretold

Paul further warned the followers of Christ who were already looking forward to His second coming, that that day would not come "except there come a falling away first." That there has been a falling away is clearly evidenced by the fact that there are hundreds of denominations and cults all professing to believe in Christ, but worshiping Him through man-made doctrines. Had there been no falling away, there would be but one Church of Jesus Christ upon the earth today. Note Paul's warning:

Now we beseech you, brethren, by the coming of our Lord Jesus Christ, and by our gathering together unto him,

That ye be not soon shaken in mind, or be troubled, neither by spirit, nor by word, nor by letter as from us, as that the day of Christ is at hand.

Let no man deceive you by any means: for that day shall not come, *except there come a falling away first*, and that man of sin be revealed, the son of perdition;

Who opposeth and exalteth himself above all that is called God, or that is worshipped; so that he as God sitteth in the temple of God, shewing himself that he is God. (II Thessalonians 2:1-4.)

Further describing this departure from the truth, Paul declared:

For the time will come when they will not endure

sound doctrine; but after their own lusts shall they heap to themselves teachers, having itching ears;

    And they shall turn away their ears from the truth, and shall be turned unto fables. (II Timothy 4:3-4.)

Satan to Overcome the Saints

The universality of this departure from the truth was proclaimed by John when he described the power which would be given to Satan:

    And it was given unto him to make war with the saints, and to overcome them: *and power was given him over all kindreds, and tongues, and nations.* (Revelation 13:7.)

While Satan was to be given power over the peoples of all nations, it should not be supposed that this would leave them without churches and religious teachings, for as the Apostle Paul stated, they would have "a form of godliness." Satan's policy seems to be to imitate the truth, i.e., when men "will not endure sound doctrine," as Paul stated, Satan sends teachers who will teach them "after their own lusts" since they have "itching ears." Such teachers Jesus referred to as "false prophets, which come to you in sheep's clothing, but inwardly they are ravening wolves." (St. Matthew 7:15.)

A Marvelous Work and a Wonder to Come Forth

Even though the prophets understood that Satan would have power to overcome the Saints, and scatter the people of the Lord, nevertheless, the Lord gave His prophets to understand that His truth would ultimately triumph in the earth, and that His kingdom would subdue all other kingdoms, powers and dominions. This kingdom would be established "in the latter days" to prepare for the second coming of the Messiah. Witness the following statement of Isaiah:

    Wherefore the Lord said, Forasmuch as this people draw near me with their mouth, and with their lips do

honour me, but have removed their heart far from me, and
their fear toward me is taught by the *precept of men*:

Therefore, behold, I will proceed to do a marvellous
work among this people, even a marvellous work and a
wonder; for the wisdom of their wise men shall perish,
and the understanding of their prudent men shall be hid.
(Isaiah 29:13-14.)

Without a full consideration of the magnitude of
this promise, it would be difficult for the layman to understand and comprehend that which, in the eyes of
the Lord, would constitute "a marvellous work and a
wonder," which would cause the wisdom of their wise
men to perish, and the understanding of their prudent
men to be hid. It should be noted that the Lord said He
would proceed to do *"a marvellous work"* among the
people. Thus it would be the work of God and not of
man.

The God of Heaven to Set Up His Kingdom

This "marvellous work and a wonder" is nothing
more nor less than the establishment of the Kingdom of
God upon the earth in the latter days in direct fulfillment of the prophecy of Daniel, quoted again for
emphasis:

But there is a God in heaven that revealeth secrets,
and maketh known to the king Nebuchadnezzar what shall
be *in the latter days. . . .*

And in the days of these kings shall the God of heaven
set up a kingdom, which shall never be destroyed: and
the kingdom shall not be left to other people, but it shall
break in pieces and consume all these kingdoms, and it
shall stand for ever. (Daniel 2:28, 44.)

Thus the God of Heaven decreed that He would set
up a kingdom, and who can prevent His doing the thing
He has decreed He would do "in the latter days?"

This, therefore, is the message we have to offer both
to the House of Judah and to the House of Joseph, or

Israel. The "marvellous work and a wonder" has been established in the earth through the prophet and seer "like unto Moses" who should "by the power of the Lord . . . bring my people unto salvation." (2 Nephi 3:15.)

An Angel to Restore the Gospel

When the Apostle John was banished upon the Isle of Patmos, in relating his experiences, he said:

> After this I looked, and behold, a door was opened in heaven; and the first voice which I heard was as it were of a trumpet talking with me; which said, Come up hither, *and I will shew thee things which must be hereafter.* (Revelation 4:1.)

After John was shown the power that would be given Satan to make war with the Saints (Revelation 13:7), he also saw the everlasting gospel brought back to the earth again by an angel of the Lord:

> And I saw another angel fly in the midst of heaven, having the everlasting gospel to preach unto them that dwell on the earth, and to every nation, and kindred, and tongue and people,
> Saying with a loud voice, Fear God, and give glory to him: for the hour of his judgment is come; and worship him that made heaven, and earth, and the sea, and the fountains of waters. (Revelation 14:6-7.)

If there had been any nation, kindred, tongue, or people upon the earth still in possession of "the everlasting gospel," the sending of an angel to restore it would have been entirely unnecessary. According to the Apostle John, the coming of this angel with "the everlasting gospel" was an event which "must be hereafter." This vision was given to John years after the crucifixion of the Lord, and at a time when "the everlasting gospel" was still upon the earth, which is but another evidence that it would be taken from the earth, else there would be no need for a restoration.

Restitution of All Things Foretold

The Apostle Peter must have understood the "marvellous work and a wonder" to be a "restitution of all things." In speaking to those who had crucified the Lord he said:

> Repent ye therefore, and be converted, that your sins may be blotted out, when the times of refreshing shall come from the presence of the Lord;
> And he shall send Jesus Christ, which before was preached unto you:
> Whom the heaven must receive until the times of restitution of all things, which God hath spoken by the mouth of all his holy prophets since the world began. (Acts 3:19-21.)

Since Peter's words were spoken following the crucifixion of Jesus Christ, they constitute a promise that the Lord will send Him to the earth again. Peter makes perfectly clear that the second coming of the Messiah cannot occur "until the times of restitution of all things, which God hath spoken by the mouth of all his holy prophets since the world began."

In his epistle to the Ephesians, the Apostle Paul must also have envisioned the "restitution of all things" as foretold by Peter:

> Having made known unto us the mystery of his will, according to his good pleasure which he hath purposed in himself:
> That *in the dispensation of the fulness of times* he might gather together in one all things in Christ, both which are in heaven, and which are on earth; even in him: (Ephesians 1:9-10.)

These statements of Peter and Paul are very comprehensive. They seem to include all that would be done to establish the Kingdom of God upon the earth to prepare the way for the second coming of the Messiah. What they beheld and foretold seems to be nothing less than " the marvellous work and a wonder," which

Isaiah saw that the Lord would establish upon the earth. Many of the prophets seemed to have been given a vision of this "marvellous work and a wonder" the Lord would accomplish in the latter days to prepare for the glorious second coming of His Son in power and great glory, as King of kings and Lord of lords (Revelation 19:16); when all men shall know Him in His true character; when "the government shall be upon his shoulder; and his name shall be called Wonderful, Counsellor, the Mighty God, the Everlasting Father, the Prince of Peace. (Isaiah 9:6.)

It was this glorious coming which the Prophet Daniel was privileged to see "in the night visions," when he saw one "like the Son of man" come "with the clouds of heaven . . . and there was given him dominion, and glory, and a kingdom, that all people, nations, and languages, should serve him: his dominion is an everlasting dominion, which shall not pass away, and his kingdom that which shall not be destroyed." (Daniel 7:13-14.)

This is the final day Jesus taught His disciples to pray for when He gave them what is known as the Lord's Prayer, as a sample of how they should pray:

"Thy kingdom come. Thy will be done in earth, as it is in heaven. (St. Matthew 6:10.)

End Declared from the Beginning

As we follow these prophecies, we can better understand what Isaiah meant when he said:

> Remember the former things of old: for I am God, and there is none else; I am God, and there is none like me, *Declaring the end from the beginning,* and from ancient times the things that are not yet done, saying, My counsel shall stand, and I will do all my pleasure. (Isaiah 46:9-10.)

Surely the Lord is able to declare "the end from the beginning." This is evidenced by the fact that the words of the prophets have been literally fulfilled. Had the Lord not had a pattern for His work, the prophets could not have made such definite statements of things which would come to pass in the distant future, "declaring the end from the beginning." The Lord's way of making known His plan to His children for their guidance is through His servants, the prophets. (Amos 3:7.)

Of the importance of prophecy, the Apostle Peter stated:

> We have also a *more sure word of prophecy;* whereunto ye do well that ye take heed, as unto a light that shineth in a dark place, until the day dawn, and the day star arise in your hearts:
>
> Knowing this first, that no prophecy of the scripture is of any private interpretation.
>
> For the prophecy came not in old time by the will of man: but holy men of God spake as they were moved by the Holy Ghost. (II Peter 1:19-21.)

Keeping in mind the Prophet Isaiah's statement that God can declare "the end from the beginning," let the sons of Judah remember the promises made unto them by the Messiah when He visited His people in America as recorded in the Stick of Joseph:

> And I will remember the covenant which I have made with my people; and I have covenanted with them that I would gather them together in mine own due time, that I would give unto them again the land of their fathers for their inheritance, which is the land of Jerusalem, which is the promised land unto them forever, saith the Father.
>
> *And it shall come to pass that the time cometh, when the fulness of my gospel shall be preached unto them:*
>
> And they shall believe in me, that I am Jesus Christ, the Son of God, and shall pray unto the Father in my name.
>
> Then shall their watchmen lift up their voice, and with the voice together shall they sing; for they shall see eye to eye.
>
> *Then will the Father gather them together again, and give unto them Jerusalem for the land of their inheritance.*

Then shall they break forth into joy — Sing together, ye waste places of Jerusalem; for the Father hath comforted his people, *he hath redeemed Jerusalem.*

The Father hath made bare his holy arm in the eyes of all the nations; *and all the ends of the earth shall see the salvation of the Father; and the Father and I are one.* (3 Nephi 20:29-35.)

In these scriptures, the Savior indicated that when the fulness of His gospel is preached to the Jews, and when they shall believe in Him, that He is Jesus Christ, the Son of God, and shall pray unto the Father in His name—then will the Father gather them together again, and give unto them Jerusalem for the land of their inheritance.

This promise was published with the coming forth of the Stick of Joseph in 1829, long before the Jews commenced to return to Jerusalem. The complete fulfillment of these promises could be greatly hastened if Judah would but accept Jesus Christ as the Son of God, if they would pray to the Father in His name. To achieve this great objective, the Lord has raised up a seer "like unto Moses" in these latter days, through whom He has brought forth the Stick of Joseph, that through the information contained therein, Judah will be influenced to accept Jesus Christ as the Son of God, their promised Messiah.

CHAPTER 9

"A CHOICE SEER . . . LIKE UNTO MOSES"

Promises Made to Joseph

In the beginning of Chapter Eight, we quoted from the Stick of Joseph the promise of the Lord that He would raise up, *in the latter days,* "a choice seer . . . like unto Moses."

The Lord has fulfilled His promise. The "choice seer" has come forth. The prophet "like unto Moses" has been raised up. "A marvellous work and a wonder" (Isaiah 29:13-14) has been set in full motion among the children of men "in the latter days."

Let us analyze the promise of the Lord concerning the divinely appointed mission of the "latter day" prophet whom the Lord said "shall be great like unto Moses:" (See, 2 Nephi 3:3-15.)

1. And unto him will I give commandment that he shall do a great work for the fruit of thy loins, his brethren, which shall be of great worth unto them, even to the bringing of them to the knowledge of the covenants which I have made with thy fathers. (Ibid, verse 7.)

2. And I will give unto him a commandment that he shall do none other work, save the work which I shall command him. *And I will make him great in mine eyes; for he shall do my work.* (Ibid, verse 8.)

Therefore, all Israel must look to him and heed his words which he shall receive of the Lord, for, said the Lord: "I will make him great in mine eyes; for he shall do my work." When one rejects a prophet sent of the Lord to do His work, he rejects the Lord Himself.

3. And he shall be great like unto Moses . . . and unto
him will I give power to bring forth my word . . .
and not to the bringing forth of my word only, saith
the Lord, *but to the convincing them of my word, which
shall have already gone forth among them.* (Ibid, verses
9, 11.)

Properly understood, this means that this "choice
seer . . . like unto Moses" would bring forth the Stick of
Joseph; that he would be able to explain to Israel the
teachings and prophecies of the Stick of Judah, the
Holy Bible, "*which shall have already gone forth among
them.*" And that, as Moses received the word of the
Lord direct from Him for the guidance of Israel in his
day, so would the Lord deliver His word to this new
prophet He promised to raise up for the guidance and
direction of latter day Israel, for, said the Lord: "unto
him will I give power to bring forth my word."

Therefore, by the power of the Lord, this new
prophet of this dispensation has given us some one
hundred and thirty revelations direct from the Lord,
which are recorded in the Doctrine and Covenants, a
book of some 250 pages. These revelations were given
to direct this prophet and his successors in the establishment of the Church and Kingdom of God upon the
earth in these latter days to prepare the way for the
second coming of the Messiah.

This "choice seer" has also given us the Pearl of
Great Price, which contains the word of the Lord to
Abraham, the friend of God; also the word of the Lord
to Moses as revealed to this latter-day prophet.

This new prophet has brought forth more of the
word of the Lord unto Israel than any other one prophet
of the past of whom we have record.

4. We should not overlook the prophecy that the
Stick of Joseph and the Stick of Judah, by the power of
God, through this promised prophet of "the latter days,"

"shall grow together, unto the confounding of false doctrines . . . and establishing peace among the fruit of thy loins," (Ibid, verse 12.)

Can one look at the spiritually divided condition of the House of Judah and the House of Joseph, without realizing how much they need a prophet sent of God, with power given him to speak in the name of the Lord, "unto the confounding of false doctrines," that all of our Father's children may come to a unity of the faith?

5. Of this new prophet, the Lord further stated to Joseph:

> And out of weakness he shall be made strong, in that day when my work shall commence among all my people, unto the restoring thee, O house of Israel, said the Lord. (Ibid, verse 13.)

Through this new prophet, the work of the Lord "shall commence among all my people." Hence all "my people" would have to look to him, and accept of the work the Lord would establish through him if they would be restored. All this new work would look "unto the restoring thee, O house of Israel, saith the Lord," or to the gathering of Israel, or the House of Joseph to their Zion of the latter days in the land of America, and the bringing in of the dispersed of Judah to the promised land of Palestine, and the rebuilding of the Holy City, Jerusalem.

> 6. And thus prophesied Joseph, saying: Behold, that seer will the Lord bless; and they that seek to destroy him shall be confounded; for this promise, which I have obtained of the Lord, of the fruit of my loins, shall be fulfilled. Behold, I am sure of the fulfilling of this promise; (Ibid, verse 14.)

The enemies of this "choice seer" did seek to destroy him as the wicked have done with many of the prophets of the past, thinking that if he were destroyed the work

he had commenced under the power and direction of
God would fail. Persecutions and imprisonment were
heaped upon him, until he was martyred at the hands of
a cruel mob, led by ministers of religion. But his enemies were confounded. The Lord had so directed this
new prophet in the establishment of His Church upon
the earth that there must be a Quorum of Twelve Apostles, who held, with this "choice seer", all the keys of the
Kingdom. Therefore, when the prophet was martyred,
June 27, 1844, the Quorum of Twelve Apostles carried
forward the great work God had established in the earth
until his successor was appointed.

7. Referring further to the promises of the Lord
concerning this new prophet the Lord promised to raise
up, Joseph said:

> *And his name shall be called after me; and it shall be
> after the name of his father.* And he shall be like unto me;
> for the thing, which the Lord shall bring forth by his hand,
> by the power of the Lord shall bring my people unto salva-
> tion. (Ibid, verse 15.)

According to this promise, the new prophet's name
was to be Joseph, and his father's name was to be Joseph
also.

This promise of the Lord has had a literal fulfillment *"in the latter days"*—the coming forth of Joseph
Smith, Jr., the "choice seer . . . like unto Moses" whose
father's name was Joseph Smith, Sr.

8. Note the final promise of the marvelous work
this new prophet would bring forth:

> . . . for the thing which the Lord shall bring forth by
> his hand, by the power of the Lord, shall bring my people
> unto salvation. (Ibid, verse 15.)

The promise has been fulfilled. The new prophet
has been raised up, and "by the power of the Lord

shall bring . . . [all Israel] unto salvation" if they will accept and participate in this "marvellous work and a wonder" established "in the latter days."

A Seer "Like Unto Moses" Has Come Forth

The Prophet Joseph Smith, Jr., by the power of the Lord, conversed with the Father and His Son Jesus Christ, in the spring of 1820. He established anew upon the earth, the Church of Jesus Christ, with all the gifts and powers that existed in the primitive Church established by the Messiah during His earthly ministry. To distinguish the Church of this last dispensation from the Church established by our Redeemer, the Prophet Joseph Smith was directed by the Lord to name the restored Church, "The Church of Jesus Christ of Latter-day Saints."

Since known unto God are all His works from the beginning, He also knew the spirit of Joseph Smith and sent him into the world at the time decreed by the Almighty to accomplish the work He had for him to do. Joseph Smith was the "choice seer . . . like unto Moses" whom the Lord promised Joseph He would raise up out of the fruit of his loins "in the latter days," and was the prophet who, *by the power of the Lord shall bring my people unto salvation.*

Prophets Known to God Before Birth

When it is understood that the spirits of all men lived in the presence of God the Eternal Father before the world was formed, it is easy to understand how the Lord could declare in such definite terms the work He would require at the hands of Joseph Smith.

We read that the Prophet Jeremiah was chosen for his ministry before he was born:

> Then the word of the Lord came unto me, saying,
> Before I formed thee in the belly I knew thee; and be-

fore thou camest forth out of the womb I sanctified thee, and ordained thee a prophet unto the nations. (Jeremiah 1:4-5.)

The Stick of Joseph affirms that when Jesus Christ, the Messiah, visited His people in the land of America, He told them that it was He who gave the law unto Moses, showing that before Jesus was born in the flesh His mission was fully assigned unto Him by the Father. He was therefore the Jehovah of the Old Testament:

> Behold, I am he that gave the law, and I am he who covenanted with my people Israel; therefore, the law in me is fulfilled, for I have come to fulfill the law; therefore it hath an end. (3 Nephi 15:5.)

We also learn from the Stick of Joseph that Jesus Christ spoke to Nephi, the son of Helaman, the day before He was born into the world, and announced that on the morrow He would come into the world to fulfill all that He had caused the holy prophets to speak concerning Him:

> Lift up your head and be of good cheer; for behold, the time is at hand, and on this night shall the sign be given, and on the morrow come I into the world, to show unto the world that I will fulfill all that which I have caused to be spoken by the mouth of my holy prophets. (3 Nephi 1:13.)

From the Book of Abraham we obtain a very clear understanding of the fact that the spirits of all men existed before they were born into this world, and that many had achieved greatness, even as had the Christ:

> Now the Lord had shown unto me, Abraham, the intelligences that were organized before the world was; and among all these there were many of the noble and great ones;
>
> And God saw these souls that they were good, and he stood in the midst of them, and he said: These I will make my rulers; for he stood among those that were spirits, and he saw that they were good; and he said unto me: Abraham,

thou art one of them; thou wast chosen before thou wast born. (Pearl of Great Price, Abraham 3:22-23.)

In the light of these few references, it is easy to understand how the Lord could inform Joseph, the son of Jacob (Israel), that the "choice seer . . . like unto Moses" would come through his lineage and bear his name, "Joseph", which would also be the name of his father. Not only did the Lord designate his greatness, and know what his name in mortality would be, but He knew that Joseph Smith would be born some 3600 years later, "in the latter days."

The Seer "Like Unto Moses" Tells His Own Story

Knowing the great work He had for His new prophet of this dispensation, the Lord put it into his heart, when but a boy, to be dissatisfied with the teachings of the various religious denominations of his day. Therefore, while but a young man in his fifteenth year, in answer to his earnest supplication for wisdom as to which of all the then existing churches he should join, the Father and His Son Jesus Christ appeared to Joseph Smith and gave him instructions to guide him in the accomplishment of the work to which the Lord had called him long before he was born. It seems proper that we should let this promised prophet from the fruit of the loins of Joseph, tell his own story of the glorious events connected with the restoration of all things *in the latter days.*

Owing to the many reports which have been put in circulation by evil-disposed and designing persons, in relation to the rise and progress of the Church of Jesus Christ of Latter-day Saints, all of which have been designed by the authors thereof to militate against its character as a Church and its progress in the world — I have been induced to write this history, to disabuse the public mind, and put all inquirers after truth in possession of the facts, as they have transpired, in relation both to myself and the Church, so far as I have such facts in my possession.

In this history I shall present the various events in relation to this Church, in truth and righteousness, as they have transpired, or as they at present exist, being now the eighth year since the organization of the said Church.

I was born in the year of our Lord one thousand eight hundred and five, on the twenty-third day of December, in the town of Sharon, Windsor county, State of Vermont. ... My father, Joseph Smith, Sen., left the State of Vermont, and moved to Palmyra, Ontario (now Wayne) county, in the State of New York, when I was in my tenth year, or thereabouts. In about four years after my father's arrival in Palmyra, he moved with his family into Manchester in the same county of Ontario —

His family consisting of eleven souls, namely, my father, Joseph Smith; my mother, Lucy Smith (whose name, previous to her marriage, was Mack, daughter of Solomon Mack); my brothers, Alvin (who died November 19th, 1824, in the 27th year of his age), Hyrum, myself, Samuel Harrison, William, Don Carlos; and my sisters, Sophronia, Catherine, and Lucy.

Some time in the second year after our removal to Manchester, there was in the place where we lived an unusual excitement on the subject of religion. It commenced with the Methodists, but soon became general among all the sects in that region of country. Indeed, the whole district of country seemed affected by it, and great multitudes united themselves to the different religious parties, which created no small stir and division among the people, some crying, "Lo, here!" and others, "Lo, there!" Some were contending for the Methodist faith, some for the Presbyterian, and some for the Baptist.

For notwithstanding the great love which the converts to these different faiths expressed at the time of their conversion, and the great zeal manifested by the respective clergy, who were active in getting up and promoting this extraordinary scene of religious feeling, in order to have everybody converted, as they were pleased to call it, let them join what sect they pleased; yet when the converts began to file off, some to one party and some to another, it was seen that the seemingly good feelings of both the priests and the converts were more pretended than real; for a scene of great confusion and bad feeling ensued — priest contending against priest, and convert against convert; so that all their good feelings one for another, if they ever had any, were entirely lost in a strife of words and a contest about opinions.

I was at this time in my fifteenth year. My father's family was proselyted to the Presbyterian faith, and four of them joined that church, namely, my mother, Lucy; my brothers Hyrum and Samuel Harrison; and my sister Sophronia.

During this time of great excitement my mind was called up to serious reflection and great uneasiness; but though my feelings were deep and often poignant, still I kept myself aloof from all these parties, though I attended their several meetings as often as occasion would permit. In process of time my mind became somewhat partial to the Methodist sect, and I felt some desire to be united with them; but so great were the confusion and strife among the different denominations, that it was impossible for a person young as I was, and so unacquainted with men and things, to come to any certain conclusion who was right and who was wrong.

My mind at times was greatly excited, the cry and tumult were so great and incessant. The Presbyterians were most decided against the Baptists and Methodists, and used all the powers of both reason and sophistry to prove their error, or, at least, to make the people think they were in error. On the other hand, the Baptists and Methodists in their turn were equally zealous in endeavoring to establish their own tenets and disprove all others.

In the midst of this war of words and tumult of opinions, I often said to myself: What is to be done? Who of all these parties are right; or, are they all wrong together? If any one of them be right, which is it, and how shall I know it?

While I was laboring under the extreme difficulties caused by the contests of these parties of religionists, I was one day reading the Epistle of James, first chapter and fifth verse, which reads: *If any of you lack wisdom, let him ask of God, that giveth to all men liberally, and upbraideth not; and it shall be given him.*

Never did any passage of scripture come with more power to the heart of man than this did at this time to mine. It seemed to enter with great force into every feeling of my heart. I reflected on it again and again, knowing that if any person needed wisdom from God, I did; for how to act I did not know, and unless I could get more wisdom than I then had, I would never know; for the teachers of religion of the different sects understood the same passages

of scripture so differently as to destroy all confidence in
settling the question by an appeal to the Bible.

At length I came to the conclusion that I must either
remain in darkness and confusion, or else I must do as
James directs, that is, ask of God. I at length came to the
determination to "ask of God," concluding that if he gave
wisdom to them that lacked wisdom, and would give liberally, and not upbraid, I might venture.

So, in accordance with this, my determination to ask
of God, I retired to the woods to make the attempt. It was
on the morning of a beautiful, clear day, early in the spring
of eighteen hundred and twenty. It was the first time in
my life that I had made such an attempt, for amidst all my
anxieties I had never as yet made the attempt to pray vocally.

After I had retired to the place where I had previously
designed to go, having looked around me, and finding myself
alone, I kneeled down and began to offer up the desire of
my heart to God. I had scarcely done so, when immediately
I was seized upon by some power which entirely overcame
me, and had such an astonishing influence over me as to
bind my tongue so that I could not speak. Thick darkness
gathered around me, and it seemed to me for a time as if
I were doomed to sudden destruction.

But, exerting all my powers to call upon God to deliver
me out of the power of this enemy which had seized me,
and at the very moment when I was ready to sink into
despair and abandon myself to destruction — not to an
imaginary ruin, but to the power of some actual being from
the unseen world, who had such marvelous power as I had
never before felt in any being — just at this moment of great
alarm, I saw a pillar of light exactly over my head, above
the brightness of the sun, which descended gradually until
it fell upon me.

It no sooner appeared than I found myself delivered
from the enemy which held me bound. When the light
rested upon me I saw two Personages, whose brightness
and glory defy all description, standing above me in the air.
One of them spake unto me, calling me by name and said,
pointing to the other — *This is My Beloved Son. Hear Him!*

My object in going to inquire of the Lord was to
know which of all the sects was right, that I might know
which to join. No sooner, therefore, did I get possession
of myself, so as to be able to speak, than I asked the Personages who stood above me in the light, which of all the
sects was right — and which I should join.

I was answered that I must join none of them, for they

were all wrong; and the Personage who addressed me said that all their creeds were an abomination in his sight; that those professors were all corrupt; that: "they draw near to me with their lips, but their hearts are far from me, they teach for doctrines the commandments of men, having a form of godliness, but they deny the power thereof."

He again forbade me to join with any of them; and many other things did he say unto me, which I cannot write at this time. When I came to myself again, I found myself lying on my back, looking up into heaven. When the light had departed, I had no strength; but soon recovering in some degree, I went home. And as I leaned up to the fireplace, mother inquired what the matter was. I replied, "Never mind, all is well — I am well enough off." I then said to my mother, "I have learned for myself that Presbyterianism is not true." It seems as though the adversary was aware, at a very early period of my life, that I was destined to prove a disturber and an annoyer of his kingdom; else why should the powers of darkness combine against me? Why the opposition and persecution that arose against me, almost in my infancy?

Some few days after I had this vision, I happened to be in company with one of the Methodist preachers, who was very active in the before mentioned religious excitement; and, conversing with him on the subject of religion, I took occasion to give him an account of the vision which I had had. I was greatly surprised at his behavior; he treated my communication not only lightly, but with great contempt, saying it was all of the devil, that there were no such things as visions or revelations in these days; that all such things had ceased with the apostles, and that there would never be any more of them.

I soon found, however, that my telling the story had excited a great deal of prejudice against me among professors of religion, and was the cause of great persecution, which continued to increase; and though I was an obscure boy, only between fourteen and fifteen years of age, and my circumstances in life such as to make a boy of no consequence in the world, yet men of high standing would take notice sufficient to excite the public mind against me, and create a bitter persecution; and this was common among all the sects — all united to persecute me.

It caused me serious reflection then, and often has since, how very strange it was that an obscure boy, of a little over fourteen years of age, and one, too, who was doomed to the necessity of obtaining a scanty maintenance

by his daily labor, should be thought a character of sufficient importance to attract the attention of the great ones
of the most popular sects of the day, and in a manner to
create in them a spirit of the most bitter persecution and
reviling. But strange or not, so it was, and it was often the
cause of great sorrow to myself.

However, it was nevertheless a fact that I had beheld
a vision. I have thought since, that I felt much like Paul,
when he made his defense before King Agrippa, and related the account of the vision he had when he saw a light,
and heard a voice; but still there were but few who believed
him; some said he was dishonest, others said he was mad;
and he was ridiculed and reviled. But all this did not destroy the reality of his vision. He had seen a vision, he
knew he had, and all the persecution under heaven could
not make it otherwise; and though they should persecute
him unto death, yet he knew, and would know to his latest
breath, that he had both seen a light and heard a voice
speaking unto him, and all the world could not make him
think or believe otherwise.

So it was with me. I had actually seen a light, and
in the midst of that light I saw two Personages, and they
did in reality speak to me; and though I was hated and
persecuted for saying that I had seen a vision, yet it was
true; and while they were persecuting me, reviling me, and
speaking all manner of evil against me falsely for so saying, I was led to say in my heart: Why persecute me for
telling the truth? I have actually seen a vision; and who
am I that I can withstand God, or why does the world
think to make me deny what I have actually seen? For I
had seen a vision; I knew it, and I knew God knew it, and
I could not deny it, neither dared I do it; at least I knew
that by so doing I would offend God, and come under
condemnation.

I had now got my mind satisfied so far as the sectarian
world was concerned — that it was not my duty to join with
any of them, but to continue as I was until further directed.
I had found the testimony of James to be true — that a man
who lacked wisdom might ask of God, and obtain, and not
be upbraided.

I continued to pursue my common vocations in life
until the twenty-first of September, one thousand eight
hundred and twenty-three, all the time suffering severe
persecution at the hands of all classes of men, both religious
and irreligious, because I continued to affirm that I had seen
a vision.

During the space of time which intervened between the time I had the vision and the year eighteen hundred and twenty-three—having been forbidden to join any of the religious sects of the day, and being of very tender years, and persecuted by those who ought to have been my friends and to have treated me kindly, and if they supposed me to be deluded to have endeavored in a proper and affectionate manner to have reclaimed me — I was left to all kinds of temptations; and, mingling with all kinds of society, I frequently fell into many foolish errors, and displayed the weakness of youth, and the foibles of human nature; which I am sorry to say, led me into divers temptations, offensive in the sight of God. In making this confession, no one need suppose me guilty of any great or malignant sins. A disposition to commit such was never in my nature. But I was guilty of levity, and sometimes associated with jovial company, etc., not consistent with that character which ought to be maintained by one who was called of God as I had been. But this will not seem very strange to any one who recollects my youth, and is acquainted with my native cheery temperament.

In consequence of these things, I often felt condemned for my weakness and imperfections; when, on the evening of the above-mentioned twenty-first of September, after I had retired to my bed for the night, I betook myself to prayer and supplication to Almighty God for forgiveness of all my sins and follies, and also for a manifestation to me, that I might know of my state and standing before him; for I had full confidence in obtaining a divine manifestation, as I previously had one.

While I was thus in the act of calling upon God, I discovered a light appearing in my room, which continued to increase until the room was lighter than at noonday, when immediately a personage appeared at my bedside, standing in the air, for his feet did not touch the floor.

He had on a loose robe of most exquisite whiteness. It was a whiteness beyond anything earthly I had ever seen; nor do I believe that any earthly thing could be made to appear so exceedingly white and brilliant. His hands were naked, and his arms also, a little above the wrists; so, also, were his feet naked, as were his legs, a little above the ankles. His head and neck were also bare. I could discover that he had no other clothing on but this robe, as it was open, so that I could see into his bosom.

Not only was his robe exceedingly white, but his whole person was glorious beyond description, and his countenance truly like lightning. The room was exceedingly light, but not so very bright as immediately around his person. When I first looked upon him, I was afraid; but the fear soon left me.

He called me by name, and said unto me that he was a messenger sent from the presence of God to me, and that his name was Moroni; that God had a work for me to do; and that my name should be had for good and evil among all nations, kindreds, and tongues, or that it should be both good and evil spoken of among all people.

He said there was a book deposited, written upon gold plates, giving an account of the former inhabitants of this [the American] continent, and the source from whence they sprang. He also said that the fulness of the everlasting Gospel was contained in it, as delivered by the Savior to the ancient inhabitants;

Also, that there were two stones in silver bows — and these stones, fastened to a breastplate, constituted what is called the Urim and Thummim — deposited with the plates; and the possession and use of these stones were what constituted "seers" in ancient or former times; and that God had prepared them for the purpose of translating the book.

After telling me these things, he commenced quoting prophecies of the Old Testament.

He first quoted part of the third chapter of Malachi; and he quoted also the fourth or last chapter of the same prophecy, though with a little variation from the way it reads in our Bibles. Instead of quoting the first verse as it reads in our books, he quoted it thus:

For behold, the day cometh that shall burn as an oven, and all the proud, yea, and all that do wickedly shall burn as stubble; for they that come shall burn them, saith the Lord of Hosts, that it shall leave them neither root nor branch.

And again, he quoted the fifth verse thus: *Behold, I will reveal unto you the Priesthood, by the hand of Elijah the prophet, before the coming of the great and dreadful day of the Lord.*

He also quoted the next verse differently: *And he shall plant in the hearts of the children the promises made to the fathers, and the hearts of the children shall turn to their fathers. If it were not so, the whole earth would be utterly wasted at his coming.*

In addition to these, he quoted the eleventh chapter of Isaiah, saying that it was about to be fulfilled. He quoted also the third chapter of Acts, twenty-second and twenty-third verses, precisely as they stand in our New Testament. He said that that prophet was Christ; but the day had not yet come when "they who would not hear his voice should be cut off from among the people," but soon would come.

He also quoted the second chapter of Joel, from the twenty-eighth verse to the last. He also said that this was not yet fulfilled, but was soon to be. And he further stated that the fulness of the Gentiles was soon to come in. He quoted many other passages of scripture, and offered many explanations which cannot be mentioned here.

Again, he told me, that when I got those plates of which he had spoken—for the time that they should be obtained was not yet fulfilled—I should not show them to any person; neither the breastplate with the Urim and Thummim; only to those to whom I should be commanded to show them; if I did I should be destroyed. While he was conversing with me about the plates, the vision was opened to my mind that I could see the place where the plates were deposited, and that so clearly and distinctly that I knew the place again when I visited it.

After this communication, I saw the light in the room begin to gather immediately around the person of him who had been speaking to me, and it continued to do so until the room was again left dark, except just around him; when, instantly I saw, as it were, a conduit open right up into heaven, and he ascended till he entirely disappeared, and the room was left as it had been before this heavenly light had made its appearance.

I lay musing on the singularity of the scene, and marveling greatly at what had been told to me by this extraordinary messenger; when, in the midst of my meditation, I suddenly discovered that my room was again beginning to get lighted, and in an instant, as it were, the same heavenly messenger was again by my bedside.

He commenced, and again related the very same things which he had done at his first visit, without the least variation; which having done, he informed me of great judgments which were coming upon the earth, with great desolations by famine, sword, and pestilence; and that these grievous judgments would come on the earth in this generation. Having related these things, he again ascended as he had done before.

By this time, so deep were the impressions made on my mind, that sleep had fled from my eyes, and I lay overwhelmed in astonishment at what I had both seen and heard. But what was my surprise when again I beheld the same messenger at my bedside, and heard him rehearse or repeat over again to me the same things as before; and added a caution to me, telling me that Satan would try to tempt me (in consequence of the indigent circumstances of my father's family) to get the plates for the purpose of getting rich. This he forbade me, saying that I must have no other object in view in getting the plates but to glorify God, and must not be influenced by any other motive than that of building his kingdom; otherwise I could not get them.

After this third visit, he again ascended into heaven as before, and I was again left to ponder on the strangeness of what I had just experienced; when almost immediately after the heavenly messenger had ascended from me for the third time, the cock crowed, and I found that day was approaching, so that our interviews must have occupied the whole of that night.

I shortly after arose from my bed, and, as usual, went to the necessary labors of the day; but, in attempting to work as at other times, I found my strength so exhausted as to render me entirely unable. My father, who was laboring along with me, discovered something to be wrong with me, and told me to go home. I started with the intention of going to the house; but, in attempting to cross the fence out of the field where we were, my strength entirely failed me, and I fell helpless on the ground, and for a time was quite unconscious of anything.

The first thing that I can recollect was a voice speaking unto me, calling me by name. I looked up, and beheld the same messenger standing over my head, surrounded by light as before. He then again related unto me all that he had related to me the previous night, and commanded me to go to my father and tell him of the vision and commandments which I had received.

I obeyed; I returned to my father in the field, and rehearsed the whole matter to him. He replied to me that it was of God, and told me to go and do as commanded by the messenger. I left the field, and went to the place where the messenger had told me the plates were deposited; and owing to the distinctness of the vision which I had had concerning it, I knew the place the instant that I arrived there.

Convenient to the village of Manchester, Ontario County, New York, stands a hill of considerable size, and the most elevated of any in the neighborhood. On the west side of this hill, not far from the top, under a stone of considerable size, lay the plates, deposited in a stone box.

This stone was thick and rounding in the middle on the upper side, and thinner towards the edges, so that the middle part of it was visible above the ground, but the edge all around was covered with earth.

Having removed the earth, I obtained a lever, which I got fixed under the edge of the stone, and with a little exertion raised it up. I looked in, and there indeed did I behold the plates, the Urim and Thummim, and the breastplate, as stated by the messenger. The box in which they lay was formed by laying stones together in some kind of cement. In the bottom of the box were laid two stones crossways of the box, and on these stones lay the plates and other things with them.

I made an attempt to take them out, but was forbidden by the messenger, and was again informed that the time for bringing them forth had not yet arrived, neither would it, until four years from that time; but he told me that I should come to that place precisely in one year from that time, and that he would there meet with me, and that I should continue to do so until the time should come for obtaining the plates.

Accordingly, as I had been commanded, I went at the end of each year, and at each time I found the same messenger there, and received instruction and intelligence from him at each of our interviews, respecting what the Lord was going to do, *and how and in what manner his kingdom was to be conducted in the last days. . . .*

At length the time arrived for obtaining the plates, the Urim and Thummim, and the breastplate. On the twenty-second day of September, one thousand eight hundred and twenty-seven, having gone as usual at the end of another year to the place where they were deposited, the same heavenly messenger delivered them up to me with this charge: that I should be responsible for them; that if I should let them go carelessly, or through any neglect of mine; I should be cut off; but that if I would use all my endeavors to preserve them, until he, the messenger, should call for them, they should be protected.

I soon found out the reason why I had received such strict charges to keep them safe, and why it was that the messenger had said that when I had done what was required at my hand, he would call for them. For no sooner was it known that I had them, than the most strenuous exertions were used to get them from me. Every stratagem that could be invented was resorted to for that purpose. The persecution became more bitter and severe than before, and multitudes were on the alert continually to get them from me if possible. But by the wisdom of God, they remained safe in my hands, until I had accomplished by them what was required at my hand. When, according to arrangements, the messenger called for them, I delivered them up to him; and he has them in his charge until this day, being the second day of May, one thousand eight hundred and thirty-eight. (Pearl of Great Price, pages 46-54.)

This account of the calling of the Prophet Joseph Smith constitutes one of the greatest and most inspiring events in the entire history of the world.

From this account it will be observed that Satan did all within his power to stop the work the Lord had set His hand to accomplish. Joseph Smith was persecuted in a most cruel and unwarranted manner. Nevertheless, the Lord sustained him and raised up friends to assist him in the great work of translating the word of the Lord engraved on the gold plates.

Stick of Joseph Translated

The Lord sent one, Martin Harris, a resident of Palmyra, New York, to the prophet, and Martin gave him $50.00 to assist in the work of translation. On the 5th day of April, 1829, Oliver Cowdery called at the home of the prophet who had never seen him before. Cowdery had been teaching school in the vicinity and had heard the report that the prophet had the gold plates, and he came to make inquiry. Two days after his arrival, April 7, 1829, Joseph Smith commenced to translate and Oliver Cowdery began to write for him. Of this experience, Oliver Cowdery gave the following account:

These were days never to be forgotten—to sit under the sound of a voice dictated by the inspiration of heaven, awakened the utmost gratitude of this bosom! Day after day I continued, uninterrupted to write from his mouth, as he translated with the Urim and Thummim, or, as the

Nephites would have said, 'Interpreters,' the history or record called "The Book of Mormon." (Times and Seasons, Vol. 2, p. 201.)

The translation of the characters on the gold plates was called the *Book of Mormon,* and is the *Stick of Joseph.*

Mormon was a prophet who made an abridgment of the many records kept by the Nephite prophets, which, together with the plates from which the abridgment was made, with other valuable articles, including the Urim and Thummim, he turned over to his son Moroni who buried them in a stone box in the hill Cumorah, in the State of New York, U. S. A., until commanded by the Lord to deliver them to Joseph Smith for translation.

Contents of the Stick of Joseph

On the fly-leaf of the Book of Mormon (Stick of Joseph) we read the following, setting forth what the record consists of, and the purpose for which it had been preserved:

The Book of Mormon, an account written by the hand of Mormon upon plates taken from the plates of Nephi. Wherefore, it is an abridgment of the record of the people of Nephi, and also of the Lamanites—Written to the Lamanites, who are a remnant of the house of Israel; and also to Jew and Gentile—Written by way of commandment, and also by the spirit of prophecy and of revelation—Written and sealed up, and hid up unto the Lord, that they might not be destroyed—To come forth by the gift and power of God unto the interpretation thereof—Sealed by the hand of Moroni, and hid up unto the Lord, to come forth in due time by way of the Gentile—The interpretation thereof by the gift of God.

An abridgment taken from the Book of Ether also, which is a record of the people of Jared, who were scattered at the time the Lord confounded the language of the people, when they were building a tower to get to heaven—Which is to show unto the remnant of the House of Israel what great things the Lord hath done for their fathers; *and that they may know the covenants of the Lord, that they are not cast off forever—and also to the convincing of the Jew and Gen-*

tile that JESUS is the CHRIST, the ETERNAL GOD, mani-
festing himself unto all nations—And now, if there are
faults they are the mistakes of men; wherefore, condemn
not the things of God, that ye may be found spotless at the
judgment-seat of Christ.

Testimony of the Three Witnesses

Also, in the forepart of the Book of Mormon are
recorded the testimonies of three witnesses to whom an
angel of the Lord showed the plates, and eight witnesses
to whom the Prophet Joseph Smith was authorized to
show the plates. Following is the testimony of the
three witnesses:

Be It Known unto all nations, kindreds, tongues, and
people, unto whom this work shall come: That we, through
the grace of God the Father, and our Lord Jesus Christ,
have seen the plates which contain this record, which is a
record of the people of Nephi, and also of the Lamanites,
their brethren, and also of the people of Jared, who came
from the tower of which hath been spoken. And we also
know that they have been translated by the gift and power
of God, for his voice hath declared it unto us; wherefore
we know of a surety that the work is true. And we also
testify that we have seen the engravings which are upon
the plates; and they have been shown unto us by the power
of God, and not of man. And we declare with words of
soberness, that an angel of God came down from heaven, and
he brought and laid before our eyes, that we beheld and
saw the plates, and the engravings thereon; and we know
that it is by the grace of God the Father, and our Lord
Jesus Christ, that we beheld and bear record that these
things are true. And it is marvelous in our eyes. Nevertheless, the voice of the Lord commanded us that we should
bear record of it; wherefore, to be obedient unto the commandments of God, we bear testimony of these things.
And we know that if we are faithful in Christ, we shall rid
our garments of the blood of all men, and be found spotless before the judgment-seat of Christ, and shall dwell
with him eternally in the heavens. And the honor be to
the Father, and to the Son, and to the Holy Ghost, which
is one God. Amen.

Oliver Cowdery
David Whitmer
Martin Harris

Testimony of the Eight Witnesses

Following is the testimony of the eight witnesses:

Be It Known unto all nations, kindreds, tongues, and people, unto whom this work shall come: That Joseph Smith, Jun., the translator of this work, has shown unto us the plates of which hath been spoken, which have the appearance of gold; and as many of the leaves as the said Smith has translated we did handle with our hands; and we also saw the engravings thereon, all of which has the appearance of ancient work, and of curious workmanship. And this we bear record with words of soberness, that the said Smith has shown unto us, for we have seen and hefted, and know of a surety that the said Smith has got the plates of which we have spoken. And we give our names unto the world, to witness unto the world that which we have seen. And we lie not, God bearing witness of it.

Christian Whitmer
Jacob Whitmer
Peter Whitmer, Jun.
John Whitmer
Hiram Page
Joseph Smith, Sen.
Hyrum Smith
Samuel H. Smith

Even though, in future years, some of these witnesses did not remain true to their friendship toward the Prophet Joseph Smith, nevertheless, not one of them ever repudiated the testimony he had given that he had seen the plates.

Aaronic Priesthood Restored by John the Baptist

While Oliver Cowdery was assisting Joseph Smith in translating from the gold plates, they went into the woods to inquire of the Lord concerning baptism for the remission of sins, which they found mentioned in the translation of the plates. Following is the prophet

Joseph Smith's account of this event and the wonderful results thereof:

> We still continued the work of translation, when, in the ensuing month (May, 1829), we on a certain day went into the woods to pray and inquire of the Lord respecting baptism for the remission of sins, that we found mentioned in the translation of the plates. While we were thus employed, praying and calling upon the Lord, a messenger from heaven descended in a cloud of light, and having laid his hands upon us, he ordained us, saying:
>
> *Upon you my fellow servants, in the name of Messiah I confer the Priesthood of Aaron, which holds the keys of the ministering of angels, and of the gospel of repentance, and of baptism by immersion for the remission of sins; and this shall never be taken again from the earth, until the sons of Levi do offer again an offering unto the Lord in righteousness.*
>
> He said this Aaronic Priesthood had not the power of laying on hands for the gift of the Holy Ghost, but that this should be conferred on us hereafter; and he commanded us to go and be baptized, and gave us directions that I should baptize Oliver Cowdery, and that afterwards he should baptize me.
>
> Accordingly we went and were baptized. I baptized him first, and afterwards he baptized me — after which I laid my hands upon his head and ordained him to the Aaronic Priesthood, and afterwards he laid his hands on me and ordained me to the same Priesthood — for so we were commanded.
>
> The messenger who visited us on this occasion and conferred this Priesthood upon us, said that his name was John, the same that is called John the Baptist in the New Testament, and that he acted under the direction of Peter, James and John, who held the keys of the Priesthood of Melchizedek, which Priesthood, he said, would in due time be conferred on us, and that I should be called the first Elder of the Church, and he (Oliver Cowdery) the second. It was on the fifteenth day of May, 1829, that we were ordained under the hand of this messenger, and baptized. (Pearl of Great Price, page 56, verses 68-72.)

Power of the Holy Ghost Made Manifest

Immediately following their baptism and ordination, the Holy Ghost fell upon Joseph Smith and Oliver Cowdery and they prophesied concerning the rise of the Church which had not yet been organized. Then Joseph Smith made this further statement:

> Our minds being now enlightened, we began to have the scriptures laid open to our understandings, and the true meaning and intention of their more mysterious passages revealed unto us in a manner which we never could attain to previously, nor ever before had thought of. . . . (Pearl of Great Price, page 57, verse 74.)

In this manner the Lord proceeded to train and qualify the new prophet of this dispensation for the work assigned to the "choice seer . . . like unto Moses." The experience Joseph Smith and Oliver Cowdery had when they received the Aaronic Priesthood from John the Baptist, and, under his direction, baptized each other, should put an end to all disputations, for all time to come, as to the proper form and purpose of baptism, and the authority necessary to perform this sacred ordinance.

Melchizedek Priesthood Restored by Peter, James and John

Not long after this glorious event transpired, Peter, James and John, Apostles of the Lord Jesus Christ, conferred upon Joseph Smith and Oliver Cowdery the Melchizedek Priesthood, as promised by John the Baptist, which included the Holy Apostleship. The Melchizedek Priesthood gave them the necessary authority to organize the Church and Kingdom of God upon the earth in this dispensation. Accordingly, The Church of Jesus Christ of Latter-day Saints was organized with six members at Fayette, Seneca County, New York, U.S.A., April 6, 1830.

In a revelation on Priesthood given through the Prophet Joseph Smith on March 28, 1835, the Lord stated:

> There are, in the Church, two priesthoods, namely, the Melchizedek and Aaronic, including the Levitical Priesthood.
>
> Why the first is called the Melchizedek Priesthood is because Melchizedek was such a great high priest.
>
> Before his day it was called the Holy Priesthood, after the Order of the Son of God.
>
> But out of respect or reverence to the name of the Supreme Being, to avoid the too frequent repetition of his name, they, the church, in ancient days, called that priesthood after Melchizedek, or the Melchizedek Priesthood.
>
> All other authorities or offices in the church are appendages to this priesthood.
>
> But there are two divisions or grand heads — one is the Melchizedek Priesthood, and the other is the Aaronic or Levitical Priesthood. (Doctrine and Covenants 107:1-6.)

Modern Revelation Given the Seer "Like Unto Moses"

Now that these two Priesthoods had been restored to the earth, and men had been given the power and authority to officiate therein, the Lord proceeded to reveal unto the Church through His prophet, the necessary steps to be taken that the establishment of His Church may achieve all its objectives as foretold by the prophets of Judah and Joseph. To accomplish this, it was necessary for the Lord to give to this "choice seer" some 130 revelations which have all been recorded in the book, Doctrine and Covenants.

Many Records of God's Word to be Kept

We have already shown that when the day should come that the Lord would proceed to do "a marvellous work and a wonder" among the children of men, as declared by Isaiah, that it would partly consist of the bringing together, in one, the Stick of Judah and the Stick of Joseph, and other records that had been kept:

> Wherefore, because that ye have a Bible ye need not suppose that it contains all my words; neither need ye suppose that I have not caused more to be written.
>
> For I command all men, both in the east and in the west, and in the north, and in the south, and in the islands of the sea, that they shall write the words which I speak unto them; for out of the books which shall be written I will judge the world, every man according to their works, according to that which is written.
>
> *For behold, I shall speak unto the Jews and they shall write it; and I shall also speak unto the Nephites and they shall write it;* and I shall also speak unto the other tribes of the house of Israel, which I have led away, and they shall write it; and I shall also speak unto all nations of the earth and they shall write it.
>
> *And it shall come to pass that the Jews shall have the words of the Nephites, and the Nephites shall have the words of the Jews;* and the Nephites and the Jews shall have the words of the lost tribes of Israel; and the lost tribes of Israel shall have the words of the Nephites and the Jews.
>
> And it shall come to pass that *my people,* which are of the *house of Israel,* shall be gathered home unto the land of their possessions; *and my word also shall be gathered in one.* And I will show unto them that fight against my word and against my people, who are of the house of Israel, that I am God, and that I covenanted with Abraham that I would remember his seed forever. (2 Nephi 29:10-14.)

While we do not now have the records of the lost tribes of Israel, we look forward to their coming in the own due time of the Lord, for so hath He promised.

Scriptures Available Today

We do, however, have the Stick of Judah, the Holy Bible; the Stick of Joseph, the Book of Mormon; the Doctrine and Covenants, or the revelations of the Lord through the Prophet Joseph Smith. We also have another volume of scripture known as the Pearl of Great Price, which, among other writings, contains the translation of certain papyrus taken from catacombs near the place where formerly stood the ancient city of Thebes, Egypt, obtained by the French Explorer, Antonio Sebolo, in 1831. In 1835 they fell into the hands of the Prophet Joseph Smith who translated some of the ancient hieroglyphic characters, which proved to be the writings of Abraham.

The Pearl of Great Price also contains the Visions of Moses as revealed to Joseph Smith, the Prophet, in June, 1830.

Since the Lord promised that "my word also shall be gathered in one," we will feel free in our further discussions to quote from each of these four records. Since the Book of Mormon (Stick of Joseph) is a record of over 500 pages, and the Doctrine and Covenants over 250 pages, and the Pearl of Great Price over 50 pages, it will be impossible to do more than refer briefly to the information and prophecies contained therein. We shall not attempt to consider details with respect to the organization of His Church with its officers and Priesthood quorums in this writing. We will confine our discussion to a consideration of the visits of heavenly messengers to the Prophet Joseph Smith. We will also consider those matters which must be understood in order that the Kingdom of Judah and the Kingdom of Israel may ultimately be brought together as the prophets have foretold, that each may contribute its part to the fulfillment of the promises of the Lord to Abraham, Isaac and Jacob.

Jesus Christ, Jehovah, Appears in this Dispensation

A week following the dedication of the Kirtland Temple in the State of Ohio, U.S.A., April 3, 1836, the Prophet Joseph Smith gave the following account of the appearance of the Lord, Jesus Christ, to Oliver Cowdery and himself:

> The veil was taken from our minds, and the eyes of our understanding were opened.
> We saw the Lord standing upon the breastwork of the pulpit, before us; and under his feet was a paved work of pure gold, in color like amber.
> His eyes were as a flame of fire; the hair of his head was white like pure snow; his countenance shone above the brightness of the sun; and his voice was as the sound of the rushing of great waters, even the voice of Jehovah, saying:
> I am the first and the last; I am he who liveth, I am he who was slain; I am your advocate with the Father. (Doctrine and Covenants, 110:1-4.)

Moses Returns with the Keys for Gathering Scattered Israel

The same day, the Prophet Moses appeared to Joseph Smith and Oliver Cowdery, and conferred upon them the keys of the gathering of Israel from the four parts of the earth. Of this visit, Joseph Smith gives this account:

> After this vision closed, the heavens were again opened unto us; and Moses appeared before us, and committed unto us the keys of the gathering of Israel from the four parts of the earth, and the leading of the ten tribes from the land of the north. (Doctrine and Covenants, 110:11.)

This commitment seems to cover all necessary keys and authority to gather all branches of the House of Israel to the lands of their inheritance, withersoever they may have been scattered, even the ten tribes from the land of the north.

Coming of Elias

The same day, April 3, 1836, Elias appeared to Joseph Smith and Oliver Cowdery in the temple, and

committed the keys as recounted by Joseph Smith in
these words:

> After this, Elias appeared, and committed the dispen-
> sation of the gospel of Abraham, saying that in us and our
> seed all generations after us should be blessed. (Doctrine
> and Covenants 110:12.)

This seems to renew to the seed of Abraham and
Isaac, through Jacob, all the promises of the Lord unto
them, as they apply to this dispensation, with their ac-
companying responsibility, that through them all generations would be blessed.

Elijah Returns with the Keys of Salvation for the Dead

When Joseph Smith was visited by Moroni, to
which we have already referred, he quoted from the
fourth chapter of Malachi in the Stick of Judah regarding the promised coming of Elijah, although his quotation was slightly different than it appears in the Holy
Bible (King James Version) saying that this promise
was about to be fulfilled:

> And again, he quoted the fifth verse thus: *Behold, I
> will reveal unto you the Priesthood, by the hand of Elijah
> the prophet, before the coming of the great and dreadful
> day of the Lord.*
>
> He also quoted the next verse differently: *And he shall
> plant in the hearts of the children the promises made to the
> fathers, and the hearts of the children shall turn to their
> fathers, if it were not so, the whole earth would be utterly
> wasted at his coming.* (Pearl of Great Price, page 51, verses
> 38-39. See also Malachi 4:5-6.)

Obviously one cannot believe the promises contained in the Holy Bible, the Stick of Judah, without
knowing that Elijah must come "before the coming of
the great and dreadful day of the Lord." This promise
was reaffirmed by Moroni when he visited Joseph Smith
three times during the night of September 21, 1823.

On April 3, 1836, following the dedication of the Kirtland Temple, Elijah the prophet appeared to Joseph Smith and Oliver Cowdery in the temple at Kirtland, Ohio. His visit followed that of the Savior, Moses and Elias. Of Elijah's coming, the Prophet Joseph Smith gives us this account:

> After this vision had closed, another great and glorious vision burst upon us; for Elijah the prophet, who was taken to heaven without tasting death, stood before us, and said:
> Behold, the time has fully come, which was spoken of by the mouth of Malachi — testifying that he [Elijah] should be sent, before the great and dreadful day of the Lord come —
> To turn the hearts of the fathers to the children, and the children to the fathers, lest the whole earth be smitten with a curse —
> Therefore, the keys of this dispensation are committed into your hands; and by this ye may know that the great and dreadful day of the Lord is near, even at the doors. (Doctrine and Covenants 110:12-16.)

The importance of Elijah's coming was emphasized by Malachi, for he stated that if Elijah failed to come and "turn the hearts of the fathers to the children, and the children to the fathers" the whole earth would be smitten "with a curse."

As far as we know, no other church than the Church of Jesus Christ of Latter-day Saints claims the fulfillment of this prophecy, nor do others seem to understand the nature of Elijah's mission. Neither would we understand had Elijah not come and conferred the keys of his mission and ministry upon Joseph Smith and Oliver Cowdery.

When the keys of this dispensation for the turning of the hearts of the fathers to the children, and the hearts of the children to their fathers, had been committed, by Elijah, into the hands of Joseph Smith and Oliver

Cowdery, they proceeded to explain the new and strange doctrine of baptism for the dead to their associates and the membership of the Church. They made it plain that those living upon the earth can be baptized for their loved ones who have passed away without enjoying this privilege. The knowledge of this great truth has caused the "hearts of the children" to turn "to their fathers," and the children to seek out their genealogy so they can be baptized for their kindred dead. It was for this purpose that the Lord sent Elijah back to this earth as promised by Malachi, and as announced by Moroni to Joseph Smith. Much more could be said on this subject, but this seems sufficient to indicate the nature of Elijah's mission.

Joseph Smith, the "Choice Seer . . . Like Unto Moses"

Surely Joseph Smith can be compared to Moses, for as the Lord appeared unto Moses and "spake unto him face to face, as a man speaketh unto his friend," (Exodus 33:11) so the Lord, with His Son Jesus Christ, appeared unto Joseph Smith when he prayed in the grove near his father's house in Palmyra, New York, in the spring of 1820.

The Lord promised Joseph, the son of Jacob, that, when He raised up "a choice seer . . . like unto Moses" in "the latter days," He would give him *power to bring forth my word* unto the seed of thy loins, for the thing which the Lord shall bring forth by his hand, by the power of the Lord shall bring my people unto salvation." (2 Nephi 3:15.) Thus the Lord gave Joseph Smith power to bring forth His word, the Stick of Joseph, containing the prophecies and teachings of the Nephite prophets. The Lord also gave him many revelations for his guidance in establishing the Kingdom of God in the earth for the last time to prepare the way for the second coming of the Messiah.

Chapter 10

TWO GATHERING PLACES FOR ISRAEL
IN THE LATTER DAYS

"And He Shall Set Up an Ensign for the Nations"

When the Angel Moroni appeared to Joseph Smith three times during the night of September 21, 1823, he quoted from the eleventh chapter of Isaiah saying that this prophecy was about to be fulfilled:

> And in that day there shall be a root of Jesse, which shall stand for an ensign of the people; *to it shall the Gentiles seek*: and his rest shall be glorious.
>
> And it shall come to pass in that day, that the Lord shall set his hand again *the second time* to recover the remnant of his people, which shall be left, from Assyria, and from Egypt, and from Pathros, and from Cush, and from Elam, and from Shinar, and from Hamath, and from the islands of the sea.
>
> *And he shall set up an ensign for the nations*, and *shall assemble the outcasts of Israel*, and *gather together the dispersed of Judah* from the four corners of the earth.
>
> *The envy also of Ephraim shall depart*, and *the adversaries of Judah shall be cut off: Ephraim shall not envy Judah*, and *Judah shall not vex Ephraim.* (Isaiah 11:10-13.)

From this prophecy we learn:

First: That the Lord would establish an ensign among *the Gentiles*.

Second: That the Lord would set his hand again *the second time* to recover the remnant of His people.

Third: It will be noted that when the Lord would set His hand *"the second time"* to gather Israel, it would be twofold in nature: (1) That He would *"assemble the outcasts of Israel,* and *gather together the dispersed of Judah.*" (2) That this great movement would have its inception among the Gentiles, the Kingdom of Israel or Ephraim.

Fourth: That "The envy also of Ephraim shall depart, and the adversaries of Judah shall be cut off: Ephraim shall not envy Judah, and Judah shall not vex Ephraim."

Since the Angel Moroni made this declaration to Joseph Smith, this work has been going forth in the earth. The Lord established His Church among the seed of Joseph scattered among the Gentile nations. In a revelation from the Lord to the Prophet Joseph Smith, March 8, 1833, on his responsibility as President of the Church, the Lord said:

> That through your administration they may receive the word, and through their administration the word may go forth unto the ends of the earth, *unto the Gentiles first,* and then, behold, and lo, *they shall turn unto the Jews.*
> And then cometh the day when the arm of the Lord shall be revealed in power in convincing the nations, *the heathen nations, the house of Joseph,* of the gospel of their salvation. (Doctrine and Covenants 90:9-10.)

This revelation was given three years after The Church of Jesus Christ of Latter-day Saints was organized. In it, the Lord clearly indicated that His word, or the Gospel, as it had been restored, would go forth unto the Gentiles first, and then unto the Jews. He further reaffirmed what the prophets had foretold that the seed of Joseph would be found among the Gentile or heathen nations.

Gentiles to Take the Gospel to Judah

In a revelation to the Prophet Joseph Smith, March 7, 1831, less than a year after the organization of His

Church, the Lord indicated the time that the Gospel would be taken by the Gentiles to the Jews:

> As ye have asked of me concerning the signs of my coming, in the day when I shall come in my glory in the clouds of heaven, to fulfill the promises that I have made unto your fathers. . . .
>
> Ye say that ye know that the end of the world cometh; ye say also that ye know that the heavens and the earth shall pass away;
>
> And in this ye say truly, for so it is; *but these things which I have told you shall not pass away until it shall be fulfilled.*
>
> And this I have told you concerning Jerusalem; and when that day shall come, shall a remnant be scattered among all nations;
>
> But they shall be gathered again; *but they shall remain until the times of the Gentiles be fulfilled.* . . .
>
> And when the times of the Gentiles is come in, *a light shall break forth among them that sit in darkness, and it shall be the fulness of my gospel;*
>
> But they receive it not; for they perceive not the light, and they turn their hearts from me because of the precepts of men.
>
> *And in that generation shall the times of the Gentiles be fulfilled.* (Doctrine and Covenants 45:16, 22-25, 28-30.)

Thus, "the times of the Gentiles" would be recognized by the fact that "a light shall break forth among them that sit in darkness, and it shall be the fulness of my gospel. . . . And in that generation shall the times of the Gentiles be fulfilled."

It would seem, therefore, that the times of the Gentiles are nearing fulfillment. The fulness of His everlasting Gospel has been established among the Gentile nations of the earth. "And then, behold, and lo, they shall turn unto the Jews." (Doctrine and Covenants 90:9.) Therefore, all that the Lord revealed to the House of Joseph in this last dispensation through the Prophet Joseph Smith, that "choice seer . . . like unto Moses," is now being offered to the Jews, according to the promise of the Lord.

Israel and Judah are being Gathered

The Father has commenced His work to accomplish the gathering of His covenant people; His Church has been established among the Gentiles since the sixth day of April, 1830. Since that time, He has been gathering to His Zion the seed of Joseph scattered among the Gentile nations. His spirit has been working with the rulers of nations which has made it possible for the Jews to commence to gather back to Palestine, the land of their inheritance, as the prophets have declared they would.

As the gathering to these two centers continues, the seed of Joseph in the Rocky Mountains of America, and the descendants of Judah to the land of Palestine, one can well understand Isaiah's words concerning this great event:

O Zion, that bringest good tidings, get thee up into the high mountain; O Jerusalem, that bringest good tidings, lift up thy voice with strength; lift it up, be not afraid; say unto the cities of Judah, Behold your God! (Isaiah 40:9.)

The prophet Jeremiah seemed to have had quite a clear vision of the time when the Lord would seek to bring together the House of Joseph, and the House of Judah, since each was to be gathered to his own land:

And the Lord said unto me, The *backsliding Israel* hath justified herself more than *treacherous Judah.*

Go and proclaim these words toward the north, and say, Return thou backsliding Israel, saith the Lord; and I will not cause mine anger to fall upon you: for I am merciful, saith the Lord, and I will not keep anger for ever.

Only acknowledge thine iniquity, that thou hast transgressed against the Lord thy God, and hast scattered thy ways to the strangers under every green tree, and ye have not obeyed my voice, saith the Lord.

Turn, O backsliding children, saith the Lord; for I am married unto you: and I will take you one of a city, and two of a family, and I will bring you to Zion:

And I will give you pastors according to mine heart, which shall feed you with knowledge and understanding.
. . .
In those days the house of Judah shall walk with the house of Israel, and they shall come together out of the land of the north to the land that I have given for an inheritance unto your fathers. (Jeremiah 3:11-15, 18.)

It is evident that, since the Lord had made a covenant with Israel, "for I am married unto you, and I will take you one of a city, and two of a family, and I will bring you to Zion," He intended to fulfill that covenant at the time when He would establish His Church among the children of Israel, the House of Joseph. He further declared: "And I will give you pastors according to mine heart, which shall feed you with knowledge and understanding." The Lord added: "In those days the House of Judah shall walk with the House of Israel." He knew that in that day Israel would take to Judah a knowledge of the restoration of the Gospel, including the bringing forth of the Stick of Joseph, which He would accomplish through the Prophet Joseph Smith.

Since therefore, the Lord made the declaration that "In those days the house of Judah shall walk with the house of Israel," Judah should realize how important it is that she listen to the message and invitation that shall come to her from Israel, to accept and listen to those the Lord promised to send: "And I will give you pastors according to mine heart, which shall feed you with knowledge and understanding."

A New Covenant with Israel and Judah

The prophet Jeremiah speaks again of the new covenant the Lord would make with the House of Israel, and with the House of Judah, realizing that they were

separate and apart from each other, and that the covenant would go from Israel to Judah:

> Behold the days come, saith the Lord, that I will make
> a new covenant with the house of Israel, and with the house
> of Judah:
> Not according to the covenant that I made with their
> fathers in the day that I took them by the hand to bring
> them out of the land of Egypt; which my covenant they
> brake, although I was an husband unto them, saith the
> Lord:
> *But this shall be the covenant that I will make with the*
> *house of Israel: After these days, saith the Lord, I will put*
> *my law in their inward parts, and write it in their hearts;*
> *and will be their God, and they shall be my people.*
> And they shall teach no more every man his neighbour,
> and every man his brother, saying, Know the Lord: for they
> shall all know me, from the least of them unto the greatest
> of them, saith the Lord; for I will forgive their iniquity,
> and I will remember their sin no more. (Jeremiah 31:31-34.)

The prophet Zechariah looked to the time that the
Lord would turn again to the House of Judah and the
House of Joseph, indicating that He realized they were
separated from each other:

> And I will strengthen *the house of Judah,* and I will
> save *the house of Joseph,* and I will bring them again to
> place them; for I have mercy upon them: and they shall
> be as though I had not cast them off: for I am the Lord
> their God, and will hear them.
> And they of Ephraim shall be like a mighty man, and
> their heart shall rejoice as through wine: yea, their children
> shall see it, and be glad; their heart shall rejoice in the
> Lord.
> I will hiss for them, and gather them; for I have re-
> deemed them: and they shall increase as they have in-
> creased.
> And I will sow them among the people: and they shall
> remember me in far countries; and they shall live with their
> children, and turn again. (Zechariah 10:6-9.)

Thus the Lord declared that He would "bring them
again to place them," for "I will strengthen the house of
Judah, and I will save the house of Joseph."

Jesus Outlines the Gathering of Israel and Judah

When Jesus appeared to the Nephites, as recorded in the Stick of Joseph, He spoke to them of the gathering of Israel in the latter days from the "face of the earth" whithersoever they had been scattered. He made it plain that the land of America had been given to the seed of Joseph, and that the Jews would be gathered to Jerusalem:

And it came to pass that when they had all given glory unto Jesus, he said unto them: Behold now I finish the commandment which the Father hath commanded me concerning this people, who are a remnant of the house of Israel.

Ye remember that I spake unto you, and said that when the words of Isaiah should be fulfilled — behold they are written, ye have them before you, therefore search them —

And verily, verily, I say unto you, that when they shall be fulfilled then is the fulfilling of the covenant which the Father hath made unto his people, O house of Israel.

And then shall the remnants, which shall be scattered abroad upon the face of the earth, be gathered in from the east and from the west, and from the south and from the north; and they shall be brought to the knowledge of the Lord their God, who hath redeemed them.

And the Father hath commanded me that *I should give unto you this land, for your inheritance.*

And I say unto you, that if the Gentiles do not repent after the blessing which they shall receive, after they have scattered my people —

Then shall ye, who are a remnant of the house of Jacob, go forth among them; and ye shall be in the midst of them who shall be many; and ye shall be among them as a lion among the beasts of the forest, and as a young lion among the flocks of sheep, who, if he goeth through both treadeth down and teareth to pieces, and none can deliver.

Thy hand shall be lifted up upon thine adversaries, and all thine enemies shall be cut off.

And I will gather my people together as a man gathereth his sheaves into the floor.

For I will make my people with whom the Father hath covenanted, yea, I will make thy horn iron, and I

will make thy hoofs brass. And thou shalt beat in pieces
many people; and I will consecrate their gain unto the
Lord, and their substance unto the Lord of the whole earth.
And behold, I am he who doeth it.

And it shall come to pass, saith the Father, that the
sword of my justice shall hang over them at that day; and
except they repent it shall fall upon them, saith the Father,
yea, *even upon all the nations of the Gentiles.*

And it shall come to pass that I will establish my people,
O house of Israel.

And behold, *this people will I establish in this land,*
unto the fulfilling of the covenant which I made with your
father Jacob; *and it shall be a New Jerusalem.* And the
powers of heaven shall be in the midst of this people; *yea,
even I will be in the midst of you.*

Behold, I am he of whom Moses spake, saying: A
prophet shall the Lord your God raise up unto your brethren, like unto me; him shall ye hear in all things whatsoever
he shall say unto you. And it shall come to pass that every
soul who will not hear that prophet shall be cut off from
among the people.

Verily I say unto you, yea, and all the prophets from
Samuel and those that follow after, as many as have
spoken, have testified of me.

And behold, ye are the children of the prophets, and
ye are of the house of Israel; and ye are of the covenant
which the Father made with your fathers, saying unto
Abraham: And in thy seed shall all the kindreds of the
earth be blessed.

The Father having raised me up unto you first, and
sent me to bless you in turning away every one of you
from his iniquities; and this because ye are the children
of the covenant —

And after that ye were blessed then fulfilleth the Father
the covenant which he made with Abraham, saying: In thy
seed shall all the kindreds of the earth be blessed — unto
the pouring out of the Holy Ghost through me upon the
Gentiles, *which blessing upon the Gentiles shall make them
mighty above all,* unto the scattering of my people, O house
of Israel.

And they shall be a scourge unto the people of this
land. Nevertheless, *when they shall have received the fulness of my gospel,* then if they shall harden their hearts
against me I will return their iniquities upon their own
heads, saith the Father.

And I will remember the covenant which I have made with my people; and I have covenanted with them that I would gather them together in mine own due time, that I would give unto them again the land of their fathers for their inheritance, which is the land of Jerusalem, which is the promised land unto them forever, saith the Father.

And it shall come to pass that the time cometh, when the fulness of my gospel shall be preached unto them;

And they shall believe in me, that I am Jesus Christ, the Son of God, and shall pray unto the Father in my name.

Then shall their watchmen lift up their voice, and with the voice together shall they sing; for they shall see eye to eye.

Then will the Father gather them together again, and give unto them Jerusalem for the land of their inheritance,

Then shall they break forth into joy — Sing together, ye waste places of Jerusalem; for the Father hath comforted his people, he hath redeemed Jerusalem.

The Father hath made bare his holy arm in the eyes of all the nations; and all the ends of the earth shall see the salvation of the Father; and the Father and I are one.

. . .

Verily, verily, I say unto you, all these things shall surely come, even as the Father hath commanded me.   Then shall this covenant which the Father hath covenanted with his people be fulfilled; and then shall Jerusalem be inhabited again with my people, and it shall be the land of their inheritance. (3 Nephi 20:10-35, 46.)

From this declaration of Jesus there can be no doubt but that the land of America was given to the descendants of Joseph for an everlasting inheritance, and that, in the Lord's own due time, He would gather again the children of Judah to the land of their fathers, which was given them for their inheritance, "which is the land of Jerusalem, which is the promised land unto them forever." Jesus further indicated that this would come to pass at the time "when the fulness of my gospel shall be preached unto them."

A New Jerusalem for the Seed of Joseph

From the Stick of Joseph, we have the words of the Prophet Ether who was privileged to see the time when the earth would pass away, and there would be a new heaven and a new earth. In his description of these glorious events, he makes it very plain that there would be two gathering places:

And now I, Moroni, proceed to finish my record concerning the destruction of the people of whom I have been writing.

For behold, they rejected all the words of Ether; for he truly told them of all things, from the beginning of man; and that after the waters had receded from off the face of this land it became a choice land above all other lands, a chosen land of the Lord; wherefore the Lord would have that all men should serve him who dwell upon the face thereof;

And that it was the place of the New Jerusalem, which should come down out of heaven, and the holy sanctuary of the Lord.

Behold, Ether saw the days of Christ, and he spake concerning a New Jerusalem upon this land.

And he spake also concerning the house of Israel, *and the Jerusalem from whence Lehi should come — after it should be destroyed it should be built up again, a holy city unto the Lord; wherefore, it could not be a new Jerusalem for it had been in a time of old; but it should be built up again, and become a holy city of the Lord; and it should be built unto the house of Israel.*

And that *a New Jerusalem should be built upon this land,* unto the *remnant of the seed of Joseph,* for which things there has been a type.

For as Joseph brought his father down into the land of Egypt, even so he died there; wherefore, the Lord brought a remnant of the seed of Joseph out of the land of Jerusalem, that he might be merciful unto the seed of Joseph that they should perish not, even as he was merciful unto the father of Joseph that he should perish not.

Wherefore, the remnant of the house of Joseph shall be built upon this land; and it shall be a land of their inheritance; and they shall build up a holy city unto the Lord, like unto the Jerusalem of old; and they shall no more be confounded, until the end come when the earth shall pass away.

And there shall be a new heaven and a new earth; and they shall be like unto the old save the old have passed away, and all things have become new.

And then cometh the New Jerusalem; and blessed are they who dwell therein, for it is they whose garments are white through the blood of the Lamb; and they are they who are numbered among *the remnant of the seed of Joseph,* who were of the house of Israel.

And then also cometh the Jerusalem of old; and the inhabitants thereof, blessed are they, for they have been washed in the blood of the Lamb; and they are they who were scattered and gathered in from the four quarters of the earth, and from the north countries, and are partakers of the fulfilling of the covenant which God made with their father, Abraham.

And when these things come, bringeth to pass the scripture which saith, *there are they who were first, who shall be last; and there are they who were last, who shall be first.* Ether 13:1-12.)

Two Gathering Places — Zion and Jerusalem

On November 3, 1831, the Prophet Joseph Smith received a revelation from the Lord explaining certain events in connection with the second coming of the Messiah; the establishment of Zion and Jerusalem; the coming of the lost tribes from the north countries to receive their blessings at the hands of Ephraim:

Wherefore, prepare ye for the coming of the Bridegroom; go ye, go ye out to meet him.

For behold, he shall stand upon the mount of Olivet, and upon the mighty ocean, even the great deep, and upon the islands of the sea, and upon the land of Zion.

And he shall utter his voice out of Zion, and he shall speak from Jerusalem, and his voice shall be heard among all people;

And it shall be a voice as the voice of many waters, and as the voice of a great thunder, which shall break down the mountains, and the valleys shall not be found.

He shall command the great deep, and it shall be driven back into the north countries, and the islands shall become one land;

And the land of Jerusalem and the land of Zion shall be turned back into their own place; and the earth shall be like as it was in the days before it was divided.

And the Lord, even the Savior, shall stand in the midst of his people, and shall reign over all flesh.

And they who are in the north countries shall come in remembrance before the Lord; and their prophets shall hear his voice, and shall no longer stay themselves; and they shall smite the rocks, and the ice shall flow down at their presence.

And an highway shall be cast up in the midst of the great deep.

Their enemies shall become a prey unto them,

And in the barren deserts there shall come forth pools of living water; and the parched ground shall no longer be a thirsty land.

And they shall bring forth their rich treasures unto the children of Ephraim, my servants.

And the boundaries of the everlasting hills shall tremble at their presence.

And there shall they fall down and be crowned with glory, even in Zion, by the hands of the servants of the Lord, even the children of Ephraim.

And they shall be filled with songs of everlasting joy.

Behold, this is the blessing of the everlasting God upon the tribes of Israel, and the richer blessing upon the head of Ephraim and his fellows.

And they also of the tribe of Judah, after their pain shall be sanctified in holiness before the Lord, to dwell in his presence day and night, forever and ever. (Doctrine and Covenants 133:19-35.)

The Lord thus made it plain to the Prophet Joseph Smith that there would be two centers or gathering places, Zion and Jerusalem, and that He would utter His voice from both: "And he shall utter his voice out of Zion, and he shall speak from Jerusalem."

Gathering to be "in the Last Days"

The Prophet Isaiah also seemed to know of these events when he said:

And it shall come to pass *in the last days,* that the mountain of the Lord's house shall be established in the top of the mountains, and shall be exalted above the hills; and all nations shall flow unto it.

And many people shall go and say, Come ye, and let us go up to the mountain of the Lord, to the house of the God of Jacob; and he will teach us of his ways, and we will walk in his paths: for *out of Zion shall go forth the law, and the word of the Lord from Jerusalem.* (Isaiah 2:2-3.)

Isaiah leaves no doubt as to when the gathering would take place: "And it shall come to pass *in the last days.*" Surely, we are living in the last days. The Lord's house has been established in the top of the mountains. For more than one hundred years, people from all nations have been coming to Zion, "to the house of the God of Jacob," that He might teach them of His ways, that they might walk in His paths. The law of His Gospel has been going forth "out of Zion," and ultimately, as the prophet Isaiah declared, "the word of the Lord" will go forth "from Jerusalem."

Chapter 11

THE GATHERING OF ISRAEL

Keys Restored for Gathering Scattered Israel

On the night of September 21, 1823, the angel Moroni told Joseph Smith many things concerning the gathering of latter-day Israel. In reporting the visits of Moroni, Joseph Smith wrote—"He quoted the eleventh chapter of Isaiah, saying *it was about to be fulfilled.*"

More than twelve years later (April 3, 1836), following the dedication of the temple in Kirtland, Ohio, Moses appeared to Joseph Smith and Oliver Cowdery and conferred upon them the keys for the gathering of scattered Israel. This glorious event marked the beginning of the fulfillment of Moroni's prediction that the prophecy of Isaiah concerning the gathering of Israel "was about to be fulfilled."

Joseph Smith's account of the visit of the ancient Prophet Moses is as follows:

> Moses appeared before us, and committed unto us the keys of the gathering of Israel from the four parts of the earth, and the leading of the ten tribes from the land of the north. (Doctrine and Covenants 110:11.)

In a revelation to the Prophet Joseph Smith in September, 1830, the Lord instructed him in regard to the gathering of His people:

> And ye are called to bring to pass the gathering of mine elect; for mine elect hear my voice and harden not their hearts;
> Wherefore the decree hath gone forth from the Father that they shall be gathered in unto one place upon the face of this land, to prepare their hearts and be prepared in all things against the day when tribulation and desolation are sent forth upon the wicked. (Doctrine and Covenants 29: 7-8.)

Thus, in the establishment of the Church and Kingdom of God on the earth in these latter days, it will be noted that from the very beginning, the "gathering of mine elect" was fully understood to be one of the great objectives to be achieved. Such was the announcement made by the angel Moroni in 1823, six and one half years before the Church was organized, and more than twelve years before Moses restored the keys for accomplishing the gathering of Israel.

Seed of Joseph to be Gathered in the Land of America

The angel Moroni gave the Prophet Joseph Smith to understand that the gathering of Israel would be two fold in nature: (1) "He shall set up an ensign for the nations;" (2) He "shall assemble the outcasts of Israel." This contemplated the organization of the Lord's Church and Kingdom here upon the earth, "in the latter-days", to which would be gathered, in this land of America, the seed of Joseph which had been scattered among the Gentile nations. The gathering of Joseph (Israel) has been going forward ever since the organization of The Church of Jesus Christ of Latter-day Saints, April 6, 1830.

Joseph Smith was given to understand that the Lord would also "gather together the dispersed of Judah from the four corners of the earth," as a part of His great latter-day Gospel dispensation, and that this gathering would be to the land of Jerusalem and Palestine. (The gathering of Judah will be discussed in the following chapter.) We will now concern ourselves with the gathering of Israel to this land of America.

In a revelation from the Lord to the Prophet Joseph

Smith, December 16, 1833, the Lord made plain that His people were to be gathered together:

Behold, it is my will, that all they who call on my name, and worship me according to mine everlasting gospel, should gather together, and stand in holy places;

And prepare for the revelation which is to come, when the veil of the covering of my temple, in my tabernacle, which hideth the earth, shall be taken off, and all flesh shall see me together. . . .

That the work of the gathering together of my saints may continue, that I may build them up unto my name upon holy places; for the time of harvest is come, and my word must needs be fulfilled.

Therefore, I must gather together my people, according to the parable of the wheat and the tares, that the wheat may be secured in the garners to possess eternal life, and be crowned with celestial glory, when I shall come in the kingdom of my Father to reward every man according as his work shall be. (Doctrine and Covenants 101:22-23, 64-65.)

The following quotations from the revelations of the Lord to the Prophet Joseph Smith are given merely to confirm the statements already made:

And even so will I gather mine elect from the four quarters of the earth, even as many as will believe in me, and hearken unto my voice. (Doctrine and Covenants 33:6; October, 1830.)

And Israel shall be saved in mine own due time; and by the keys which I have given shall they be led, and no more be confounded at all. (Doctrine and Covenants 35:25; December, 1830.)

And again, I say unto you, I give unto you a commandment, that every man, both elder, priest, teacher, and also member, go to with his might, with the labor of his hands, to prepare and accomplish the things which I have commanded.

And let your preaching be the warning voice, every man to his neighbor, in mildness and in meekness.

And go ye out from among the wicked. Save yourselves. Be ye clean that bear the vessels of the Lord. . . . (Doctrine and Covenants 38:40-42; January 1831.)

That my covenant people may be gathered in one in that day when I shall come to my temple. And this I do for the salvation of my people. (Doctrine and Covenants 42:36; February 1831.)

And again, the Lord shall utter his voice out of heaven, saying: Hearken, O ye nations of the earth, and hear the words of that God who made you.

O, ye nations of the earth, how often would I have gathered you together as a hen gathereth her chickens under her wings, but ye would not! (Doctrine and Covenants 43:23-24; February, 1831.)

And it shall come to pass that the righteous shall be gathered out from among all nations, and shall come to Zion, singing with songs of everlasting joy. (Doctrine and Covenants 45:71; March 1831.)

Wherefore, prepare ye, prepare ye, O my people; sanctify yourselves; gather ye together, O ye people of my church, upon the land of Zion, all you that have not been commanded to tarry.

Go ye out from Babylon. Be ye clean that bear the vessels of the Lord.

Call your solemn assemblies, and speak often one to another. And let every man call upon the name of the Lord.

Yea, verily I say unto you again, the time has come when the voice of the Lord is unto you: Go ye out of Babylon; gather ye out from among the nations, from the four winds, from one end of heaven to the other.

Send forth the elders of my church unto the nations which are afar off; unto the islands of the sea; send forth unto foreign lands; call upon all nations, *first upon the Gentiles, and then upon the Jews.*

And behold, and lo, this shall be their cry, and the voice of the Lord unto all people: Go ye forth unto the land of Zion, that the borders of my people may be enlarged, and that her stakes may be strengthened and that Zion may go forth unto the regions round about. (Doctrine and Covenants 133:4-9; November 1831.)

It will be noted that these revelations were all given within two years after the Church was organized. There is no question but what the Lord had in mind that the seed of Joseph would be gathered out of the nations and be gathered together in one place, as the above quotations so clearly indicate.

Gathering of Joseph (Israel) Already in Progress

While the Lord has indicated that His Zion of the latter days would be established in the land of America, and that the new Jerusalem would be built upon this land, it is obvious that Israel would be gathered to more than one city in Zion. In fulfillment of the command of the Lord in this matter, the Latter-day Saints have built over six hundred cities, to which have been gathered converts to the new faith from many countries.

At the first gathering place of the saints in this dispensation which was Kirtland, Ohio, they erected their first temple to the Most High.

The second gathering was in the State of Missouri where they laid the cornerstones for two temples, one at Independence and the other at Far West. But the saints were compelled to leave Missouri because of cruel persecutions. However, until this day, the Church anticipates the time when its members will return and build a temple and the city of Zion to the Most High, at Independence, Missouri, in the land of Joseph (America).

From Missouri, the saints went to Nauvoo, Illinois, where they built a city of some 20,000 souls, and erected a beautiful temple to their God. It was while they were located here that the Prophet Joseph Smith and his brother, Hyrum, were martyred in cold blood, by a wicked mob, in Carthage jail, Illinois, on June 27, 1844. Soon after this, the saints were compelled to leave Nauvoo. Their homes were devasted; their beautiful new temple was burned by their enemies. From Illinois they turned their faces to the valleys of the Rocky Mountains, stopping at Winter Quarters, Iowa, only long enough to make preparations for their journey across the plains. The first main company arrived in what is now Salt Lake

City, Utah, July 24, 1847, the headquarters of The Church of Jesus Christ of Latter-day Saints to this day.

In a revelation to Joseph Smith under date of March 8, 1833, the Lord referred to the House of Joseph as "the heathen nations":

> And then cometh the day when the arm of the Lord shall be revealed in power in convincing the nations, the *heathen nations, the house of Joseph,* of the gospel of their salvation. (Doctrine and Covenants 90:10.)

The prophet Amos had declared that the House of Israel would be sifted among the nations, and this accounts for the fact that the seed of Joseph would be gathered from among "the heathen nations":

> I will not utterly destroy the house of Jacob, saith the Lord.
>
> For, lo, I will command, and I will sift the house of Israel among all nations, like as corn is sifted in a sieve, yet shall not the least grain fall upon the earth. (Amos 9: 8-9.)

Predictions Concerning the Gathering of Israel

In the translation of the Book of Mormon (Stick of Joseph), the Prophet Joseph Smith learned much concerning the plan of the Lord to gather Israel in the latter days, and to establish His Zion in the land of Joseph.

We quote the words of Jesus Christ to the Nephites when He visited them in America following His resurrection:

> And verily I say unto you, I give unto you a sign, that ye may know the time when these things shall be about to take place — *that I shall gather in, from their long dispersion, my people, O house of Israel, and shall establish again among them my Zion;*
>
> And behold, this is the thing which I will give unto you for a sign — for verily I say unto you that when these things which I declare unto you, and which I shall declare unto you hereafter of myself, and by the power of the Holy

Ghost which shall be given you of the Father, shall be made known unto the Gentiles that they may know concerning this people who are a remnant of the house of Jacob, and concerning this my people who shall be scattered by them;

Verily, verily, I say unto you, when these things shall be made known unto them of the Father, and shall come forth of the Father, from them unto you;

For it is wisdom in the Father that *they should be established in this land,* and be set up as a free people by the power of the Father, that these things might come forth from them unto a remnant of your seed, that the covenant of the Father may be fulfilled which he hath covenanted with his people, O house of Israel;

Therefore, when these works and the works which shall be wrought among you hereafter shall come forth *from the Gentiles,* unto your seed which shall dwindle in unbelief because of iniquity;

For thus it behooveth the Father that it should come forth from the Gentiles, that he may show forth his power unto the Gentiles, for this cause that the Gentiles, if they will harden not their hearts, that they may repent and come unto me and be baptized in my name and know of the true points of my doctrine, that they may be numbered among my people, O house of Israel;

And when these things come to pass that thy seed shall begin to know these things — it shall be a sign unto them, that they may know that the work of the Father hath already commenced unto the fulfilling of the covenant which he hath made unto the people who are of the house of Israel. . . .

For in that day, *for my sake shall the Father work a work, which shall be a great and marvelous work among them;* and there shall be among them those who will not believe it, although a man shall declare it unto them. . . .

And my people who are a remnant of Jacob shall be among the Gentiles, yea, in the midst of them as a lion among the beasts of the forest, as a young lion among the flocks of sheep, who, if he go through both treadeth down and teareth in pieces, and none can deliver. . . .

But if they will repent and hearken unto my words, and harden not their hearts, *I will establish my church among them,* and they shall come in unto the covenant and be numbered among this the remnant of Jacob, *unto whom I have given this land for their inheritance;*

And they shall assist my people, the remnant of Jacob,

and also as many of the house of Israel as shall come, *that they may build a city, which shall be called the New Jerusalem.*

And then shall they assist my people that they may be gathered in, *who are scattered upon all the face of the land,* in unto the New Jerusalem.

And then shall the power of heaven come down among them; *and I also will be in the midst.*

And then shall the work of the Father commence at that day, even when this gospel shall be preached among the remnant of this people. Verily I say unto you, at that day shall the work of the Father commence among all the dispersed of my people, yea, even the tribes which have been lost, *which the Father hath led away out of Jerusalem.*

Yea, the work shall commence among all the dispersed of my people, with the Father, to prepare the way whereby they may come unto me, that they may call on the Father in my name.

Yea, and then shall the work commence, with the Father, among all nations, in preparing the way whereby his people may be gathered home to the land of their inheritance.

And they shall go out from all nations; and they shall not go out in haste, nor go by flight, for I will go before them, saith the Father, and I will be their rearward. (3 Nephi 21:1-7, 9, 12, 22-29.)

In considering this scripture, it should be remembered that the Book of Mormon (Stick of Joseph) was published and given to the world in 1829, a year before the Church was organized. Joseph Smith was only twenty-four years old. And yet this statement from that inspired record covers all the essential points with respect to the gathering of latter-day Israel, to-wit:

1. That the New Jerusalem would be established in the land of America.
2. That The Church of Jesus Christ would be established in the land of America.
3. That the Church would be established among the Gentiles (We have pointed out how Israel would be scattered among the Gentile nations).
4. That at the time His Church would be established among the Gentiles in this land of America, it would

be a sign that the time had arrived, "That I shall
gather in, from their long dispersion, my people,
O house of Israel, and shall establish among them
my Zion."

5. That the accomplishment of these things would
precede the second coming of the Christ: "And I
also will be in the midst."

6. That at that time, the Lord would set His hand to
gather His people from among all nations: "Yea, and
then shall the work commence, with the Father,
among all nations, in preparing the way whereby His
people may be gathered home to the land of their
inheritance."

7. These declarations of the Savior confirm the statements of the prophets that Israel would be sifted
among all nations.

The Prophet Ether, as recorded in the Stick of
Joseph, had a clear understanding of the gathering of
Israel in the latter days and of the establishment of a
New Jerusalem in this land of America, and the rebuild-
ing of the Jerusalem of old by the Jews. (Ether 13:1-13.)

Predictions of the Prophets of Judah Concerning the Gathering of Israel

The prophet Jeremiah was privileged to see how
complete would be the gathering of Israel to the lands
the Lord had given "unto their fathers":

Therefore, behold, the days come, saith the Lord, that
it shall no more be said, The Lord liveth, that brought up
the children of Israel out of the land of Egypt;

But, The Lord liveth, that brought up the children of
Israel from the land of the north, and from all the lands
whither he had driven them: and I will bring them again
into their land that I gave unto their fathers.

Behold, I will send for many fishers, saith the Lord, and
they shall fish them; and after will I send for many hunters,
and they shall hunt them from every mountain, and from
every hill, and out of the holes of the rocks. (Jeremiah 16:
14-16.)

This latter-day gathering, as seen by Jeremiah, was to exceed in magnitude the leading of Israel out of the land of Egypt, when, by the power of God, they passed through the Red Sea on dry ground.

At the time of this writing it is evident that the Lord has made bare His arm to fulfill His promise made by the Prophet Jeremiah with respect to the gathering of Israel in the latter days. The prophet indicated that the Lord would send fishers and hunters to "hunt them from every mountain, and from every hill, and out of the holes in the rocks," showing how completely He would fulfill His promise, that after Israel was sifted among the nations, "yet shall not the least grain fall upon the earth." (Amos 9:8-9.)

In the establishment of The Church of Jesus Christ of Latter-day Saints upon the earth in these latter days, the Lord has provided therein a great missionary program, through which a great many male members of the Church give two years or more of their lives, at their own expense, to preach the message of the restored gospel to all the inhabitants of the earth. Up to the present time, it is estimated that over 70,000 missionaries have filled such missions for the Church to acquaint the world with the "marvelous work and a wonder" the Lord has established in the earth in these latter days according to the promises of the prophets. These are the "fishers" and "hunters" the Lord promised to send. It is apparent that the Lord did not intend any should be overlooked.

Through Jeremiah, the Lord makes this further promise to Israel:

> Turn, O backsliding children, saith the Lord; for I am married unto you: and I will take you one of a city, and two of a family, and I will bring you to Zion:
> And I will give you pastors according to mine heart, which shall feed you with knowledge and understanding. (Jeremiah 3:14-15.)

From these prophecies it will be seen that Jeremiah realized that as Israel had been "sifted among the nations," the Lord would gather them, not in great multitudes, but "one of a city and two of a family," and that when He should bring them to Zion, He would give them "pastors according to mine heart, which shall feed you with knowledge and understanding." In other words, He would lead them to Zion where He had established His Church and Kingdom, restored His Priesthood, that they may be fed "with knowledge and understanding."

Jeremiah gave a vivid and detailed description of the gathering of the seed of Joseph or Ephraim, who were given the land of America for their inheritance:

> For there shall be a day, that the watchmen upon the mount Ephraim shall cry, Arise ye, and let us go up to Zion unto the Lord our God.
>
> For thus saith the Lord; Sing with gladness for Jacob, and shout among the chief of the nations: publish ye, praise ye, and say, O Lord, save thy people, the remnant of Israel.
>
> Behold, I will bring them from the north country, and gather them from the coasts of the earth, and with them the blind and the lame, the woman with child and her that travaileth with child together: a great company shall *return thither*.
>
> They shall come with weeping, and with supplications will I lead them: I will cause them to walk by the rivers of waters in a straight way, wherein they shall not stumble: *for I am a father to Israel, and Ephraim is my firstborn.*
>
> Hear the word of the Lord, O ye nations, and declare it in the isles afar off, and say, He that scattered Israel will gather him, and keep him, as a shepherd doth his flock.
>
> For the Lord hath redeemed Jacob, and ransomed him from the hand of him that was stronger than he.
>
> Therefore they shall come and sing in the height of Zion, and shall flow together to the goodness of the Lord, for wheat, and for wine, and for oil, and for the young of the flock and of the herd: and their soul shall be as a watered garden; and they shall not sorrow any more at all.

Then shall the virgin rejoice in the dance, both young men and old together: for I will turn their mourning into joy, and will comfort them, and make them rejoice from their sorrow.

And I will satiate the soul of the priests with fatness, and my people shall be satisfied with my goodness, saith the Lord. (Jeremiah 31:6-14.)

Prophecies of Jeremiah Fulfilled

It would appear that Jeremiah wrote a portion of the history of The Church of Jesus Christ of Latter-day Saints approximately 2500 years before it occurred.

This was a cry from "the watchmen upon mount Ephraim. . . . Arise ye and let us go up to Zion unto the Lord our God." This has nothing to do with Judah as the prophet further indicated: "For I am a father to Israel, and Ephraim is my firstborn."

Recall that the birthright was taken from Reuben, the firstborn of the twelve sons of Israel, or Jacob, and was given to Joseph, and from him to his sons Ephraim and Manasseh, (I Chronicles 5:1-2.) Thereafter, the Lord regarded Ephraim as his "firstborn." (Jeremiah 31:9.) Therefore, this was to be a gathering of the descendants of Joseph and Ephraim, "to Zion unto the Lord our God."

"Sing with gladness for Jacob." Why? Because the day of his redemption was nigh.

"Shout among the chief of the nations." The Elders of this Church had been sent to Great Britain (1846), the Scandinavian countries, Germany, etc., the chief nations, and had gathered in many converts to Nauvoo, Illinois.

"I will bring them . . . a great company shall return *thither*." This was something the Lord was going to do. Note that Jeremiah does not say that they will return *hither*, or to the place where this prediction was made, but *thither*, or to a distant place. He understood that

Joseph was to be given a new land in the "utmost bound of the everlasting hills." (See Genesis 49:22-26; Deuteronomy 33:13-17.)

A "great company" was to "return thither," and with them "the blind and the lame, the woman with child and her that travaileth with child together," and "they shall come with weeping, and with supplications will I lead them." About twenty thousand Latter-day Saints were driven out of Nauvoo, and with them "the blind and the lame, the woman with child." They did not leave their beautiful homes because they wanted to, hence they came "weeping" and with "supplications" unto the Lord, and He led them as He had promised.

"I will cause them to walk by the rivers of waters in a straight way, wherein they shall not stumble." In their trek from Nauvoo, Illinois, across the great American desert to the Salt Lake Valley, the saints traveled about six hundred miles along the North Platte River, as Jeremiah had seen.

"Therefore they shall come and sing in the height of Zion." At this writing (1954) the Tabernacle Choir, at Salt Lake City, Utah, consisting of approximately 375 unpaid voices broadcasts weekly "from the crossroads of the west." They are in their twenty-sixth year of weekly nation-wide broadcasts. This represents but a small part of the singing that is done "in the height of Zion."

" . . . and shall flow together to the goodness of the Lord, for wheat, and for oil, and for wine, and for the young of the flock and of the herd." Compare this promise with the blessing pronounced upon the head of Joseph by Moses, when he referred to the land of Joseph:

> And of Joseph he said, Blessed of the Lord be his land, for the precious things of heaven, for the dew, and for the deep that coucheth beneath.

And for the precious fruits brought forth by the sun,
and for the precious things put forth by the moon.

And for the chief things of the ancient mountains, and
for the precious things of the lasting hills,

And for the precious things of the earth and fulness
thereof. . . . (Deuteronomy 33:13-16; For Jacob's blessing
to Joseph, see Genesis 49:22-26.)

It is easy to believe that Joseph's land was to be
"choice above all other lands," as the Stick of Joseph
indicates, when one recalls how many times Moses used
the word "precious" in describing the land and its blessings. One will find these predictions in actual fulfillment as he travels among the Latter-day Saints in the
valleys of the Rocky Mountains.

Continuing our analyses of the prophecy of Jeremiah: "And they shall not sorrow any more at all. Then
shall the virgin rejoice in the dance, both young men and
old together: for I will turn their mourning into joy, and
will comfort them, and make them rejoice from their sorrow." To understand how completely this has been fulfilled, one needed but to attend the testimony meetings of
the Latter-day Saints, after their arrival in the valleys of
the Rocky Mountains, and hear them express their gratitude to the Lord for having brought them here. To
attend their dances and see how both young and the
old "rejoice in the dance," is a revelation. Practically
every organized ward or branch of Latter-day Saints
have, adjoining their chapel, a recreation hall where the
young and the old do rejoice together in the dance, and
where other activities are carried on for their enjoyment.
Surely the Lord has turned "their mourning into joy,"
and has comforted them and made "them to rejoice from
their sorrow."

"And I will satiate the soul of the priests with fatness, and my people shall be satisfied with my goodness."
While the members of the Priesthood in The Church of

Jesus Christ of Latter-day Saints are not paid for their services, and thousands of them have left their families for years at a time to do missionary work in the nations of the earth, paying their own expenses and without remuneration from the Church, yet, in their hearts, they feel they are better paid than any other religious leaders in the world, because of the joy and satisfaction the Lord plants in their hearts, which could not possibly be purchased with money. Thus He has satiated "the soul of the priests with fatness," and His people are satisfied with His goodness.

The Prophet Jeremiah speaks again of the gathering of Israel and of Judah when the Messiah shall make His second advent to judge His people, and to reign "as King of kings and Lord of lords:"

> And I will gather the remnants of my flock out of all countries whither I have driven them, and will bring them again to their folds; and they shall be fruitful and increase.
>
> And I will set up shepherds over them which shall feed them; and they shall fear no more, nor be dismayed, neither shall they be lacking, saith the Lord.
>
> Behold, the days come, saith the Lord, that I will raise unto David a righteous Branch, and a King shall reign and prosper, and shall execute judgment and justice in the earth.
>
> *In his days Judah shall be saved, and Israel shall dwell safely*: and this is his name whereby he shall be called, THE LORD OF RIGHTEOUSNESS.
>
> Therefore, behold, the days come, saith the Lord, that they shall no more say, The Lord liveth, which brought up the children of Israel out of the land of Egypt;
>
> But, the Lord liveth, which brought up and which led the seed of the house of Israel out of the north country, and from all countries whither I had driven them; and they shall dwell in their own land. (Jeremiah 23:3-8.)

In this prophecy, it is plain that Jeremiah saw the gathering of the House of Israel, and the House of Judah, in the days preceding the second coming of the Messiah.

Prophecies of Isaiah Concerning the Gathering of Israel

Only those who are associated with The Church of Jesus Christ of Latter-day Saints can understand how literally the following prophecy of Isaiah has been fulfilled:

> And it shall come to pass in the last days, that the mountain of the Lord's house shall be established in the top of the mountains and shall be exalted above the hills; and all nations shall flow unto it.
>
> And many people shall go and say, Come ye, and let us go up to the mountain of the Lord, to the house of the God of Jacob; and he will teach us of his ways, and we will walk in his paths; for out of Zion shall go forth the law, and the word of the Lord from Jerusalem. (Isaiah 2:2-3.)

In order that the saints may enjoy the privileges of the sealing ordinances performed in the "house of the God of Jacob," many have gathered from the nations of the earth where the missionaries have carried the message of the restored gospel of the Lord Jesus Christ. The law of the Lord (His Gospel) is going forth out of Zion, as will the "word of the Lord from Jerusalem" when the Messiah comes to reign as King of kings and Lord of lords.

This establishment of the "Lord's house" in the "top of the mountains," and the gathering of all nations unto it, must be "in the last days," as Isaiah declared, and would precede the judgments of the Lord which will be followed by a day when, "nation shall not lift up sword against nation, neither shall they learn war any more." (Isaiah 2:4.) With the close of World War II we are all hopeful that we are approaching the day when the condition Isaiah foretold may be anticipated. At least we know that it has not yet been fulfilled.

Isaiah Foresees the Coming of the Railroad and Airplane

In fixing the time of the great gathering, Isaiah seemed to indicate that it would take place in the day of the railroad train and the airplane:

> And he will lift up an ensign to the nations from far, and will hiss unto them from the end of the earth: and, behold, *they shall come with speed swiftly:*
>
> None shall be weary nor stumble among them; none shall slumber nor sleep; neither shall the girdle of their loins be loosed, nor the latchet of their shoes be broken:
>
> Whose arrows are sharp, and all their bows bent, their horses' hoofs shall be counted like flint, and their wheels like a whirlwind:
>
> Their roaring shall be like a lion, they shall roar like young lions: yea, they shall roar, and lay hold of the prey, and shall carry it away safe, and none shall deliver it. (Isaiah 5:26-29.)

Since there were neither trains nor airplanes in that day, Isaiah could hardly have mentioned them by name. However, he seems to have described them in unmistakable words. How better could "their horses' hoofs be counted like flint, and their wheels like a whirlwind" than in the modern train? How better could "their roaring . . . be like a lion" than in the roar of the airplane? Trains and airplanes do not stop for night. Therefore, was not Isaiah justified in saying: "none shall slumber nor sleep; neither shall the girdle of their loins be loosed, nor the latchet of their shoes be broken"? With this manner of transportation the Lord can really "hiss unto them from the end of the earth," that "they shall come with speed swiftly." Indicating that Isaiah must have foreseen the airplane, he stated: "Who are these that fly as a cloud, and as the doves to their windows?" (Isaiah 60:8.)

Isaiah Predicts the Desert Shall Blossom as the Rose

Isaiah also understood that this gathering of Joseph (Israel) would be to the mountains, and that the Lord would cause the desert to rejoice and blossom as the rose. In this respect, it is remarkable what part "water" was to play in redeeming the desert and the wilderness as the gathering place of latter-day Israel:

> The wilderness and the solitary place shall be glad for them; and the desert shall rejoice, and blossom as the rose.
> It shall blossom abundantly, and rejoice even with joy and singing: the glory of Lebanon shall be given unto it, the excellency of Carmel and Sharon, they shall see the glory of the Lord, and the excellency of our God. . . .
> Then the eyes of the blind shall be opened, and the ears of the deaf shall be unstopped.
> Then shall the lame man leap as an hart, and the tongue of the dumb sing: *for in the wilderness shall waters break out, and streams in the desert.*
> *And the parched ground shall become a pool, and the thirsty land springs of water*: in the habitation of dragons, where each lay, shall be grass with reeds and rushes. . . .
> And the ransomed of the Lord shall return, and come to Zion with songs of everlasting joy upon their heads: they shall obtain joy and gladness, and sorrow and sighing shall flee away. (Isaiah 35:1-2, 5-7, 10.)

This has, in part at least, been fulfilled. The desert has been made to "rejoice and blossom as the rose." Waters have broken out "in the wilderness." (flowing wells) "and streams in the desert," (irrigation canals) "and the ransomed of the Lord" have returned, "and come to Zion with songs and everlasting joy upon their heads."

Isaiah continued his description of the gathering of Israel and the reclaiming of the wilderness:

> Fear not: for I am with thee: I will bring thy seed from the east, and gather thee from the west;
> I will say to the north, Give up; and to the south, Keep not back; bring my sons from far, and my daughters from the ends of the earth;

Even every one that is called by my name; for I have created him for my glory, I have formed him; yea, I have made him. . . .

Behold, *I will do a new thing;* now it shall spring forth; shall ye not know it? I will even make a way in the wilderness, *and rivers in the desert.*

The beasts of the field shall honour me, the dragons and the owls: because *I give waters in the wilderness,* and *rivers in the desert,* to give drink to my people, my chosen.

This people have I formed for myself; they shall shew forth my praise. (Isaiah 43:5-7, 19-21.)

Introduction of Irrigation may Fulfill Isaiah's Prophecy

"Behold, I will do a new thing." What is this new thing the Lord speaks of through the Prophet Isaiah? Could it not be the great system of "irrigation" which the Lord inspired His servants to teach to His people when they entered the valleys of the mountains? It was irrigation which caused the desert to "rejoice, and blossom as the rose;" to "make a way in the wilderness, and rivers in the desert." The great irrigation canals are larger than many rivers as they flow through the desert, bringing tens of thousands of acres of otherwise arid lands under profitable cultivation.

Even the beasts of the field—and the dragons and the owls shall honor Him, "because I give waters in the wilderness, and rivers in the desert, to give drink to my people, my chosen." What the Lord has thus done, in this "new thing" has blessed His "people," His "chosen" with such measure of prosperity that they have been able to send most of their old and young men on missions to the peoples of all nations at their own expense, bearing witness of the restoration of the gospel in this dispensation. No doubt this is what the Lord had in mind for them to do, when He said, "This people have I formed for myself; they shall shew forth my praise." They become the "fishers" and "hunters" whom the Lord said He would send out to hunt Israel "from every mountain, and from every hill, and out of the holes of the rocks." (Jeremiah 16:14-16.)

The Prophet Isaiah continued:

> *I will open rivers in high places,* and fountains in the midst of the valleys: *I will make the wilderness a pool of water,* and the dry land springs of water.
> I will plant in the wilderness the cedar, the shittah tree, and the myrtle, and the oil tree; I will set in the desert the fir tree, and the pine, and the box tree together:
> That they may see, and know, and consider, and understand together, that the hand of the Lord hath done this, and the Holy One of Israel hath created it. (Isaiah 41:18-20.)

"Rivers in high places" could have reference to the reservoirs built in the canyons to impound the winter run-off of water so it may be used for summer irrigation.

"And fountains in the midst of the valleys." If you have seen some of the flowing wells that have been drilled in some of the dry valleys, you can understand this part of the prophecy. All these fulfillments of prophecy have so changed the wilderness, that it has been possible to plant the various types of trees that otherwise would not grow.

"That they may see, and know, and consider, and understand together, that the hand of the Lord hath done this, and the Holy One of Israel hath created it." All this, therefore, may be regarded as the work of the Holy One of Israel, for the benefit of gathered Israel in the latter days.

President Brigham Young Meets Jim Bridger

The Lord must have had a great deal to do with the development of this western empire, for when Brigham Young and the Latter-day Saints were en route to the Salt Lake Valley, they met Jim Bridger, an early western trapper, who said: "Mr. Young, I would give a thousand dollars if I knew an ear of corn could be ripened in the Great Basin." (See Discourses of Brigham Young, p. 481.)

Statement of Senator McDuffie and Joseph Smith's Prophecy

As late as 1843, two years before the exodus of the Latter-day Saints from Illinois, the opinion held by the majority in the United States was that the whole territory of the Rocky Mountains was not worth a "pinch of snuff." Such was the expression made by Senator George H. McDuffie, of South Carolina, in the Senate that year. Discussing the settlement of Oregon, he said:

> Who are to go there, along the line of military posts, and take possession of the only part of the territory fit to occupy — that part upon the seacoast, a strip less than one hundred miles in width. Why, sir, of what use will this be for agricultural purposes? I would not for that purpose give a pinch of snuff for the whole territory. I wish to God we did not own it. (Congressional Globe, 27th Congress, 3rd Session, pp. 198-201.)

About the time Senator McDuffie made this statement, the Prophet Joseph Smith made the following statement:

> I prophesied that the Saints would continue to suffer much affliction, and would be driven to the Rocky Mountains, many would apostatize, others would be put to death by our persecutors or lose their lives in consequence of exposure or disease, and some of you will live to go and assist in making settlements and build cities, and see the Saints become a mighty people in the midst of the Rocky Mountains. (Documentary History of the Church, Vol. 5, p. 85.)

Since the Lord could make such a worthless land as described by Senator McDuffie to "blossom as a rose," and make the saints "become a mighty people in the midst of the Rocky Mountains," surely these are even greater accomplishments than when the Lord parted the Red Sea and led Israel of old through on dry land.

In the light of these prophecies, it seems logical that, in the restoration of the gospel in these latter days, Moses would be sent by the Father to restore the keys for the gathering of Israel to Joseph Smith "a choice seer . . . like unto Moses." In and of itself, the restoration of these keys of gathering constitutes " a marvellous work and a wonder," as promised by Isaiah. (Isaiah 29:13-14.)

Why did the prophets make such predictions, if we are not to look for their fulfillment? Have they been fulfilled? If so, when, and where, and by what people, if not by The Church of Jesus Christ of Latter-day Saints?

Nephite Prophets Promise Understanding

The Nephite prophets, as recorded in the Stick of Joseph, understood the value of the prophecies of Isaiah, and that it would be given to the Lord's people to understand them in the day when they would be fulfilled:

> For the eternal purposes of the Lord shall roll on, until all his promises shall be fulfilled.
> Search the prophecies of Isaiah. . . . (Mormon 8:22-23.)

> But behold, I proceed with mine own prophecy, according to my plainness; in the which I know that no man can err, nevertheless, *in the days that the prophecies of Isaiah shall be fulfilled men shall know of a surety, at the times when they shall come to pass.*
> Wherefore, they are of worth unto the children of men, and he that supposeth that they are not, unto them will I speak particularly, and confine the words unto mine own people; *for I know that they shall be of great worth unto them in the last days; for in that day shall they understand them; wherefore, for their good have I written them.* (2 Nephi 25:7-8.)

It should be remembered that these words of prophecy were published in the Stick of Joseph (The Book of Mormon) in 1829, before the Church was organized in 1830. They were published before any of the prophecies with respect to the establishment of "a marvellous work and a wonder" or the gathering of latter-day Israel had been fulfilled. Many of us today have lived to see almost a complete fulfillment of the promises made.

From this study of the prophecies of Isaiah, it would appear that he almost lived more in our day than in the day when he was actually upon the earth because of the wonderful visions given him concerning the things the Lord promised to do in the latter days. Isaiah fully understood that all the promises of the Lord would be fulfilled:

> The grass withereth, the flower fadeth: but the word of our God shall stand for ever. (Isaiah 40:8.)

He saw with great plainness the establishment of Zion in the land of Joseph (America), to which the seed of Joseph would be gathered. He beheld the rebuilding of Jerusalem by the Jews to which they would be gathered in the latter days. He loved to speak of Zion and Jerusalem:

> O Zion, that bringest good tidings, get thee up into the high mountain; O Jerusalem, that bringest good tidings, lift up thy voice with strength; lift it up, be not afraid; say unto the cities of Judah, Behold your God! (Isaiah 40:9.)

> Awake, awake; put on thy strength, O Zion; put on thy beautiful garments, O Jerusalem. . . . (Isaiah 52:1.)

Chapter 12

THE GATHERING OF JUDAH

Nephite Prophets Predict the Gathering of Judah

Moroni, sent from the presence of God, quoted these words of Isaiah three times, during the night of September 21, 1823, to impress them upon the mind of Joseph Smith:

> *And he shall set up an ensign for the nations, and shall assemble the outcasts of Israel, and gather together the dispersed of Judah from the four corners of the earth.* (Isaiah 11:12.)

There probably was no fact established more definitely in the mind of Joseph Smith than that the Lord was about to "assemble the outcasts of Israel and gather together the dispersed of Judah."

In the translation of the records contained in the gold plates, the Stick of Joseph, this fact was confirmed in a very definite manner through the Nephite prophets who had lived in this land of America. We will, therefore, quote from a few of the prophecies of these Nephite prophets, indicating how unmistakably it was given them to understand that not only would this land of America be the gathering place of the seed of Joseph, but that "in the latter days" the seed of Judah would be gathered back to the land of Palestine to rebuild Jerusalem and to reclaim her waste places:

> But behold, thus saith the Lord God: When the day cometh that they shall believe in me, that I am Christ, then have I covenanted with their fathers that they shall be restored in the flesh, upon the earth, unto the lands of their inheritance.

> And it shall come to pass that they shall be gathered in from their long dispersion, from the isles of the sea, and from the four parts of the earth; *and the nations of the Gentiles shall be great in the eyes of me, saith God, in carrying them forth to the lands of their inheritance.* (2 Nephi 10:7-8.)

The Prophet Nephi was given to know that Jesus Christ would come in the flesh six hundred years from the time his father left Jerusalem with his family, and that the inhabitants of Jerusalem would be scourged and scattered. Then he added:

> And because they turn their hearts aside, saith the prophet, and have despised the Holy One of Israel, they shall wander in the flesh, and perish, and become a hiss and a by-word, and be hated among all nations.
>
> Nevertheless, when that day cometh, saith the prophet, that they no more turn aside their hearts against the Holy One of Israel, then will he remember the covenants which he made to their fathers.
>
> Yea, then will he remember the isles of the sea; yea, and all the people who are of the house of Israel, will I gather in, saith the Lord, according to the words of the prophet Zenos, from the four quarters of the earth.
>
> Yea, and all the earth shall see the salvation of the Lord, saith the prophet; every nation, kindred, tongue and people shall be blessed. (I Nephi 19:14-17.)

The seed of Judah cannot help but recognize in these words of Nephi a complete account of what has happened to the Jews. Surely they have wandered in the flesh; they have perished; they have become a hiss and a by-word, and have been hated among all nations. Yet the Lord promised that He would remember the covenant He made with their fathers, and gather them in from the isles of the sea, and from the four quarters of the earth.

Promises of the Messiah to Judah

When the Messiah appeared to the Nephites, following His resurrection, He spoke of the promises of the Lord to the fathers, and then said:

> And I will remember the covenant which I have made with my people; and I have covenanted with them that I *would give them again the land of their fathers for their inheritance, which is the land of Jerusalem,* which is the promised land unto them forever, saith the Father.
>
> *And it shall come to pass that the time cometh, when the fulness of my gospel shall be preached unto them;*
>
> And they shall believe in me, that I am Jesus Christ, the Son of God, and shall pray unto the Father in my name.
>
> Then shall their watchmen lift up their voice, and with the voice together shall they sing; for they shall see eye to eye.
>
> Then will the Father gather them together again, *and give unto them Jerusalem for the land of their inheritance.*
>
> Then shall they break forth into joy — Sing together, *ye waste places of Jerusalem;* for the Father hath comforted his people, *he hath redeemed Jerusalem.* (3 Nephi 20:29-34.)

This is a very definite promise that the Lord would gather again His people to Jerusalem, that He would redeem her waste places, and at a time when "the fulness of my gospel shall be preached unto them." There is nothing indefinite about this promise.

In speaking to the Nephites, Jesus Christ made this further statement in regard to His promises to the Jews:

> *Yea, and ye need not any longer hiss, nor spurn, nor make game of the Jews,* nor any of the remnant of the house of Israel; for behold, the Lord remembereth his covenant unto them, and he will do unto them according to that which he hath sworn.
>
> Therefore ye need not suppose that ye can turn the right hand of the Lord unto the left, that he may not execute judgment unto the fulfilling of the covenant which he hath made unto the house of Israel. (3 Nephi 29:8-9.)

It should be a great comfort to the Jews to know that the day of their afflictions shall cease, "for behold, the Lord remembereth his covenant unto them."

Modern Revelations Concerning Judah

In a revelation from the Lord Jesus Christ to the Prophet Joseph Smith, given at Kirtland, Ohio, March 7, 1831, He makes reference to the predictions made to His disciples of former days:

> And ye have asked of me concerning the signs of my coming, in the day when I shall come in my glory in the clouds of heaven, to fulfil the promises that I have made unto your fathers,
>
> For as ye have looked upon the long absence of your spirits from your bodies to be a bondage, I will show unto you how the day of redemption shall come, and also the restoration of the scattered Israel.
>
> And now ye behold this temple which is in Jerusalem, which ye call the house of God, and your enemies say that this house shall never fall.
>
> But, verily I say unto you, that desolation shall come upon this generation as a thief in the night, and this people shall be destroyed and scattered among all nations.
>
> And this temple which ye now see shall be thrown down that there shall not be left one stone upon another.
>
> And it shall come to pass, that this generation of Jews shall not pass away until every desolation which I have told you concerning them shall come to pass.
>
> Ye say that ye know that the end of the world cometh; ye say also that ye know that the heavens and the earth shall pass away;
>
> And in this ye say truly, for so it is; but these things which I have told you shall not pass away until all shall be fulfilled.
>
> And this I have told you *concerning Jerusalem;* and when that day shall come, shall a remnant be scattered among all nations;
>
> *But they shall be gathered again; but they shall remain until the times of the Gentiles be fulfilled.*
>
> And in that day shall be heard of wars and rumors of wars, *and the whole earth shall be in commotion,* and men's hearts shall fail them, and they shall say that Christ delayeth his coming until the end of the earth.
>
> And the love of men shall wax cold, and iniquity shall abound

And when the times of the Gentiles is come in, a light shall break forth among them that sit in darkness, and it shall be the fulness of my gospel;

But they receive it not; for they perceive not the light, and they turn their hearts from me because of the precepts of men.

And in that generation shall the times of the Gentiles be fulfilled. (Doctrine and Covenants 45:16-30.)

Most of these predictions have been fulfilled. "Desolation" did come to the inhabitants of Jerusalem and the people were "destroyed and scattered among all nations." Their temple was "thrown down" that there was not one stone left upon another. But Jesus reassured them: "But they shall be gathered again; but they shall remain until the times of the Gentiles be fulfilled . . . and when the times of the Gentiles is come in, a light shall break forth among them that sit in darkness, and it shall be the fulness of my gospel."

The promised "light" has broken forth among the Gentiles, the seed of Joseph, through the restoration of "the fulness of my gospel" which was restored through the "choice seer . . . like unto Moses" the Lord promised to raise up in the latter days through the loins of Joseph the son of Jacob. The Lord promised that this seer of the latter days would bring forth His word, and added: "for the thing which the Lord shall bring forth by his hand, by the power of the Lord, shall bring my people unto salvation." (2 Nephi 3:15.)

It would seem that the "times of the Gentiles" are nearing fulfillment and that the time of the redemption of the Jews is drawing near when the "fulness of my Gospel" must be preached unto them, and they shall gather again unto the land of their inheritance and again rebuild the city of Jerusalem.

On March 27, 1836, the Prophet Joseph Smith dedicated the Temple at Kirtland, Ohio. According to the prophet's own statement, the prayer he offered was given by revelation. Note the words of the prayer which relate directly to Judah:

> But thou knowest that thou hast a great love for the children of Jacob, who have been scattered upon the mountains for a long time, in a cloudy and dark day.
>
> We therefore ask thee to have mercy upon the children of Jacob, *that Jerusalem, from this hour, may begin to be redeemed;*
>
> And the yoke of bondage may begin to be broken off from the house of David;
>
> *And the children of Judah may begin to return to the lands which thou didst give Abraham, their father.* (Doctrine and Covenants 109:61-64.)

It was made plain to the prophet of this dispensation, early in his ministry, that the return of the Jews to their Promised Land, and the rebuilding of Jerusalem was a very definite part of the Lord's plan in establishing His Kingdom upon the earth in these latter days to prepare the way for His second coming.

Holy Land Dedicated for the Gathering of the Jews

In preparation for the gathering of the Jews, the Prophet Joseph Smith and his counselors, as the Presidency of the Church, sent Elder Orson Hyde, a descendant of Judah, one of the Twelve Apostles of the Church, on a mission to Jerusalem, to dedicate the Holy Land for the ultimate return of Judah's scattered remnant according to the predictions of ancient prophets, for the rebuilding of Jerusalem. In keeping with this special assignment, on Sunday morning, October 24, 1841, Apostle Orson Hyde went up on the Mount of Olives and there performed the ceremony of dedication which had been assigned him. Following are excerpts from

Elder Hyde's dedicatory prayer which should touch the heart of every living Jew, the world over:

O Thou! who art from everlasting to everlasting, eternally and unchangeably the same, even the God who rules in the heavens above, and controls the destinies of men on the earth, wilt Thou not condescend, through thine infinite goodness and royal favor, to listen to the prayer of Thy servant which he this day offers up unto Thee in the name of Thy holy child Jesus, upon this land, where the Sun of Righteousness set in blood, and thine Anointed One expired. . . .

Now, O Lord! Thy servant has been obedient to the heavenly vision which Thou gavest him in his native land; and under the shadow of Thine outstretched arm, he has safely arrived in this place to dedicate and consecrate this land unto Thee, for the gathering together of Judah's scattered remnants, according to the predictions of the holy Prophets — for the building up of Jerusalem again after it has been trodden down by the Gentiles so long, and for rearing a Temple in honor of Thy name. . . .

O Thou, Who didst covenant with Abraham, Thy friend, and Who didst renew that covenant with Isaac, and confirm the same with Jacob with an oath, that Thou wouldst not only give them this land for an everlasting inheritance, but that Thou wouldst also remember their seed forever. Abraham, Isaac, and Jacob have long since closed their eyes in death, and made the grave their mansion. Their children are scattered and dispersed abroad among the nations of the Gentiles like sheep that have no shepherd, and are still looking forward for the fulfillment of these promises which Thou didst make concerning them; and even this land, which once poured forth nature's richest bounty, and flowed, as it were, with milk and honey, has, to a certain extent, been smitten with barrenness and sterility since it drank from murderous hands the blood of Him who never sinned.

Grant, therefore, O Lord, in the name of Thy wellbeloved Son, Jesus Christ, to remove the barrenness and sterility of this land, and let springs of living water break forth to water its thirsty soil. Let the vine and olive produce in their strength, and the fig-tree bloom and flourish. Let the land become abundantly fruitful when possessed by its rightful heirs; let it again flow with plenty to feed the returning prodigals who come home with a spirit of grace and supplication; upon it let the clouds distil virtue and richness, and let the fields smile with plenty. Let the flocks and the herds greatly increase and multiply upon the mountains and the hills; and let Thy great kindness conquer and subdue the unbelief of Thy people. Do Thou take from them their stony heart, and give them a heart of flesh; and may the Sun of Thy favor dispel the cold mists of darkness which have beclouded their atmosphere. *Incline them to gather in upon this land according to Thy word.* Let them come like clouds and like doves to their windows. Let the large ships of the nations bring them from the distant isles; and let kings become their nursing fathers, and queens with motherly fondness wipe the tear of sorrow from their eye.

Thou, O Lord, did once move upon the heart of Cyrus to show favor unto Jerusalem and her children. Do Thou now also be pleased to inspire the hearts of kings and the powers of the earth to look with a friendly eye towards this place, and with a desire to see Thy righteous purposes executed in relation thereto. Let them know that it is Thy good pleasure to restore the kingdom unto Israel—raise up Jerusalem as its capital, *and constitute her people a distinct nation and government,* with David Thy servant, even a descendant from the loins of ancient David to be their king.

Let that nation or that people who shall take an active part in behalf of Abraham's children, and in the raising up of Jerusalem, find favor in Thy sight. Let not their enemies prevail against them, neither let pestilence or famine overcome them, but let the glory of Israel overshadow them, and the power of the Highest protect them; while that nation or kingdom that will not serve Thee in this glorious work must perish, according to Thy word—"yea, those nations shall be utterly wasted." (*Joseph Smith,* Documentary History of the Church, Vol. 4, pp. 456-457.)

Concerning his visit to Jerusalem, Elder Hyde reported:

I have found many Jews who listened with intense interest. The idea of the Jews being restored to Palestine is gaining ground in Europe almost every day. . . . Many of the Jews who are old go to this place to die, and many are coming from Europe into this eastern world. The great wheel is unquestionably in motion, and the word of the Almighty has declared that it shall roll. (Ibid, page 459.)

Elder Hyde further stated:

> In the early part of March last (1840), I retired to my
> bed one evening as usual, and while contemplating and
> enquiring out, in my own mind, the field of my ministerial
> labors for the then coming season, the vision of the Lord,
> like clouds of light, burst upon my view. The cities of
> London, Amsterdam, Constantinople, and Jerusalem all
> appeared in succession before me; and the Spirit said unto
> me, "Here are many of the children of Abraham whom I
> will gather to the land that I gave to their fathers, and here
> also is the field of your labors. (*Joseph S. Hyde*, Orson
> Hyde, p. 5.)

Prophets to be Raised Up to Judah

In March 1832, the Prophet Joseph Smith received
a revelation explaining part of the revelation of John:

> What is to be understood by the two witnesses, in the
> eleventh chapter of Revelations?
> They are two prophets that are to be raised up to the
> Jewish nation in the last days, at the time of the restoration,
> and to prophesy to the Jews after they are gathered and
> have built the city of Jerusalem in the land of their fathers.
> (Doctrine and Covenants 77:15.)

Therefore, as the Jews gather and rebuild the city
of Jerusalem in the land of their fathers, they have the
promise of the Lord that two prophets shall be raised up
unto them, "at the time of the restoration." No doubt
these prophets will be called and ordained and sent by
the First Presidency of The Church of Jesus Christ of
Latter-day Saints, for the Lord's house is a house of
order, and true prophets are never self sent—they must
be called and sent of God. That is why the Lord sent
Holy Prophets of old back to this earth to confer upon
Joseph Smith the keys of the authority they held, which
keys and authority are in the Church today.

Descendants of Judah to Flee to Jerusalem

In a revelation given through the Prophet Joseph
Smith at Hiram, Ohio, November 3, 1831, in response to

questions by Elders of the Church regarding the preaching of the gospel and the gathering of scattered Israel, the Lord said:

> Send forth the elders of my church unto the nations which are afar off; unto the islands of the sea; send forth unto foreign lands; call upon all nations, *first upon the Gentiles, and then upon the Jews.*
>
> And behold, and lo, this shall be their cry, and the voice of the Lord unto all people: Go ye forth unto the land of Zion, that the borders of my people may be enlarged, and that her stakes may be strengthened, and that Zion may go forth unto the regions round about.
>
> Yea, let the cry go forth among all people: Awake and arise and go forth to meet the Bridegroom; behold and lo, the Bridegroom cometh; go ye out to meet him. Prepare yourselves for the great day of the Lord.
>
> Watch, therefore, for ye know neither the day nor the hour.
>
> Let them, therefore, who are among the Gentiles flee unto Zion.
>
> *And let them who be of Judah flee unto Jerusalem,* unto the mountains of the Lord's house. (Doctrine and Covenants 133:8-13.)

In this revelation, the Lord makes plain the fact that the Gentiles would be gathered to Zion, and that the Jews would "flee unto Jerusalem."

After discussing this matter further in this revelation, the Lord adds:

> And he shall utter his voice out of Zion, and he shall speak from Jerusalem, and his voice shall be heard among all people. (Doctrine and Covenants 133:21.)

It is not difficult to understand how His voice would "be heard among all people," for we listen daily to voices over the radio coming from all nations of the earth. Then the Lord adds:

> And they also of the tribe of Judah, after their pain shall be sanctified in holiness before the Lord, to dwell in his presence day and night, forever and ever. (Doctrine and Covenants 133:35.)

What a glorious promise to the tribe of Judah, and remember, all His promises shall be fulfilled.

To our brethren, the seed of Judah, we call attention to the fact that all these Promises concerning the gathering of the Jews to the land of Jerusalem in this dispensation, as quoted from the Stick of Joseph, and from the revelations of the Lord to the "choice seer . . . like unto Moses", were translated, published, and given to the world over one hunderd and fifteen years ago, when such a thing would have seemed more than a remote possibility. And yet the prophets spoke in most definite terms—no uncertainty whatsover about their promises.

Prophets of Judah Predict the Gathering of the Jews

These things were also foretold by the prophets of Judah, as recorded in the Stick of Judah, the Old Testament, centuries ago.

These are the words of the Prophet Zechariah:

> Sing and rejoice, O daughter of Zion: for, lo, I come, and I will dwell in the midst of thee, saith the Lord.
> And many nations shall be joined to the Lord in that day, and shall be my people: and I will dwell in the midst of thee, and thou shalt know that the Lord of hosts hath sent me unto thee.
> *And the Lord shall inherit Judah his portion in the holy land, and shall choose Jerusalem again.* (Zechariah 2:10-12.)

Even though these words were spoken approximately three thousand years ago, there is no uncertainty about the promises given since all of God's works are known unto Him from the beginning—He works to a definite program.

Again, the Prophet Zechariah describes the restoration of Judah to her land of promise:

> The burden of the word of the Lord for Israel, saith the Lord, which stretcheth forth the heavens, and layeth the

foundation of the earth, and formeth the spirit of man within him.

Behold, *I will make Jerusalem a cup of trembling* unto all the people round about, when they shall be in the siege both *against Judah* and *against Jerusalem.*

And in that day will I make Jerusalem a burdensome stone for all people: all that burden themselves with it shall be cut in pieces, though all the people of the earth be gathered together against it.

In that day, saith the Lord, I will smite every horse with astonishment, and his rider with madness: *and I will open mine eyes upon the house of Judah,* and will smite every horse of the people with blindness.

And the *governors of Judah* shall say in their heart, The *inhabitants of Jerusalem* shall be my strength in the Lord of hosts their God.

In that day *will I make the governors of Judah* like an hearth of fire among the wood, and like a torch of fire in a sheaf; and they shall devour all the people round about, on the right hand and on the left: *and Jerusalem shall be inhabited again in her own place, even in Jerusalem.*

The Lord also shall save the tents of Judah first, that the glory of the house of David and the glory of the inhabitants of Jerusalem do not magnify themselves against Judah.

In that day shall the Lord defend the inhabitants of Jerusalem; and he that is feeble among them at that day shall be as David; and the house of David shall be as God, as the angel of the Lord before them.

And it shall come to pass in that day, that I will seek to destroy all the nations that come against Jerusalem.

And I will pour upon the *house of David,* and upon the *inhabitants of Jerusalem,* the spirit of grace and of supplications: *and they shall look upon me whom they have pierced,* and they shall mourn for him, as one mourneth for his only son, and shall be in bitterness for him, as one that is in bitterness for his firstborn. (Zechariah 12:1-10.)

A careful reading of the last verse quoted indicates that the Lord has definitely fixed the time for the fulfillment of these promises, "And they shall look upon me whom they have pierced," showing that it would be at the time of His *second coming.*

The Prophet Zechariah particularly refers to those

things which will happen at the time of the coming of our Lord:

> Behold, the day of the Lord cometh, and thy spoil shall be divided in the midst of thee.
> For I will gather all nations against Jerusalem to battle; and the city shall be taken, and the houses rifled, and the women ravished; and half of the city shall go forth into captivity, and the residue of the people shall not be cut off from the city.
> Then shall the Lord go forth, and fight against those nations, as when he fought in the day of battle. . . .
> *And the Lord shall be king over all the earth: in that day shall there be one Lord, and his name one. . . .*
> And men shall dwell in it, and there shall be no more utter destruction; but Jerusalem shall be safely inhabited. . . .
> And Judah also shall fight at Jerusalem; and the wealth of all the heathen round about shall be gathered together, gold, and silver, and apparel, in great abundance. (Zechariah 14:1-3, 9, 11, 14.)

The Prophet Jeremiah speaks a forthright prophecy concerning both Judah and Israel:

> In those days the house of Judah shall walk with the house of Israel, and they shall come together out of the land of the north to the land that I have given for an inheritance unto your fathers. (Jeremiah 3:18.)

It must be understood that when "the house of Judah shall walk with the house of Israel," that it will be at a time when the Lord would bring them together through the restoration of His gospel, as we have pointed out.

The word of the Lord to Jeremiah continues:

> The word that came to Jeremiah from the Lord, saying,
> Thus speaketh the Lord God of Israel, saying, Write thee all the words that I have spoken unto thee in a book.
> For, lo, the days come, saith the Lord, that I will bring again the captivity of my people Israel and Judah, saith the Lord: and I will cause them to return to the land that I gave to their fathers, and they shall possess it. . . .
> Therefore fear thou not, O my servant Jacob, saith the Lord; neither be dismayed, O Israel: for, lo, I will save thee from afar, and thy seed from the land of their captivity;

and Jacob shall return, and shall be in rest, and be quiet, and none shall make him afraid. . . .

Thus saith the Lord; Behold, I will bring again the captivity of Jacob's tents, and have mercy on his dwelling-places; *and the city shall be builded upon her own heap,* and the palace shall remain after the manner thereof. . . .

The fierce anger of the Lord shall not return, until he have done it, and until he have performed the intents of his heart: *in the latter days* ye shall consider it. (Jeremiah 30:1-3, 10, 18, 24.)

At the same time, saith the Lord, will I be the God of all the families of Israel, and they shall be my people. (Jeremiah 31:1.)

It is worthy of emphasis that "in the latter days . . saith the Lord, will I be the God of all the families of Israel, and they shall be my people."

The Prophet Jeremiah further declared how the Lord at that time would "make a new covenant with the house of Israel, and with the house of Judah":

Behold, the days come, saith the Lord, that *I will make a new covenant with the house of Israel, and with the house of Judah:*

Not according to the covenant that I made with their fathers in the day that I took them by the hand to bring them out of the land of Egypt; which my covenant they brake, although I was an husband unto them, saith the Lord:

But this shall be the covenant that I will make with the house of Israel; After those days, saith the Lord, I will put my law in their inward parts, and write it in their hearts; and will be their God, and they shall be my people.

And they shall teach no more every man his neighbour, and every man his brother, saying, Know the Lord: for they shall all know me, from the least of them unto the greatest of them, saith the Lord: for I will forgive their iniquity, and I will remember their sin no more. (Jeremiah 31:31-34.)

Jeremiah provides a vivid description of how the Lord will proceed to gather His people; "every man to his land":

Thus saith the Lord against all mine evil neighbours, that touch the inheritance which I have caused my people

Israel to inherit; Behold, I will pluck them out of their land, *and pluck out the house of Judah* from among them.

And it shall come to pass, after that I have plucked them out I will return, and have compassion on them, and will bring them again, every man to his heritage, and every man to his land. (Jeremiah 12:14-15.)

The Lord, through Jeremiah, reassures Judah concerning the gathering into the promised land from which they shall no more be driven:

And now therefore thus saith the Lord, the God of Israel, concerning this city, whereof ye say, It shall be delivered into the hand of the king of Babylon by the sword, and by the famine, and by the pestilence;

Behold, I will gather them out of all countries, whither I have driven them in mine anger, and in my fury, and in great wrath; and I will bring them again unto this place, and *I will cause them to dwell safely*:

And they shall be my people, and I will be their God:

And I will give them one heart, and one way, that they may fear me for ever, for the good of them, and of their children after them:

And *I will make an everlasting covenant with them,* that I will not turn away from them, to do them good; but I will put my fear in their hearts, that they shall not depart from me.

Yea, I will rejoice over them to do them good, and *I will plant them in this land assuredly with my whole heart and with my whole soul.*

For thus saith the Lord; Like as I have brought all this great evil upon this people, so will I bring upon them all the good that I have promised them.

And *fields shall be bought in this land, whereof ye say, It is desolate without man or beast;* it is given into the hand of the Chaldeans.

Men shall buy fields for money, and subscribe evidences, and seal them, and take witnesses in the land of Benjamin, and *in the places about Jerusalem,* and *in the cities of Judah,* and in the cities of the mountains, and in the cities of the valley, and in the cities of the south: for I will cause their captivity to return, saith the Lord. (Jeremiah 32:36-44.)

The Prophet Amos saw the day when Judah would return again and reconstruct the waste cities of their land:

> And I will bring again the captivity of my people of Israel, and they shall build the waste cities, and inhabit them; and they shall plant vineyards, and drink the wine thereof; they shall also make gardens, and eat the fruit of them.
>
> *And I will plant them upon their land, and they shall no more be pulled up out of their land which I have given them, saith the Lord thy God.* (Amos 9:14-15.)

The prophets often spoke of the House of Judah and the House of Israel in the same sense as the Prophet Amos in this quotation: "my people of Israel." This prophecy, can only have reference to the latter-day gathering when "they shall no more be pulled up out of their land."

The Prophet Isaiah referred to the time when the Lord would make new heavens and a new earth, at which time He would gather the seed of Israel from all nations:

> And they shall bring all your brethren for an offering unto the Lord out of all nations upon horses, and in chariots, and in litters, and upon mules, and upon swift beasts, *to my holy mountain Jerusalem,* saith the Lord, as the children of Israel bring an offering in a clean vessel into the house of the Lord.
>
> And I will also take of them for priests and for Levites, saith the Lord.
>
> For as *the new heavens and the new earth,* which I will make, shall remain before me, saith the Lord, so shall your seed and your name remain. (Isaiah 66:20-22.)

Mourning of the Jews to End

Isaiah makes it clear that in preparation for the second coming of the Messiah, the Jews would be gathered home to their own land, and that even the kings of the Gentiles would assist in this gathering:

> Arise, shine; for thy light is come, and the glory of the Lord is risen upon thee.

For, behold, the darkness shall cover the earth, and gross darkness the people: but the Lord shall arise upon thee, and his glory shall be seen upon thee.

And the Gentiles shall come to thy light, and kings to the brightness of thy rising.

Lift up thine eyes round about, and see: all they gather themselves together, they come to thee: thy sons shall come from far, and thy daughters shall be nursed at thy side.

Then thou shalt see, and flow together, and thine heart shall fear, and be enlarged; because the abundance of the sea shall be converted unto thee, the forces of the Gentiles shall come unto thee. . . .

Who are these that fly as a cloud, and as the doves to their windows?

Surely the isles shall wait for me, and the ships of Tarshish first, to bring thy sons from far, their silver and their gold with them, unto the name of the Lord thy God, and to the Holy One of Israel, because he hath glorified thee.

And the sons of strangers shall build up thy walls, *and their kings shall minister unto thee*: for in my wrath I smote thee, but in my favour have I had mercy on thee.

Therefore thy gates shall be open continually; they shall not be shut day nor night; that men may bring unto thee the forces of the Gentiles, and that their kings may be brought.

For the nation and kingdom that will not serve thee shall perish; yea, those nations shall be utterly wasted.

The glory of Lebanon shall come unto thee, the fir tree, the pine tree, and the box together, to beautify the place of my sanctuary; and I will make the place of my feet glorious.

The sons also of them that afflicted thee shall come bending unto thee; and all they that despised thee shall bow themselves down at the soles of thy feet; and they shall call thee, The city of the Lord, The Zion of the Holy One of Israel.

Whereas thou hast been forsaken and hated, so that no man went through thee, I will make thee an eternal excellency, a joy of many generations.

Thou shalt also suck the milk of the Gentiles, and shalt suck the breast of kings: and *thou shalt know that I the Lord am thy Saviour and thy Redeemer, the mighty One of Jacob.*

For brass I will bring gold, and for iron I will bring silver, and for wood brass, and for stones iron: I will also make thy officers peace, and thine exactors righteousness.

Violence shall no more be heard in thy land, wasting

nor destruction within thy borders; but thou shalt call thy walls Salvation, and thy gates Praise.

The sun shall be no more thy light by day; neither for brightness shall the moon give light unto thee: but the Lord shall be unto thee an everlasting light, and thy God thy glory.

Thy sun shall no more go down; neither shall thy moon withdraw itself: for the Lord shall be thine everlasting light, *and the days of thy mourning shall be ended.* (Isaiah 60:1-5, 8-20.)

New Nation of Israel Fulfills Prophecy

The Jews will understand how literally this prophecy has been in the course of fulfillment in the establishment of the Nation of Israel, and the help that has been given by the Gentile nations. The part that Great Britain played in the liberation of Palestine from Turkish rule is a matter of history which occurred during World War I, in a remarkable manner. The issuance of the Balfour Declaration on November 2, 1917 had great significance. The text reads:

> His Majesty's Government view with favor the establishment in Palestine of a National Home for the Jewish people, and will use their best endeavors to facilitate the achievement of this object, it being clearly understood that nothing shall be done which may prejudice the civil and religious rights of the existing non-Jewish communities in Palestine or the rights and political status enjoyed by Jews in any other country. (*The Autobiography of Chaim Weizmann*, Trial and Error, Harper and Brothers, publishers, page 208.)

On October 16, 1918, Colonel House, acting for President Woodrow Wilson of the United States, cabled the British Government, America's support of the substance of the declaration. This led to the approval of the League of Nations, and finally, after the close of World War II, to the recognition of a Jewish State in Palestine by the United States on May 14, 1948:

> This Government has been informed that a Jewish State has been proclaimed in Palestine, and recognition

has been requested by the Provisional Government itself.
The United States recognizes the Provisional Government
as the de facto authority of the new State of Israel. (Ibid,
page 478.)

A few days later Chaim Weizmann received word
while in New York that the Provisional Council of the
State of Israel had elected him as its president. When
Mr. Weizmann received word of this recognition on the
part of the United States, he wired the Provincial Council as follows:

My heartiest greetings to you and your colleagues in
this great hour. May God give you strength to carry out
the task which has been laid upon you and to overcome the
difficulties still ahead. Please accept and transmit the
following message to the Yishuv in my name: "On the
memorable day *when the Jewish State arises again after two
thousand years, I send expressions of love and admiration*
to all sections of the Yishuv and warmest greetings to its
Government now entering on its grave and inspiring responsibility. Am fully convinced that all who have and
will become citizens of the Jewish State will strive their
utmost to live up to the new opportunity which history has
bestowed upon them. It will be our destiny to create
institutions and values of a free community in the spirit
of the great traditions which have contributed so much
to the thought and spirit of mankind." (Ibid, p. 479.)

Thus the man who was to assume the responsibility
of becoming the first President of the "Jewish State"
acknowledged the fulfillment of the promises of the
prophets in these words: "on the memorable day when
the Jewish State arises again after two thousand years."

While there may be troublesome times ahead, even
as there have been up to the present time, yet Isaiah
promised that "they shall inherit the land for ever, the
branch of my planting, the work of my hands, that I may
be glorified." (Isaiah 60:21.)

The Prophet Isaiah further declared that which the

Lord gave him to see and understand with respect to
the redemption of the Promised Land:

> And they shall build the old wastes, they shall raise up
> the former desolations, and they shall repair the waste
> cities, the desolations of many generations.
>
> And strangers shall stand and feed your flocks, and the
> sons of the alien shall be your plowmen and your vine-
> dressers.
>
> But ye shall be named the Priests of the Lord: men
> shall call you the Ministers of our God: ye shall eat the
> riches of the Gentiles, and in their glory shall ye boast your-
> selves. (Isaiah 61:4-6.)

When Isaiah stated: "they shall repair the waste
cities, the desolations of many generations," he only
wrote history in advance as evidenced when Chaim
Weizmann acknowledged that in the establishment of
the Jewish State it is the first "after two thousand years."
Isaiah further declared the help that would be received
from the Gentiles, a fact which history has fully vindicated.

The Lord spoke through Isaiah: "I will direct their
work in truth, and I will make an everlasting covenant
with them." (Ibid, verse 8.)   The "everlasting covenant"
is the establishment of the "fulness of my everlasting
Gospel" among the Jews through the House of Joseph.
(See 3 Nephi 20:30.)

We may then look for the fulfillment of the promise
of the Lord through His Prophet Ezekiel:

> Thus saith the Lord God; In the day that I shall have
> cleansed you from all your iniquities I will also cause you to
> dwell in the cities, and the wastes shall be builded.
>
> And the desolate land shall be tilled, whereas it lay
> desolate in the sight of all that passed by.
>
> And they shall say, *This land that was desolate is become
> like the garden of Eden;* and the waste and desolate and
> ruined cities are become fenced, and are inhabited.
>
> Then the heathen that are left round about you shall
> know that I the Lord build the ruined places, and plant

that that was desolate: I the Lord have spoken it, and I will do it. (Ezekiel 36:33-36.)

The Messiah, the Jehovah of the Jews, even Jesus Christ the Son of God declared to His disciples nearly two thousand years ago how the descendants of Judah would be scattered and persecuted "until the times of the Gentiles be fulfilled:"

> But woe unto them that are with child, and to them that give suck, in those days! for there shall be great distress in the land, and wrath upon this people.
> And they shall fall by the edge of the sword, and shall be led away captive into all nations: *and Jerusalem shall be trodden down of the Gentiles, until the times of the Gentiles be fulfilled.* (St. Luke 21:23-24.)

Two thousand years are nearly ended—"the times of the Gentiles" are being fulfilled. The Jews are now being gathered back to their own land. The "Jewish State" has been acknowledged by the nations. The Jews have commenced to rebuild their cities and waste places—the nations and wealth of the Gentiles are greatly assisting them.

The next and most important matter is that they accept the "choice seer. . . . Like unto Moses," Joseph Smith, the prophet, whom the Lord has raised up through the loins of Joseph "in the latter days"; that they accept the "word of the Lord," which He has brought forth in the Stick of Joseph (the Book of Mormon); that they accept the revelations of the Lord to His prophet "like unto Moses" as contained in the Doctrine and Covenants; that they accept the Pearl of Great Price, containing the sacred writings of Abraham and the Visions of Moses as revealed to the Prophet Joseph Smith in June 1830.

God is calling to the Jews. He invites them into the fold of Christ. He wants them to come and take their place in The Church of Jesus Christ of Latter-day Saints, the Kingdom of God which "shall stand forever." (Daniel 2:44.)

CHAPTER 13

SUMMARY

End Known from the Beginning

We have endeavored to establish the fact that when a contractor has completed the erection of a building according to plans and specifications, he only brings into actual existence that which the architect has already created in his own mind. When the Lord created this earth, and placed man upon it, He only followed a plan He had previously worked out in His mind for the benefit of His children. He knew in advance how they would react to the circumstances and conditions they would be required to meet in mortality. He knew "the end from the beginning."

> Remember the former things of old: for I am God, and there is none else; I am God, and there is none like me,
> Declaring the end from the beginning, and from ancient times the things that are not yet done, saying, My counsel shall stand, and I will do all my pleasure: (Isaiah 46:9-10.)

The Lord Works Only Through His Prophets

The Lord's way of making known to His children what His purposes and plans are, is through His prophets. He gave His children prophets from time to time, unto whom He revealed His mind and will:

> Surely the Lord God will do nothing, but he revealeth his secret unto his servants the prophets. (Amos 3:7.)

Purposes of the Lord Fail Not

The Apostle Peter understood the importance of the word of prophecy to guide us:

> We have also a more sure word of prophecy; whereunto ye do well that ye take heed, as unto a light that

shineth in a dark place, until the day dawn, and the day
star arise in your hearts:

Knowing this first, that no prophecy of the scripture is
of any private interpretation.

For the prophecy came not in old time by the will of
man: but holy men of God spake as they were moved by the
Holy Ghost. (II Peter 1:19-21.)

Therefore, when we have the Stick of Judah (Holy
Bible), and the Stick of Joseph (Book of Mormon), we
"do well" that we "take heed, as unto a light that shineth
in a dark place, until the day dawn, and the day star
arise in your hearts."

The Prophet Mormon gave us to understand that all
the promises of the Lord would be fulfilled:

For the eternal purposes of the Lord shall roll on, *until
all his promises shall be fulfilled.* (Mormon 8:22.)

In a revelation to the Prophet Joseph Smith given
at Hiram, Ohio, February 16, 1832, the Lord gave the
prophet to understand that "his purposes fail not:"

Hear, O ye heavens, and give ear, O earth, and rejoice
ye inhabitants thereof, for the Lord is God, and beside him
there is no Savior.

Great is his wisdom, marvelous are his ways, and the
extent of his doings none can find out.

*His purposes fail not, neither are there any who can
stay his hand.*

From eternity to eternity he is the same, and his years
never fail. (Doctrine and Covenants 76:1-4.)

In light of these declarations, it is not difficult to
understand how the Prophet Isaiah could declare, one
hundred and seventy years in advance, the destruction
of the great city Babylon, the greatest city in all the world
at that time, and declare in positive terms that it should
never be rebuilt. (See Isaiah 13:19-22.) And it never
has been rebuilt. While at or near the same time, being
over seven hundred years before the destruction of
Jerusalem, and nearly twenty-seven hundred years in

advance, he declared in equally positive terms that Jerusalem would be rebuilt together with her cities and waste places. (See Isaiah 61:4.)

It was because the Prophet Isaiah understood the importance of the word of God when given through His prophets, that he declared:

> The grass withereth, the flower fadeth: but the word of our God shall stand for ever. (Isaiah 40:8.)

Since, "For the eternal purposes of the Lord shall roll on, until all his promises shall be fulfilled," (Mormon 8:22) the promises of the Lord through His prophets are but history in reverse.

Summary of the Promises of the Lord to Israel

We shall, therefore, summarize the promises of the Lord unto the house of Israel:

> For thou art an holy people unto the Lord thy God: the Lord thy God hath chosen thee to be a special people unto himself, above all people that are upon the face of the earth. (Deuteronomy 7:6.)

Inasmuch as the Lord chose Israel "to be a special people unto himself," the reason for such preferment should be understood. The Lord made this reason plain in the covenant He made with Abraham, Isaac, and Jacob:

> And the Lord said, Shall I hide from Abraham that thing which I do;
> Seeing that Abraham shall surely become a great and mighty nation, and *all the nations of the earth shall be blessed in him?* (Genesis 18:17-18.)

With the promises of the Lord, therefore, came unto Israel the responsibility to become a blessing to all the nations of the earth.

This responsibility has been discharged, at least in part, through the prophets of Israel, both of Judah and

Joseph. We have the word of the Lord as recorded in the Stick of Joseph; in the Doctrine and Covenants; and in the Pearl of Great Price. These three latter volumes of scripture have come to us through the "choice seer . . . like unto Moses", even Joseph Smith, the prophet of "the latter days."

Of even greater importance in fulfilling this responsibility, as promised unto Abraham that "all the nations of the earth shall be blessed in him," (Genesis 18:18), was the coming of the Messiah, the Jehovah of the Jews, the giver of the law unto Moses, even Jesus Christ, the Son of God, the Redeemer of the world. Jesus Christ placed the gift of eternal life and resurrection from the grave within reach of all our Father's children who ever have lived, or who ever shall live, upon the face of the earth: "For as in Adam all die, even so in Christ shall all be made alive." (I Corinthians 15:22.)

The Jehovah of the Jews gave unto the seed of Judah His gospel, with the keys and powers of the Holy Priesthood, saying:

> Verily I say unto you, Whatsoever ye shall bind on earth shall be bound in heaven: and whatsoever ye shall loose on earth shall be loosed in heaven. (Matthew 18:18.)

The Last Shall be First and the First Shall be Last

The Lord inspired His servants, the prophets and apostles, to inform the people that after He would come first to the Jews and then to the Gentiles, He would then manifest Himself first to the Gentiles and then to the Jews:

> And the time cometh that he shall manifest himself unto all nations, both unto the Jews and also unto the Gentiles; and after he has manifested himself unto the Jews and also unto the Gentiles, then he shall manifest himself unto the Gentiles and also unto the Jews, and the last shall be first, and the first shall be last. (I Nephi 13:42.)

A Falling Away Foretold

The Apostle Paul predicted a falling away from the truth:

> For the time will come when they will not endure sound doctrine; but after their own lusts shall they heap to themselves teachers, having itching ears;
> And they shall turn away their ears from the truth, and shall be turned unto fables. (II Timothy 4:3-4.)

It is easy to understand that when the conditions mentioned by Apostle Paul came to pass, there would be many varieties of churches. The people would not "endure sound doctrine, but after their own lusts shall they heap to themselves teachers, having itching ears, and they shall turn away their ears from the truth, and shall be turned unto fables." Had they not turned away their ears from the truth, there never would have been more than one church, for God is not divided, neither is His truth.

The prophets of Judah were also given to see this time when the Lord would cease to send prophets among His people:

> Behold, the days come, saith the Lord God, that I will send a famine in the land, not a famine of bread, nor a thirst for water, but of hearing the words of the Lord:
> And they shall wander from sea to sea, and from the north even to the east, they shall run to and fro to seek the word of the Lord, and shall not find it. (Amos 8:11-12.)

Thus, both the House of Joseph and the House of Judah would be left without the leadership of true prophets sent of God:

> Thus saith the Lord concerning the prophets that make my people err, that bite with their teeth, and cry, Peace; and he that putteth not into their mouths, they even prepare war against him.
> Therefore night shall be unto you, that ye shall not have a vision; and it shall be dark unto you, that ye shall

not divine; and the sun shall go down over the prophets, and the day shall be dark over them.

Then shall the seers be ashamed, and the diviners confounded: yea, they shall all cover their lips; for there is no answer of God. . . .

The heads thereof judge for reward, and the priests thereof teach for hire, and the prophets thereof divine for money: yet will they lean upon the Lord, and say, Is not the Lord among us? none evil can come upon us. (Micah 3:5-7, 11.)

It is evident that the Lord permitted His prophets to see the time when there would be no divine leadership in the earth, either in the House of Judah or in the House of Joseph.

A Marvelous Work and a Wonder to Come Forth

Because of these apostate conditions, and the lack of divine leadership when there would be "no answer of God" the Lord decreed that He would again proceed to set up His work upon the earth:

Wherefore the Lord said, Forasmuch as this people draw near me with their mouth, and with their lips do honour me, but have removed their heart far from me, and their fear toward me is taught by the precept of men:

Therefore, behold, I will proceed to do a marvellous work among this people, even a marvellous work and a wonder: for the wisdom of their wise men shall perish, and the understanding of their prudent men shall be hid. (Isaiah 29:13-14.)

In light of such a declaration, how can one who believes that Isaiah was a prophet *of God*, doubt that the Lord would proceed to do this "marvelous work and a wonder"—so marvelous, in fact, that "the wisdom of their wise men shall perish, and the understanding of their prudent men shall be hid"?

The God of Heaven to Set Up His Kingdom

Daniel, the prophet, was given to see our day and to see the kingdom which the "God of Heaven" would

set up on the earth which would subdue all other kingdoms:

> Daniel answered in the presence of the king, and said,
> The secret which the king hath demanded cannot the wise
> men, the astrologers, the magicians, the soothsayers, shew
> unto the king;
> But there is a God in heaven that revealeth secrets, and
> maketh known to the king Nebuchadnezzar *what shall be
> in the latter days.* Thy dream, and the visions of thy head
> upon thy bed, are these;
> As for thee, O king, thy thoughts came into thy mind
> upon thy bed, *what should come to pass hereafter:* and he
> that revealeth secrets maketh known to thee what shall come
> to pass. . . .
> Thou sawest till that a stone was cut out without hands,
> which smote the image upon his feet that were of iron and
> clay, and brake them to pieces.
> Then was the iron, the clay, the brass, the silver, and the
> gold, broken to pieces together, and became like the chaff
> of the summer threshingfloors; and the wind carried them
> away, that no place was found for them: *and the stone that
> smote the image became a great mountain, and filled the
> whole earth.* (Daniel 2:27-29, 34-35.)

What a great destiny was decreed for the Lord's
"latter day" Kingdom. This was to be the Kingdom of
God as the Prophet Daniel further described:

> And in the days of these kings shall the God of heaven
> set up a kingdom, which shall never be destroyed: and the
> kingdom shall not be left to other people, but it shall break
> in pieces and consume all these kingdoms, and it shall
> stand for ever. (Daniel 2:44.)

Daniel further beheld the glory and destiny of this
kingdom:

> I saw in the night visions, and, behold, one like the
> Son of man came with the clouds of heaven, and came to
> the Ancient of days, and they brought him near before him.
> And there was given him dominion, and glory, and a
> kingdom, that all people, nations, and languages, should
> serve him: his dominion is an everlasting dominion, which
> shall not pass away, and his kingdom that which shall not
> be destroyed. (Daniel 7:13-14.)

Gospel Sent First to the Gentiles and
Then to the Jews

With the setting up of this Kingdom in the earth came the responsibility to the entire House of Israel to carry its message of truth to all peoples of all nations, inviting them to join in establishing the Kingdom in the earth preparatory to His coming to claim the Kingdom for Himself. In what other way could "all people, nations, and languages" serve Him? (See Daniel 7:14.)

The Lord directed the Prophet Joseph Smith as to how this great responsibility should be discharged:

> Send forth the elders of my church unto the nations which are afar off; unto the islands of the sea; send forth unto foreign lands; call upon all nations, *first upon the Gentiles, and then upon the Jews.* (Doctrine and Covenants 133:8.)

Prophecies Concerning the Latter Days and
Their Fulfillment

Knowing the end from the beginning, the Lord revealed unto Lehi, a Nephite prophet, the promise He made to Joseph, who was sold into Egypt, that in the latter days He would raise up a "choice seer . . . like unto Moses" to accomplish the very thing He revealed unto Daniel:

> Wherefore, Joseph truly saw our day. And he obtained a promise of the Lord, that out of the fruit of his loins the Lord God would raise up a righteous branch unto the house of Israel; not the Messiah, but a branch which was to be broken off, nevertheless, to be remembered in the covenants of the Lord that the Messiah should be made manifest unto them *in the latter days,* in the spirit of power, unto the bringing of them out of darkness unto light—yea, out of hidden darkness and out of captivity unto freedom.
>
> For Joseph truly testified, saying: A seer shall the Lord my God raise up, who shall be a choice seer unto the fruit of my loins.
>
> Yea, Joseph truly said: Thus saith the Lord unto me: *A choice seer* will I raise up out of the fruit of thy loins;

and he shall be esteemed highly among the fruit of thy loins. And unto him will I give commandment that he shall do a work for the fruit of thy loins, his brethren, which shall be of great worth unto them, even to the bringing of them to the knowledge of the covenants which I have made with thy fathers.

And I will give unto him a commandment that he shall do none other work, save the work which I shall command him. *And I will make him great in mine eyes; for he shall do my work.*

And he shall be great like unto Moses, whom I have said I would raise up unto you, to deliver my people, O house of Israel.

And Moses will I raise up, to deliver thy people out of the land of Egypt.

But a seer will I raise up out of the fruit of thy loins; and unto him will I give power to bring forth my word unto the seed of thy loins—and not to the bringing forth my word only, saith the Lord, but to the convincing them of my word, which shall have already gone forth among them.

Wherefore, the fruit of thy loins shall write; and the fruit of the loins of Judah shall write; and that which shall be written by the fruit of thy loins, and also that which shall be written by the fruit of the loins of Judah, shall grow together, unto the confounding of false doctrines and laying down of contentions, and establishing peace among the fruit of thy loins, and bringing them to the knowledge of their fathers *in the latter days,* and also to the knowledge of my covenants, saith the Lord.

And out of weakness he shall be made strong, in that day when my work shall commence among all my people, unto the restoring thee, O house of Israel, saith the Lord.

And thus prophesied Joseph, saying: Behold, that seer will the Lord bless; and they that seek to destroy him shall be confounded; for this promise, which I have obtained of the Lord, of the fruit of my loins, shall be fulfilled. Behold, I am sure of the fulfilling of this promise;

And his name shall be called after me; and it shall be after the name of his father. And he shall be like unto me; *for the thing, which the Lord shall bring forth by his hand, by the power of the Lord shall bring my people unto salvation.* (2 Nephi 3:5-15.)

With the calling of such a prophet, the Lord was prepared to bring into fulfillment many promises made through His prophets concerning His Kingdom in the latter days. For instance: "Behold, the days come, saith the Lord, that I will make a new covenant with the house of Israel, and with the house of Judah:" (Jeremiah 31:31.) Peter promised a "restitution of all things, which God hath spoken by the mouth of all his holy prophets since the world began," before Christ's second coming. (See Acts 3:19-21.)

In fulfillment of these predictions, we remind the reader that the Father and His Son, Jesus Christ, did not only visit the new prophet of this dispensation in the spring of 1820, but the Lord sent the Angel Moroni, a former prophet of the Nephites, who had lived in the land of America about four hundred years A.D., who delivered to Joseph Smith the gold plates upon which was engraven the Stick of Joseph, together with the Urim and Thummim by which, with the power of God, he was able to translate the records. The translated record, The Book of Mormon, is the Stick of Joseph.

May 15, 1829, God sent John the Baptist to the earth and he conferred upon Joseph Smith and Oliver Cowdery the Aaronic Priesthood, giving them authority to baptive by immersion for the remission of sins.

About one month later, Joseph Smith and Oliver Cowdery, as promised by John the Baptist, were visited by the Apostles Peter, James and John who ordained them to the Melchizedek Priesthood, and conferred upon them the keys of this High Priesthood.

April 3, 1836, following the dedication of the Kirtland Temple, in the State of Ohio, the Prophet Joseph Smith recorded the experiences he and Oliver Cowdery enjoyed together:

> The veil was taken from our minds, and the eyes of our understanding were opened.
> *We saw the Lord standing upon the breastwork of the pulpit*, before us; and under his feet was a paved work of pure gold, in color like amber.

His eyes were as a flame of fire; the hair of his head was white like the pure snow; his countenance shone above the brightness of the sun; and his voice was as the sound of the rushing of great waters, even the voice of Jehovah, saying:

I am the first and the last; I am he who liveth, I am he who was slain; I am your advocate with the Father. . . .

After this vision closed, the heavens were again opened unto us; and *Moses appeared before us,* and committed unto us the keys of the gathering of Israel from the four parts of the earth, and the leading of the ten tribes from the land of the north.

After this, *Elias appeared,* and committed the dispensation of the gospel of Abraham, saying that in us and our seed all generations after us should be blessed.

After this vision had closed, another great and glorious vision burst upon us; for *Elijah the prophet,* who was taken to heaven without tasting death, *stood before us,* and said:

Behold, the time has fully come, which was spoken of by the mouth of Malachi—testifying that he (Elijah) should be sent, before the great and dreadful day of the Lord come—

To turn the hearts of the fathers to the children, and the children to the fathers, lest the whole earth be smitten with a curse—

Therefore, the keys of this dispensation are committed into your hands; and by this ye may know that the great and dreadful day of the Lord is near, even at the doors. (Doctrine and Covenants 110:1-4, 11-16.)

The appearance of the Father and His Son, Jesus Christ; the Angel Moroni; John the Baptist; Peter, James and John; the Savior, Moses, Elias and Elijah, gives meaning and fulfillment to the words of the Apostle Peter:

And he shall send Jesus Christ, which before was preached unto you:

Whom the heaven must receive until the times of restitution of all things, which God hath spoken by the mouth of all his holy prophets since the world began. (Acts 3:20-21.)

Their visits also fulfill the words of the Apostle John declaring what the Lord permitted him to behold when banished upon the Isle of Patmos:

> After this I looked, and, behold, a door was opened in heaven: and the first voice which I heard was as it were of a trumpet talking with me; which said, Come hither, *and I will shew thee things which must be hereafter.* . . .
>
> And I saw another angel fly in the midst of heaven, having the everlasting gospel to preach unto them that dwell on the earth, and to every nation, and kindred, and tongue, and people,
>
> Saying with a loud voice, Fear God, and give glory to him: for the hour of his judgment is come: and worship him that made heaven, and earth, and the sea, and the fountains of waters. (Revelations 4:1; 14:6-7.)

There can only be one gospel acceptable unto the Lord, and that is "the everlasting gospel." If the gospel were upon the earth, there certainly would have been no need for an angel to bring it back to this earth that it may be preached to "every nation, and kindred, and tongue, and people."

The Dispensation of the Fullness of Times

The Apostle Paul declared what the Lord had made known unto him concerning the work of final preparation for the dispensation in which we now live:

> Having made known unto us the mystery of his will, according to his good pleasure which he hath purposed in himself:
>
> That in *the dispensation of the fulness of times* he might gather together in one all things in Christ, both which are in heaven, and which are on earth; even in him: (Ephesians 1:9-10.)

It is evident that it would be through the restoration of His everlasting gospel in the latter days, that all things might be gathered together in Christ.

Israel No Longer to be Two Nations

From the Stick of Joseph, we learn that America was given to Joseph's posterity; that it is a land "choice above all other lands;" that upon it is to be established the New Jerusalem in this dispensation; and that the House of Joseph will be established in this land in this dispensation, while the House of Judah will be gathered to the land of Palestine to rebuild her waste places and to rebuild the city of Jerusalem.

There is much valuable information Judah may obtain from the Stick of Joseph. Judah and Joseph are brothers, and the Lord has promised to bring them together in these latter days, even as he has brought their two records together, that they shall no longer be two nations:

> At the same time, saith the Lord, will I be the God of all the families of Israel, and they shall be my people. . . .
> Behold, the days come, saith the Lord, that I will make a new covenant with the house of Israel, and with the house of Judah: (Jeremiah 31:1, 31.)

> And I will make them one nation in the land upon the mountains of Israel; and one king shall be king to them all: and they shall be no more two nations, neither shall they be divided into two kingdoms any more at all: (Ezekiel 37:22.)

Knowledge From the Stick of Joseph

The Stick of Joseph removes all doubt as to the fact that Jesus Christ was the promised Messiah; that His coming was made so plain through the Nephite prophets that there is no possible chance for misunderstanding, particularly after reading the account of Christ's visit to the Nephites following his crucifixion, resurrection and ascension.

Jesus the Giver of the Law of Moses

From the Stick of Joseph we also learn that Jesus Christ was the giver of the law of Moses, therefore, the Jehovah of the Jews:

> Behold, *I am he that gave the law,* and I am he who covenanted with my people Israel; therefore, the law in me is fulfilled, for I have come to fulfill the law; therefore it hath an end. (3 Nephi 15:5.)

Christ's Message to the Descendants of Judah

The Messiah spoke to the Jews through the Stick of Joseph when He visited the Nephites in this land of America:

> And I will remember the covenant which I have made with my people; and I have covenanted with them that I would gather them together in mine own due time, that I would give unto them again the land of their fathers for their inheritance, *which is the land of Jerusalem,* which is the promised land unto them forever, saith the Father.
> And it shall come to pass that the time cometh, *when the fulness of my gospel shall be preached unto them;*
> *And they shall believe in me, that I am Jesus Christ, the Son of God, and shall pray unto the Father in my name.*
> Then shall their watchmen lift up their voice, and with the voice together shall they sing; for they shall see eye to eye.
> Then will the Father *gather them together again,* and *give unto them Jerusalem* for the land of their inheritance.
> Then shall they break forth into joy—Sing together, *ye waste places of Jerusalem;* for the Father hath comforted his people, he hath redeemed Jerusalem.
> The Father hath made bare his holy arm in the eyes of all the nations; and all the ends of the earth shall see the salvation of the Father; *and the Father and I are one.* (3 Nephi 20:29-35.)

This is a definite promise that Judah will be gathered to the land of Jerusalem, "which is the promised land unto them forever."

We quote further from the words of Jesus :

> And as surely as the Lord liveth, will he gather in from the four quarters of the earth all the remnant of the seed of Jacob, who are scattered abroad upon all the face of the earth.
>
> And as he hath covenanted with all the house of Jacob, even so shall the covenant wherewith he hath covenanted with the house of Jacob be fulfilled in his own due time, unto the restoring all the house of Jacob unto the knowledge of the covenant that he hath covenanted with them.
>
> And then shall they know their Redeemer, who is Jesus Christ, the Son of God; and *then shall they be gathered in from the four quarters of the earth unto their own lands, from whence they have been dispersed;* yea, as the Lord liveth so shall it be. Amen. (3 Nephi 5:24-26.)

Jesus made it plain that Judah would be gathered to her own promised land in the latter days when they are willing to accept Him as the Son of God. It should be remembered that these statements were made nearly two thousand years ago, and were published to the world through the translation of the Stick of Joseph, (The Book of Mormon) in 1829.

Remnants of Israel to be Grafted

The Prophet Lehi was shown many things pertaining to the house of Israel:

> And after the house of Israel should be scattered they should be gathered together again; or, in fine, *after the Gentiles had received the fulness of the Gospel,* the natural branches of the olive-tree, or the remnants of the house of Israel,*should be grafted in,* or come to the knowledge of the true Messiah, their Lord and their Redeemer. (I Nephi 10:14.)

This was shown to Lehi nearly six hundred years before the birth of Jesus Christ or nearly twenty-six hundred years ago, and yet these words have been fulfilled to the very letter. Now the Gentiles are offering the "fulness of the Gospel" to the Jews. As they accept, they shall "be grafted in" to the Kingdom which the Lord has established in the earth in this dispensation, through the Gentiles.

The Nephite Prophet Jacob spoke of the covenant the Lord made with the House of Israel, and then with the House of Judah:

> And now, my beloved brethren, I have read these things that ye might know concerning the covenants of the Lord that he has covenanted with all the house of Israel—
>
> That *he has spoken unto the Jews*, by the mouth of his holy prophets, even from the beginning down, from generation to generation, *until the time comes that they shall be restored to the true church and fold of God;* when they shall be gathered home to the lands of their inheritance, and shall be established in all their lands of promise. (2 Nephi 9:1-2.)

Judah to Believe in Christ

The Prophet Nephi foretold the time when the Jews in their scattered condition would begin to believe in Christ:

> And it shall come to pass that the Jews which are scattered also shall begin to believe in Christ; and they shall begin to gather in upon the face of the land; and as many as shall believe in Christ shall also become a delightsome people. (2 Nephi 30:7.)

The Prophet Nephi beheld the destruction of Jerusalem, after the Messiah had risen from the dead, and the consequent scattering of the Jews among all nations, and that after they had been scourged from generation to generation, "until they shall be persuaded to believe in Christ," the Lord would "set his hand again the second time to restore his people from their lost and fallen state:"

> And behold it shall come to pass that after the Messiah hath risen from the dead, and hath manifested himself unto his people, unto as many as will believe on his name, behold, Jerusalem shall be destroyed again; for wo unto them that fight against God and the people of his church.

Wherefore, the Jews shall be scattered among all nations; yea, and also Babylon shall be destroyed; wherefore, the Jews shall be scattered by other nations.

And after they have been scattered, and the Lord God hath scourged them by other nations for the space of many generations, yea, even down from generation to generation *until they shall be persuaded to believe in Christ, the Son of God, and the atonement*, which is infinite for all mankind—and when that day shall come that they shall believe in Christ, and worship the Father in his name, with pure hearts and clean hands, *and look not forward any more for another Messiah*, then, at that time, the day will come that it must needs be expedient that they should believe these things.

And the Lord will set his hand again the second time to restore his people from their lost and fallen state. *Wherefore, he will proceed to do a marvelous work and a wonder among the children of men.*

Wherefore, he shall bring forth his words unto them, which words shall judge them at the last day, for they shall be given them for the purpose of convincing them of the true Messiah, who was rejected by them; and unto the convincing of them that they need not look forward any more for a Messiah to come, for there should not any come, save it should be a false Messiah which should deceive the people; *for there is save one Messiah spoken of by the prophets, and that Messiah is he who should be rejected of the Jews.* (2 Nephi 25:14-18.)

The Nephite Prophet Jacob spoke of the Jews and their rejection of the Messiah when He would come among them at Jerusalem, and of the renewal of the covenant made with their fathers:

But because of priestcrafts and iniquities, they at Jerusalem will stiffen their necks against him, that he be crucified.

Wherefore, because of their iniquities, destructions, famines, pestilences, and bloodshed shall come upon them; and they who shall not be destroyed shall be scattered among all nations.

But behold, thus saith the Lord God: When the day cometh that they shall believe in me, *that I am Christ,* then have I covenanted with their fathers that they shall be restored in the flesh, upon the earth, unto the lands of their inheritance. (2 Nephi 10:5-7.)

In the Prophet Mormon's abridgment of the records of the Nephite prophets, he wrote:

> Now these things are written unto the remnant of the house of Jacob; and they are written after this manner, because it is known of God that wickedness will not bring them forth unto them; and they are to be hid up unto the Lord that they may come forth in his own due time.
>
> And this is the commandment which I have received; and behold, they shall come forth according to the commandment of the Lord, when he shall see fit, in his wisdom.
>
> *And behold, they shall go unto the unbelieving of the Jews;* and for this intent shall they go—*that they may be persuaded that Jesus is the Christ, the Son of the living God;* that the Father may bring about, through his most Beloved, his great and eternal purpose, *in restoring the Jews,* or all the house of Israel, to the land of their inheritance, which the Lord their God hath given them, unto the fulfilling of his covenant: (Mormon 5:12-14.)

The Jews should be grateful that in the providences of the Lord He caused this record "to be hid up" to come forth "in his own due time . . . to go unto the unbelieving of the Jews;" for the glorious purpose of persuading them that "Jesus is the Christ, the Son of the living God."

In a revelation given to the Prophet Joseph Smith at Kirtland, Ohio, March 7, 1831, the Lord spoke of His second coming in these words:

> And then shall *the Jews* look upon me and say: What are these wounds in thine hands and in thy feet?
>
> Then shall they know that I am the Lord; for I will say unto them: *These wounds are the wounds with which I was wounded in the house of my friends.* I am he who was lifted up. I am Jesus that was crucified. I am the Son of God.
>
> And then shall they weep because of their iniquities; then shall they lament because they persecuted their king. (Doctrine and Covenants 45:51-53.)

Notwithstanding the things Jesus suffered at the hands of Judah, He still called them "my friends." Great are His promises to them when they are persuaded to accept Him as their Messiah.

In a revelation to the Prophet Joseph Smith given at Hiram, Ohio, November 3, 1831, the Lord spoke of the gathering of the ten tribes from the land of the north with their prophets to receive their blessings at the hands of the children of Ephraim, then added:

> And they shall be filled with songs of everlasting joy.
>
> Behold, this is the blessing of the everlasting God upon the tribes of Israel, and the richer blessing upon the head of Ephraim and his fellows:
>
> *And they also of the tribe of Judah,* after their pain shall be sanctified in holiness before the Lord, to dwell in his presence day and night, forever and ever. (Doctrine and Covenants 133:33-35.)

From all these prophecies, it is evident that the Lord stands ready to keep the covenants and promises made with their fathers, if the children of Judah will but turn unto Him and acknowledge Him as their Savior and Redeemer, the Son of God, the Holy One of Israel.

Of the time when the Jews shall "be restored to the true church and fold of God," the Nephite Prophet Jacob declared:

> And now, my beloved brethren, I have read these things that ye might know concerning the covenants of the Lord that he has covenanted with all the house of Israel—
>
> That he has spoken unto the Jews, by the mouth of his holy prophets, even from the beginning down, from generation to generation, *until the time comes that they shall be restored to the true church and fold of God; when they* shall be gathered home to the lands of their inheritance, and shall be established in all their lands of promise. (2 Nephi 9:1-2.)

The Lord to Fight Judah's Battles

The Lord has even declared that He would fight their battles, for He has said, through His Prophet Zechariah:

> Behold, I will make Jerusalem a cup of trembling unto all the people round about, when they shall be in the seige both against Judah and against Jerusalem.
>
> And in that day will I make Jerusalem a burdensome stone for all people: all that burden themselves with it shall be cut in pieces, though all the people of the earth be gathered together against it. . . .
>
> *In that day shall the Lord defend the inhabitants of Jerusalem;* and he that is feeble among them at that day shall be as David; and the house of David shall be as God, as the angel of the Lord before them.
>
> And it shall come to pass in that day, that I will seek to destroy all the nations that come against Jerusalem.
>
> And I will pour upon the house of David, and upon the inhabitants of Jerusalem, the spirit of grace and of supplications: and *they shall look upon me whom they have pierced*, and they shall mourn for him, as one mourneth for his only son, and shall be in bitterness for him, as one that is in bitterness for his firstborn. (Zechariah 12:2-3, 8-10.)

This clearly has reference to the events which shall precede the second coming of the Messiah, when the Jews shall again be gathered to Jerusalem, for the Lord said: "they shall look upon me whom they have pierced."

Of interest is the following quotation from an article by Arthur U. Michelson which was published in "The Jewish Hope," Issue No. 9, Vol. 22, September, 1950. The article suggests how the Lord may, even now, be fulfilling the prophecy of Zechariah, "In that day shall the Lord defend the inhabitants of Jerusalem . . .":

> On my recent trip to Palestine I saw with my own eyes how God's prophecy is being fulfilled. In Gen. 17:8 God promised Abraham that he would give this land to him and his seed for an everlasting possession. The Jews waited

2,500 years for the fulfillment of this promise. **After World War II**, England, which had mandatory power over Palestine, suddenly gave it up and the Jews marched in. This was marvelous, for Palestine was one of the strongest fortresses England had in the Mediterranean Sea. Many contend today that the day of miracles is past, and that God does not intervene any more on behalf of His people, but they have learned through the events in Israel that they were mistaken.

It was marvelous what God did for the Jews, especially in Jerusalem, during the fighting with the Arabs. Though quite a few months had passed since the victory of Israel's army in Israel, they were still talking about what had taken place. Everywhere I went I heard how God had intervened in their behalf, and how He helped them to win the battles. One of the officials told me how much the Jews had to suffer. They had hardly anything with which to resist the heavy attacks of the Arabs, who were well organized and equipped with the latest weapons. Besides, they had neither food nor water because all their supplies were cut off.

The Arabs, who had a great army in strong position, were determined to destroy the Jews, while the Jews were few in number, without any arms and ammunition. The two or three guns they possessed had to be rushed from one point to another, to give the Arabs the impression that they had many of them. The Jews had quite a few tin cans which they beat as they shot the guns, giving the impression of many shots. But as the pressure was too great, they were unable to hold the lines any longer and finally decided to give up the city. At this critical moment God showed them that He was on their side, for He performed one of the greatest miracles that ever happened. The Arabs suddenly threw down their arms and surrendered. When their delegation appeared with the white flag, they asked, "Where are the three men that led you, and where are all the troops we saw?" The Jews told them that they did not know anything of the three men, for this group was their entire force. *The Arabs said that they saw three persons with long beards and flowing white robes, who warned them not to fight any longer, otherwise they would all be killed.* They became so frightened that they decided to give up. What an encouragement this was for the Jews, who realized that God was fighting for them.

The Lord moves in a mysterious way His wonders to perform. The Jews did not understand who the "three persons with long beards and flowing white robes" were who warned the Arabs "not to fight any longer, otherwise they would all be killed." The Stick of Joseph may throw some light upon this matter.

When Jesus Christ appeared to the Nephites in America, following His resurrection, He organized His Church among them, calling and appointing twelve disciples, as He had done in Jerusalem. Before leaving them, He permitted each of them to express his heart's desire:

> And it came to pass when Jesus had said these words, he spake unto his disciples, one by one, saying unto them: What is it that ye desire of me, after that I am gone to the Father?
>
> And they all spake, save it were three, saying: We desire that after we have lived unto the age of man, that our ministry, wherein thou hast called us, may have an end, that we may speedily come unto thee in thy kingdom.
>
> And he said unto them: Blessed are ye because ye desired this thing of me; therefore, after that ye are seventy and two years old ye shall come unto me in my kingdom; and with me ye shall find rest.
>
> And when he had spoken unto them, *he turned himself unto the three,* and said unto them: What will ye that I should do unto you, when I am gone unto the Father?
>
> And they sorrowed in their hearts, for they durst not speak unto him the thing which they desired.
>
> And he said unto them: *Behold, I know your thoughts, and ye have desired the thing which John, my beloved, who was with me in my ministry, before that I was lifted up by the Jews, desired of me.*
>
> Therefore, more blessed are ye, for *ye shall never taste of death;* but ye shall live to behold all the doings of the Father unto the children of men, even until all things shall be fulfilled according to the will of the Father, when I shall come in my glory with the powers of heaven.
>
> And ye shall never endure the pains of death, but when I shall come in my glory ye shall be changed in the twinkling of an eye from mortality to immortality; and then shall ye be blessed in the kingdom of my Father.
>
> And again, ye shall not have pain while ye shall dwell in the flesh, neither sorrow save it be for the sins of **the**

world; and all this will I do because of the thing which ye
have desired of me, for *ye have desired that ye might bring
the souls of men unto me, while the world shall stand.* . . .

And behold they will be among the Gentiles, and the
Gentiles shall know them not.

*They will also be among the Jews, and the Jews shall
know them not.*

And it shall come to pass, when the Lord seeth fit in
his wisdom that they shall minister unto all the scattered
tribes of Israel, and unto all nations, kindreds, tongues and
people, and shall bring out of them unto Jesus many souls,
that their desire may be fulfilled, and also because of the
convincing power of God which is in them.

And they are as the angels of God, and if they shall
pray unto the Father in the name of Jesus they can show
themselves unto whatsoever man it seemeth them good.

Therefore, great and marvelous works shall be wrought
by them, before the great and coming day when all people
must surely stand before the judgment-seat of Christ; (3
Nephi 28:1-9; 27-31.)

Therefore, "the three persons with long beards and
flowing white robes" could have been these three
Nephite disciples, for Jesus said: "And behold they will
be among the Gentiles, and the Gentiles shall know them
not; they will also be among the Jews, and the Jews
shall know them not."

We quote further from the article by Arthur U.
Michelson:

> God performed the same miracles on other fighting
> fronts, for He wanted to show the nations that He had turned
> to the Jews again, and like in the olden days, would help
> them to conquer the land. The Arabs were especially
> strong in the Negev District, not far from Beersheba, for
> they were backed by a large Egyptian army. The Jews
> were encircled by the Egyptians, and humanly speaking,
> had absolutely no chance to escape. One morning to the
> amazement of the Jews, the Arabs and the Egyptians sud-
> denly gave up the fighting and surrendered. The Jews were
> at first very skeptical, because they couldn't believe that the
> Arabs and Egyptians would give up their strong position
> and surrender. But when they saw how the Arabs threw
> down their arms, they learned that God had intervened for

them. When they asked the Arabs and Egyptians for the cause of their surrender, they told them that they saw an old man with a long beard who was dressed in a white robe, and who warned them not to fight any longer, otherwise they would all perish. This man was seen and heard by almost all the enemy troops. A great fear came over them and they decided to give up the fight. These and other stories I heard from various Jews who fought on the battle fronts. They said to me, "If God had not intervened we would all have been killed. We could never have conquered Palestine because we were so few and without arms and ammunition."

The man referred to "with a long beard who was dressed in a white robe," who warned the Arabs and Egyptians "not to fight any longer, otherwise they would all be killed" could have been one of these Nephite disciples, or he could have been the Apostle John who was with the Savior in Jerusalem, for Jesus explained unto the three Nephite disciples that they desired of him the same thing "which John, my beloved, who was with me in my ministry, before that I was lifted up by the Jews, desired of me." (3 Nephi 28:6.)

A "Mystical Force" Seems to be Working with Judah

That there is a "mystical force" working with the Jews was attested by Dr. Chaim Weizmann, President of both the Jewish Agency for Palestine and the World Zionist Organization, at Jerusalem when visited by members of the Anglo-American Committee on Palestine, appointed by President Harry S. Truman of the United States, when that committee visited Palestine in 1945. Of this fact, Bartley C. Crum ,a member of that committee, reports in his book, "Behind the Silken Curtain," published in 1947 by Simon and Schuster, Inc., that when the committee visited with Dr. Chaim Weizmann, they were told by him that it was their belief in a "mystical force" that would return the Jews to the land of

Israel, that had kept them alive. This "mystical force" can only be accounted for through the coming of the Prophet Moses with the keys of the gathering of Israel in these latter days.

In Mr. Crum's book, he tells of the four months the committee, of which he was a member, spent visiting the camps of displaced persons, consisting principally of Jews, in the principal cities of Europe. In answer to questionnaires, they found that most of the remaining million Jews (six million having been put to death during the World War II) were desirous of returning to Palestine. In one city, for instance, a poll of 18,311 displaced Jews was taken with the following results: Thirteen said they wished to remain in Europe; 17,712 said they wished to go to Palestine. Some were asked to indicate their second choice, if they could not go to Palestine and hundreds answered: "Crematorium."

The suffering and persecutions which have been heaped upon the Jews in recent years are unparalleled in the history of the world, but are in fulfillment of the words of the prophets, nevertheless.

A Modern Prophet Reassures the Jews

In 1879 Wilford Woodruff, then an apostle of the Lord Jesus Christ, who later became the President of the Church of Jesus Christ of Latter-day Saints, made the following statement concerning the gathering of the Jews to their promised land:

> I wish in this testimony to say that the time is not far distant when the rich men among the Jews will be called upon to use their abundant wealth to gather the dispersed of Judah, and purchase the ancient dwelling places of their fathers in and about Jerusalem, and rebuild the holy city and temple.
>
> For the fullness of the Gentiles has come in, and the Lord has decreed that the Jews should be gathered from all the Gentile nations where they have been driven, into

their own land, in fulfillment of the words of Moses their law-giver. And this is the will of your great Elohim, O house of Judah, and whenever you shall be called upon to perform this work, the God of Israel will help you. You have a great future and destiny before you and you cannot avoid fulfilling it; you are the royal chosen seed, and the God of your father's house has kept you distinct as a nation for eighteen hundred years, under all the oppression of the whole Gentile world. You may not wait until you believe on Jesus of Nazareth, but when you meet with Shiloh your king, you will know him; your destiny is marked out, you cannot avoid it. It is true that after you return and gather your nation home, and rebuild your City and Temple, that the Gentiles may gather together their armies to go against you to battle, to take you a prey and to take you as a spoil, which they will do, for the words of your prophets must be fulfilled; but when this affliction comes, the living God, that led Moses through the wilderness, will deliver you, and your Shiloh will come and stand in your midst and will fight your battles; and you will know him, and the afflictions of the Jews will be at an end, while the destruction of the Gentiles will be so great that it will take the whole house of Israel who are gathered about Jerusalem, seven months to bury the dead of their enemies, and the weapons of war will last them seven years for fuel, so that they need not go to any forest for wood. These are tremendous sayings—who can bear them? Nevertheless they are true, and will be fulfilled, according to the sayings of Ezekiel, Zechariah and other prophets. Though the heavens and the earth pass away, not one jot or tittle will fall unfulfilled. (Matthias F. Cowley, *The Life of Wilford Woodruff*, page 509.)

A Prophet of the Latter Days Speaks of Judah

On October 19, 1952, David O. McKay, President of The Church of Jesus Christ of Latter-day Saints, with headquarters in Salt Lake City, Utah, delivered an address which we commend to all Judah:

I invite your attention, young people, today, to this book, [Book of Mormon] because if it is what it purports to be, you may rest assured that Joseph Smith was inspired.

I shall have time this afternoon to take only one point for your consideration. I take it because I can give some personal experiences in regard to it, and I believe you will accept my word as coming, at least, from a sincere heart.

Just one prophecy. You will find it in I Nephi 19:14, 15: "And because they [that means the Jews] turn their hearts aside, saith the prophet, and have despised the Holy One of Israel, they shall wander in the flesh, and perish, and become a hiss and a by-word, and be hated among all nations. Nevertheless, when that day cometh, saith the prophet, *that they no more turn aside their hearts against the Holy One of Israel,* then will he remember the covenants which he made to their fathers."

And if we turn to II Nephi, the tenth chapter, we shall find what that promise is. Commencing with the eighth verse: "And it shall come to pass that they shall be gathered in from their long dispersion, from the isles of the sea, and from the four parts of the earth; and the nations of the Gentiles shall be great in the eyes of me, saith God, in carrying them forth to the lands of their inheritance. Yea, the kings of the Gentiles shall be nursing fathers unto them, and their queens shall become nursing mothers: wherefore, the promises of the Lord are great unto the Gentiles, for he hath spoken it, and who can dispute?"

Now, that was printed in what is now known as the Book of Mormon in the year 1829. It is either Joseph Smith's guess or idea, or it is what it purports to be, a prophecy written about 500 years before Christ came. If it is Joseph Smith's writing, he could have known that the Jews were scattered and that they were persecuted (you and I knew that when we were boys), but he could not have known about a change of their hearts, because in 1829, I want to tell you that they were pretty bitter.

Sir Walter Scott depicts that persecution in several of his books, particularly in "Ivanhoe." It was manifested a way back in 1055 when the Normans came over to England, and even before that, and in the terrible massacres in Russia and other places. Now, Joseph Smith could have known about those persecutions; but, I repeat: He said, "When they no more *turn aside* their hearts against the Holy One"— it does not say *believe*, although it does in another place, but when they begin to *look with favor*—then he will remember the covenants which he made to their fathers.

That was in 1829. As an example of what intense bitterness existed even when this book was printed, I want to read to you a statement made by a Jew in California who printed a book in 1902, over 72 years after the Book of Mormon was printed. Mr. Harris Weinstock wrote a book entitled "Jesus, the Jew." It was put in my hands when I visited the California Mission for the first time, about 1912. This is what he says about the attitude of the Jews when he, the author of "Jesus, the Jew," was a boy.

"I recall that on one occasion one of the pupils by some chance brought [that would be about 1870] into the religious school a book containing the name of Jesus. I remember how wrought and excited the Rabbi became when he was made aware of its presence in the school room. 'Sacrilege! Sacrilege!' he cried indignantly, and seemed afraid to touch it. I remember how he delivered an impassioned discourse to his pupils upon the terrible sufferings to which the Jews had been subjected because of Jesus.

"He told them how the Jews had been made outcasts and wanderers over the face of the earth, how for hundreds of years they had been robbed and pillaged, tortured and plundered; how their beards had been torn from their roots, their teeth drawn from their jaws, their bodies cast into foul dungeons; how time and again they had been put on the rack, subjected to the thumbscrew and burned at the stake, all on account of Jesus.

"I remember how aroused and impassioned he became while recounting the frightful sufferings and calamities which had been inflicted upon the Jews, for all of which, in his opinion, Jesus was primarily responsible. 'How, then,' he concluded, 'can any self-respecting loyal Jew take into his hand a book containing the name of Jesus? How can the name of Jesus be thought of without connecting it, in the minds of the Jew, with the centuries of inhuman outrage and persecution heaped upon him by the followers of Jesus?' "

Mr. Weinstock comments: "His (Jesus') wisdom and gentleness, his unselfishness of spirit and his love for humanity, his desire to live in the spirit of the early Jewish prophets and to practice in his daily life the ethics of Judaism, are becoming better understood, so that the modern Jew looks upon Jesus as one of the greatest gifts that Israel has given to the world, and he is, therefore, proud to call Jesus his very own: blood of his blood, flesh of his flesh."

Keep in mind what was prophesied when *"they no more turn aside their hearts from the Holy One."* Note it, young man. "When that day cometh that they no more turn aside their hearts from the Holy One of Israel, then will he remember the covenants which he made with their fathers." I have read to you what those covenants are.

In 1830, Jerusalem was a waste. For over 400 years it had been under the domination of the Turks and the Arabs, principally the Turks. Bedouins in their camps could be seen. They oppressed the poor; one man who visited about that time tells how he was held up by bandits. You and I knew that when we were boys, just from the little geography we had read. I recall a conversation my father had with a friend who was visiting us, in which my father mentioned this prophecy, and he said, "The day will come when they will be returned to their homeland." I was about 12 or 14 years of age, and I said to myself:

"If I live to see that day, I'll know that Joseph Smith was a prophet." I didn't say it to father, but I think the Lord heard me say it.

I am going to tell you a personal experience this afternoon. In 1829, when that was written (so there is no getting around it), Jerusalem was a waste, and the Jews were not back there. For 1,500 years or more they had wandered homeless. A hiss and a by-word! Some would go back and drive nails in the old wall of the temple and then bewail their fate and pray for deliverance, and so on.

On November 2, 1917, following the World War, just five weeks after Lord Allenby entered Jerusalem, and the Turkish Army marched out of the opposite gate without firing a gun, Lord Balfour, at that time foreign secretary, had made, on behalf of the British Government, the following historic declaration (I will not have time to develop it, but you keep in mind this other statement, that the "Gentiles shall be great in mine eyes," in restoring them. How did Joseph Smith know?):

"His Majesty's Government [Great Britain] view with favor the establishment in Palestine of a national home for the Jewish people, and will use their best endeavours to facilitate the achievement of this object, it being clearly understood that nothing shall be done which may prejudice the civil and religious rights of existing non-Jewish communities in Palestine, or the rights and political status enjoyed by Jews in any other country."

The declaration (this is history) was endorsed by the principal Allied powers (the Gentiles) and embodied in the treaty of Sevres, where it was provided that the country should be entrusted to a mandatory power with a mandate to be approved by the League of Nations. After the Balfour declaration, the Zionist organization sent a commission, subsequently constituted as a part of the Zionist executive, to Palestine, to act as a link between the British authorities and the Jewish population. That was November 2, 1917.

Four years later, to the day, November 2, 1921, Brother Hugh J. Cannon and I found ourselves in Jerusalem, filling an appointment by the Church to visit the missions of the Church. We were then on our way to the Turkish Mission, as it was then. Michael, our guide, had promised to take us down to the Dead Sea on November 2, but he changed his plan and said, "Tomorrow, the second, we shall visit Jerusalem, instead." As we started out from the Allenby Hotel, which is outside the wall of Jerusalem, he said, "I will tell you as we go down, why I have changed."

Michael, who seemed apprehensive, motioned to us to follow him. We entered the gate and stood for awhile under David's Tower, off on our right, the Jewish quarter. There were about 45,000 Jews there then. Not a store open, nobody on those streets selling wares. Last night we had seen a busy town, donkeys heavily laden, walking up these stone steps; camels, also. That morning, Nov. 2, however, we didn't see a donkey; not a camel. The only store open was a stationery store kept by an Englishman. I said, "Michael, what does all this mean?"

He answered, "This means that today the Mohammedans and the Arabs, and some Christians, are protesting against Lord Balfour's declaration that the Holy Land should be set aside as a homeland for the Jews."

"Don't you believe that the Jews are coming back? You're a Christian."

"Yes, but the time hasn't come!" said Michael.

"Well," I said, "the time has come, and they will be coming back."

He replied, with vehemence, "Never! These stones will be bathed in blood first!"

"Well," I said, "Michael, these stones may be bathed in blood, but they are coming back!"

"Never!"

We walked down the stone steps, the three of us. We passed the old Wailing Wall, which is part of the old temple of Solomon. Not a Jew there that day, not one! We came up the steps to Mount Moriah and stood on the alleged spot where Abraham built his altar when he was about to offer Isaac. As we stood there, we heard a crowd, which sounded to me like students giving college yells. I said, "What is that?"

Michael said, "There is going to be trouble!"

"Well," I said, "Let's see it!" Brother Cannon and I started toward it, but there came round a street corner a crowd, crying:

"There is no God but Allah, and Mohammed is his prophet! There is no God but Allah, and Mohammed is his prophet!"

Michael said, "There will be trouble today!"

The crowd passed us, and we continued our visit of historical places, returning to David's street at about 11:30 a.m. Then we saw, coming towards us, fleeing from a mob, two women and a man, one woman clasping a child in her arms. I saw one of the pursuers throw a rock and hit the man in the back. Jews persecuted in Jerusalem because they wanted to come back to their homeland! Luckily, policemen were coming up, who stopped the mob, using a lash to whip them back, permitting the Jews to escape.

We followed those policemen as they whipped those fellows back, and came back again under David's Tower to a street leading up to the houses under that tower. There were the Jews, hiding for fear of the mob. They looked at us stealthily from behind curtains; we could see them through the doors left ajar, and by their dress we concluded that many were immigrant Jews. We wanted to find somebody to whom we could speak, for I forgot to tell you that Michael would not go up. He said, "If you go up there you go alone."

I said, "All right, Michael, here is where you and we part company. We shall see you this afternoon at 2 o'clock." And he let us go alone!

Beckoning, we found a young man who could speak English, and I said, "What does this all mean?"

Almost in the same words that Michael had used in the morning, he answered, "This means that the Mohammedans and the Christians are uniting, in protest against Lord Balfour's declaration that we should come back to our Holy Land. They won't fight us openly; we can't fight women and children." At that juncture, a gentleman who had been standing near by spoke in Yiddish or Jewish, whatever it was, evidently protesting to this young man.

I said, "Is he objecting to your speaking to us?"

The young man said, "Yes."

"Well, you tell him that we are Americans, and that we believe in the restoration of the Jews to the Holy Land."

A little boy about 14, who had been standing by, said, "Then why do you wear that?" and he pointed to a stick-pin, the "star and crescent," that had been given me by Sister McKay. The older one looked at it and said, "That is all right." I learned afterwards that the four-point star and crescent is a Mohammedan sign, the five-point star and crescent a Jewish sign, and this happened to be five, and I was happy.

I cite these incidents merely to show you how tense and bitter was the feeling in Jerusalem that day.

As we came out of the street and saw the British soldiers with helmets on their heads, rifles in their hands, bayonets fixed, I said, "Boys, I am glad to see you here."

"Oh," said one, "I think we can hold them." And they did.

As Brother Cannon and I walked toward our hotel, he said, "And the Gentiles shall be great in the eyes of me in carrying them back."

The few Jews, approximately 45,000, who had returned to Jerusalem, were under the protecting care of the British government, backed by the League of Nations.

Young man, tell me: Who wrote that prophecy? Was it a guess by Joseph Smith? No! He was merely the trans-lator. Through the eyes of prophecy, Jacob had looked down through the annals of time to the day when the Jews would persecute the Savior and He would be crucified, when they would be banished, would become a hiss and a by-word without a home for 1,600 years, and *when they no more turned aside their hearts from the Holy One,* then would he remember the promise he made to their fathers.

When we returned to the hotel and met Michael, I said, "Well, Michael, you see we are all right."

"Don't you laugh at me," he said. "When I left you, one man was killed and several injured by a bomb."

To verify this statement, I called up Governor Samuels' office (by the way, the first Jew to govern Palestine for hundreds of years). We received word from his office, "Yes, one man was killed, others were injured, and two other men beaten to death at the Jaffa gate."

Reference to that uprising you will find in the encyclo-pedia today.

Another item: On May 11, 1950, with a vote of 37 to 12, nine being absent, the State of Israel, the Jewish nation, was admitted to the United Nations in fulfillment of a prophecy made 2,000 years before.

I have taken only one point, two elements in it: One,

the change of heart that must come and did come, beginning about 1860, 30 years after the statement; the other, that the Gentiles should help them to return to Palestine. Zionist rule began about 1870; in 1917 the Gentiles declared that they should go, and protected them, and in 1950 they were given a home for the first time since before Christ. (Published in The Church News Section of The Deseret News, Salt Lake City, Utah, October 25, 1952.)

Conclusion of the Summary

It should be obvious in light of all the promises of the Lord unto the entire House of Israel, Judah and Joseph, that these promises cannot find their fulfillment until the descendants of Judah and Joseph are brought together:

> And I will make them one nation in the land upon the mountains of Israel; and one king shall be king to them all: *and they shall be no more two nations, neither shall they be divided into two kingdoms any more at all:* (Ezekiel 37:22.)

It is because the Lord declared that He would bring these two kingdoms together that we of the House of Joseph, the Kingdom of Israel, extend to the House of Judah an invitation to join us. We must come together into one kingdom, the Kingdom which, God declared through His Prophet Daniel (Daniel 2:44), would be established in the earth in the latter days to prepare for the second coming of Jesus Christ, the Messiah. The quicker we unite under the leadership of the prophets of the Lord whom He has raised up *in the latter days,* the earlier can the kingdom be prepared for His coming. This is the great work the Lord had in mind for us to accomplish when He promised Abraham, Isaac, and Jacob, that through them and their seed would all the nations of the earth be blessed.

We have made it plain that Judah would have to look to Joseph for the establishment of the Church and

Kingdom of God in the earth *in the latter days,* and that it would be taken by Joseph to Judah when the times of the Gentiles would be fulfilled.

Therefore, in the words of Isaiah, we say to our brethren, the House of Judah: "Come now and let us reason together." (Isaiah 1:18.)

The Angel Moroni fully understood this when he quoted to Joseph Smith, the "choice seer . . . like unto Moses":

> The envy also of Ephraim shall depart, and the adversaries of Judah shall be cut off: *Ephraim shall not envy Judah, and Judah shall not vex Ephraim.* (Isaiah 11:13.)

What a glorious day to anticipate! We of the House of Ephraim are ready. Will you join us, Judah, our brethren? For the coming of this day we humbly and earnestly pray, and offer to you our hand in fellowship in the great work of the God of Israel in establishing His Kingdom in the earth, and the gathering of the whole House of Israel. This is our mutual task. It is a God-given assignment. The Messiah pleaded in the meridian of time, and he is pleading today:

> O Jerusalem, Jerusalem, thou that killest the prophets, and stonest them which are sent unto thee, how often would I have gathered thy children together, even as a hen gathereth her chickens under her wings, and ye would not!
>
> Behold, your house is left unto you desolate.
>
> For I say unto you, Ye shall not see me henceforth, till ye shall say, *Blessed is he that cometh in the name of the Lord.* (Matthew 23:37-39.)

Judah, do not procrastinate your acceptance of His loving call—accept the Elders of Israel when they come to you "in the name of the Lord," with the message of the restored Gospel of Jesus Christ, "in the latter days."

INDEX

cerning restoration of Gospel, 118

John, the Baptist, messenger sent to prepare for first coming, 110
restoration of Aaronic Priesthood by, 143
Lord sent, to earth to confer Aaronic Priesthood on Joseph Smith and Oliver Cowdery, 219

Jordan, "whereunto ye go over J.," 17

Joseph Smith (see Smith, Joseph)

Joseph, son of Jacob, receives choice blessings, 10
we are descendants of, 31

Joseph, Stick of, 2
turn to Lord, 23
one record of, 25
reign of Zedekiah, 30
stick of, sealed, 39
message to Judah by, 41
and Judah walk together, 45
dreams of, 47
name foretold, 126-129
seed of J. gathered in America, 159-188, 222
gathering of seed of, 176

Judah and Israel, must come together, 3
"and they shall be no more two nations . . . ," 22
to be brought together, 22

Judah and Joseph walk together, 45

Judah, son of Jacob, receives choice blessings, 9-10
men of, drew swords, 13
Lord commanded, 14
house of, 16-24
restored, 20
temple rebuilt, 20
population of Jews in 1946, 21
Jacob's promise to, 91
through Judah came "chief ruler," 94
kingdom of, 153-161
being gathered, 156-161
predictions concerning gathering of, 189-190
Lord to fight J. battles, 229

K

Keys, for gathering, restored, 149
of salvation of dead returned, 150-151

Kingdom, of Ephraim (men of Ephraim), 13

of Israel (men of Ephraim), 13
of God will be established, 16
of Israel, sifted among the nations, 22
promise to descendants of, 22
of Judah (see Judah)

Kirtland, first gathering place, 170

Kirtland Temple, appearance of Jesus Christ, 148-149
appearance of Moses, 149, 166
appearance of Elias, 149-150
appearance of Elijah, 151

Knowledge from Stick of Joseph, 222
descendants of Judah, will be gathered to Jerusalem, 223-224
Jesus giver of Law of Moses, 223
remnants of Israel to be grafted, 224
Jews to believe in Christ, 225-227
blessings on tribe of Judah, 228

L

Laban, sons of Lehi obtain record of Jews from, 28, 32

Laman and Lemuel, Lord instructed, 33
Lord placed a curse upon, 36

Lamanite prophet Samuel's prophecy, 60-62

Lamanites (see American Indians), 36-37

Lamb of God, going forth, 52
" . . . last shall be first . . . ," 55

Law of Moses, to be fulfilled, 57-58
fulfilled, 71

League of Nations, 206

Lehi, prays unto Lord and receives vision, 27
prophesies destruction of Jerusalem, 28
led out of Jerusalem, 30
and descendants called Nephites, 36
promise of Lord recorded in Stick of Joseph, 110-111

Levi, son of Jacob, not to share equally, 9

Levites to build house of Lord, 20

Levitical Priesthood (Aaronic), 146

Lord's covenant with Abraham, 5

Lost Tribes of Israel, shall have words of Nephites, 43